Base of the Pyramid Markets in Africa

This book focuses on the Base of the Pyramid (BOP) in Africa and examines the role of the private sector in the fight against poverty.

The BOP concept, which is a market-based approach to poverty eradication, presents a great avenue for businesses to develop opportunities and new business models that enable and empower those in the BOP population in Africa to raise their socio-economic welfare and well-being. The BOP market and the business interest in the BOP in Africa is rising. This book furthers our understanding of the characteristics of BOP markets in Africa, and the challenges and opportunities to address poverty and development in a sustainable manner. The book covers various themes of BOP markets and their embeddedness in social-cultural settings in Africa. The different chapters employ a variety of theoretical and methodological approaches to advance research and practice of BOP in Africa. The book chapters reflect multiple diversities that characterise sub-Saharan Africa based on studies in 13 country contexts and from five industry sectors.

This book is recommended reading for managers and policy makers, as well as students and academics interested in Base of the Pyramid markets.

Judy N. Muthuri is Associate Professor of Corporate Social Responsibility at Nottingham University Business School (NUBS), UK, and chairs the Social and Environmental Responsibility Group leading the School's UN Principles for Responsible Management Education work.

Marlen Gabriele Arnold is a professor in the field of sustainability. Currently, she holds the Chair for Corporate Environmental Management and Sustainability at the Chemnitz University of Technology, Germany.

Stefan Gold is Professor and Chair of Sustainability Management at the University of Kassel, Germany.

Ximena Rueda is Associate Professor at the School of Management at the Universidad de los Andes, Colombia.

Innovation and Sustainability in Base of the Pyramid Markets

Series Editors:
Marlen Gabriele Arnold, Chemnitz University of Technology, Germany
Stefan Gold, Kassel University, Germany
Judy N. Muthuri, University of Nottingham, UK
Ximena Rueda, Universidad de los Andes, Colombia

Base of the Pyramid Markets in Asia
Innovation and Challenges to Sustainability
Edited by Marlen Gabriele Arnold, Stefan Gold, Judy N. Muthuri, and Ximena Rueda

Base of the Pyramid Markets in Africa
Innovation and Challenges to Sustainability
Edited by Judy N. Muthuri, Marlen Gabriele Arnold, Stefan Gold, and Ximena Rueda

For more information about this series, please visit:
www.routledge.com/Frugal-Innovation-in-Base-of-the-Pyramid-Markets/book-series/FINNBOP

Base of the Pyramid Markets in Africa

Innovation and Challenges to Sustainability

**Edited by Judy N. Muthuri,
Marlen Gabriele Arnold, Stefan Gold,
and Ximena Rueda**

LONDON AND NEW YORK

First published 2021
by Routledge
2 Park Square, Milton Park, Abingdon, Oxon OX14 4RN

and by Routledge
605 Third Avenue, New York, NY 10017

First issued in paperback 2022

Routledge is an imprint of the Taylor & Francis Group, an informa business

British Library Cataloguing-in-Publication Data
A catalogue record for this book is available from the British Library

Library of Congress Cataloging-in-Publication Data
Names: Muthuri, Judy N., editor, author. | Arnold, Marlen Gabriele, editor. |
Gold, Stefan, editor. | Rueda, Ximena, editor.
Title: Base of the pyramid markets in Africa : innovation and challenges
to sustainability / edited by Judy N. Muthuri, Marlen Gabriele Arnold,
Stefan Gold and Ximena Rueda.
Other titles: Innovation and sustainability in base of the pyramid markets.
Description: New York : Routledge, 2020. |
Series: Innovation and sustainability in base of the pyramid markets |
Includes bibliographical references and index.
Identifiers: LCCN 2020007925 (print) | LCCN 2020007926 (ebook)
Subjects: LCSH: Social entrepreneurship–Africa, Sub-Saharan. |
Poverty–Africa, Sub-Saharan. | Low-income consumers–Africa,
Sub-Saharan. | Sustainable development–Africa, Sub-Saharan.
Classification: LCC HC800.Z9.E5 B37 2020 (print) |
LCC HC800.Z9.E5 (ebook) | DDC 338.9670905–dc23
LC record available at https://lccn.loc.gov/2020007925
LC ebook record available at https://lccn.loc.gov/2020007926

ISBN 13: 978–0–367–50957–6 (pbk)
ISBN 13: 978–1–138–38911–3 (hbk)
ISBN 13: 978–0–429–42417–5 (ebk)

DOI: 10.4324/9780429424175

Typeset in Bembo
by Newgen Publishing UK

Contents

Acknowledgements

The editors take this opportunity to acknowledge the help of all those who in one way or another contributed to the development of this edited collection on the Base of the Pyramid markets in Africa. The book has benefited enormously from the scholarly input of the contributors – we are indebted! We appreciate the generous time of the anonymous reviewers whose invaluable and constructive feedback contributed to the development of the chapters. Finally, we would like to thank the team at Routledge for their support at various stages of the book's development and its publishing.

Preface

The Africa edition comes second in the Base of the Pyramid (BOP) book series that discusses the BOP markets around the globe, following the Asia edition and preceding the South America & the Caribbean and Affluent Countries editions. The BOP Africa edition is important in a number of ways. First, the World Bank and the Sustainable Development Goals Centre for Africa have confirmed in their numerous publications since 2018 that more than half of the global poor living in extreme poverty and surviving on less than $2 a day are found in Africa. Second, despite global progress towards the Sustainable Development Goals (SDGs), Africa continues to lag behind most of the world on poverty eradication and socio-economic development. Poverty is becoming more entrenched, especially in sub-Saharan Africa, making it harder to root out. Third, many countries in Africa are experiencing a rising population growth amidst slowed economic growth, resulting in a huge BOP market that needs to be served. Fourth, the dominance of informal economies in Africa, in contexts often characterised by institutional voids, means that a large BOP population is not integrated into the formal market economy. This population is least likely to reap the benefits of global trade and value creation. Against this backdrop, more effort is needed to understand how best to identify and exploit the opportunities at the BOP so as to improve shared prosperity and to move people out of poverty.

Certainly, the private sector actors, such as multinational organizations, small and medium enterprises and entrepreneurs, together with actors in the public and the non-profit sectors have a role to play in addressing the socio-economic and development challenges experienced in Africa. The BOP is an important market-based approach to poverty that presents a great avenue for business organizations to act as agents of development through developing opportunities and creating new business models that enable and empower those in the BOP population to raise their socio-economic welfare and well-being. Businesses ought to collaborate with other BOP stakeholders to find sustainable solutions that transform market systems and processes to become more productive, efficient, and inclusive. These BOP stakeholders can support businesses to play their larger societal role as agents of development.

For example, the African governments should provide an enabling environment and institutional support for BOP markets to thrive. The non-profit organizations can capitalise on their networks and utilise their high degree of social embeddedness to raise awareness of and develop, implement, and evaluate the impact of BOP strategies.

The BOP markets book series is organized into four main sections:

A. BOP markets

BOP markets have specific characteristics: core innovations, inclusive business models, main stakeholders, and actors involved. BOP markets are related to frugal, reverse, and inclusive innovations that can foster (sustainable) development and initiate new business models and value streams from which other countries can also profit. Still, the sustainability of related performance is not always clear and warrants critical reflection.

B. Drivers and barriers of BOP markets

Institutional voids and mechanisms strongly influence BOP markets, both positively and negatively. Moreover, governmental and international interventions play pivotal roles in progressing BOP markets. Often, business models fill in institutional gaps as strategies to scaling social and economic impact, trade-offs, and unanticipated outcomes.

C. Roles, cooperation, and structure in BOP markets

The configuration of BOP markets is closely linked to cooperation, structure, roles, relations, and patterns. Inclusive approaches, for instance, aim at participation, involvement or cooperation between various market actors along the entire value chain. Hence, analysis of (frugal) innovation networks, consumer behaviour, value co-creation, and cross-sector collaboration, the role of multinationals, innovation, and knowledge capabilities and empowerment of women is pivotal for an understanding of BOP markets.

D. Design, integration, innovation, and change of BOP markets

The capabilities of BOP markets aim at the differences of key success factors of networks, the interactions concerning the management of design; production, procurement, and logistics; sustainable supply chains; and integration. The transformation of BOP markets is often accompanied by renewal, innovation, learning, intellectual property and global standards, social business, inclusive corporate social responsibility, circular business models, and approaches integrating sustainability.

As evident in the chapters in this book, the BOP market and the business interest in the BOP in Africa is rising. This book furthers our understanding of the BOP phenomenon. It examines the characteristics of BOP markets in Africa and the challenges and opportunities to address poverty and development in a sustainable manner. The book covers various themes of BOP markets and their embeddedness in social-cultural settings in Africa. The various chapters employ an assortment of theoretical and methodological approaches to advance research and practice of BOP in Africa. They also reflect multiple diversities that characterise sub-Saharan Africa based on studies in 13 country contexts (Burkina Faso, Ethiopia, Ghana, Kenya, Malawi, Mozambique, Nigeria, Rwanda, Tanzania, Uganda, Somalia, South Africa, and Zimbabwe) and from five industry sectors (fashion, technology, construction, agriculture, and finance). All chapters yield valuable recommendations for researchers, managers, and policy makers.

The first chapter – **The Base of the Pyramid markets in Africa: opportunities and challenges** – by Muthuri and Farhoud provides background details on poverty, development, and the BOP in Africa, which sets the tone for the entire book. It features three interviews with experts on the BOP market in Africa, who provide great insights into the drivers, barriers, and future of BOP enterprises in Africa.

Lashitew and van Tulder demonstrate in the second chapter – **Why do firms choose to fight poverty? The motivation behind inclusive business practices in Africa** – how the nature of motivations by firms choosing to fight poverty leads to variations in strategies towards addressing social issues. The authors conclude that intrinsic rather than extrinsic motivations are important drivers of inclusive business performance.

The third chapter – **Juxtaposing supply- and demand-side drivers and barriers of technology adoption at the Base of the Pyramid markets in Uganda** – by Ebong, Giacomo, Kinoti, Nakagwa, and Adeola, explores how the adoption of technology is impacted by demand-side drivers and barriers (e.g. digital illiteracy, attitudes towards use) and supply-side drivers and barriers (e.g. service failure, costs of smartphones) in agribusiness.

Arslan, Gölgeci, Kontkanen, and Leposky discuss in Chapter 4 – **Risk and social value creation in volatile BOP markets: a case study from Somalia** – how social value might be created by foreign companies operating in volatile BOP markets in contexts characterised by significant institutional voids.

In Chapter 5 – **BOP business models and partnerships in the context of state failure** – Hanson employs the Alliance Framework to demonstrate how social partnerships for institutional capacity building can help address institutional failures in Africa.

Beyer, in Chapter 6 – **Addressing social sustainability on Base of the Pyramid markets through business model innovations: a comparative study within Africa's fashion industry** – explores how social value can be created by integrating sustainability in business strategies to advance a sustainable fashion industry in Africa.

In Chapter 7 – ***Women's economic empowerment and agricultural value chain development: evidence from Mashonaland West Province in Zimbabwe*** – Derera discusses challenges that are exacerbated by deep-rooted socio-cultural factors that hinder women's economic empowerment in the agricultural value chains, such as lack of access to technology, poor infrastructure, and lack of agricultural extension services, and makes strategic recommendations for all stakeholders in value chain development.

Ciambotti, Littlewood, Sottini, and M'ithiria examine in Chapter 8 – ***Building and scaling social enterprise business models for BOP markets in Kenya*** – how social enterprises build and scale business models and the challenges the enterprises face in doing so. The authors share insights into how these challenges might be overcome.

In Chapter 9 – ***From informal to formal and back: theoretical reflections on the formal – informal divide in the Base of the Pyramid markets*** – Vallino, Navarra, and Lanzano advance the formal – informal debates in the BOP markets by demonstrating how informal and formal markets are structurally interdependent, and how this, in turn, has various consequences for BOP players and for systems as a whole.

December 2019

Judy N. Muthuri, Nottingham University Business School, United Kingdom
Marlen Gabriele Arnold, Chemnitz University of Technology, Germany
Stefan Gold, University of Kassel, Germany
Ximena Rueda Fajardo, Universidad de los Andes, Colombia

Contributors

Ogechi Adeola, Associate Professor in Marketing, Lagos Business School, Pan-Atlantic University, Ajah – Lagos, Nigeria.

Ahmad Arslan, Associate Professor of International Business, Department of Marketing, Management & International Business, Oulu Business School, University of Oulu, Finland.

Katja Beyer, Research Assistant, Faculty of Economics and Business Administration, Corporate Environmental Management and Sustainability, Chemnitz University of Technology, Germany.

Giacomo Ciambotti, PhD Candidate, Management and Innovation, Università Cattolica del Sacro Cuore, Milan, Italy.

Evelyn Derera, Senior Lecturer in Management and Entrepreneurship, School of Management, Information Technology and Governance, College of Law and Management Studies, University of KwaZulu-Natal, South Africa.

Jimmy Ebong, Research Specialist, Financial Sector Deepening Uganda, Kampala, Uganda.

Mohamed Farhoud, PhD Candidate, Management and Entrepreneurship Department, Unit for Entrepreneurship, University of Turku, School of Economics, Turku, Finland.

Ismail Gölgeci, Associate Professor of Marketing Strategy, Department of Business Technology, Aarhus University, Denmark.

Margaret Hanson, Clinical Professor of Business Administration, Tuck School of Business, Dartmouth College, USA.

Abel Kinoti, Associate Professor of Entrepreneurship/Business Management, School of Business, Riara University, Nairobi, Kenya.

Minnie Kontkanen, University Lecturer of International Business, School of Marketing & Communications, University of Vaasa, Finland.

Cristiano Lanzano, Senior Researcher, The Nordic Africa Institute, Uppsala, Sweden.

Addisu A. Lashitew, Post-doctoral Research Fellow, Beedie School of Business, Simon Fraser University, Canada.

Tiina Leposky, Assistant Professor of International Business, School of Marketing & Communications, University of Vaasa, Finland.

David Littlewood, Senior Lecturer in Strategic Management, Sheffield University Management School, Sheffield, United Kingdom.

Esther Nkatha M'ithiria, Lecturer of Finance and Accounting, Department of Accounting & Finance, School of Business, Catholic University of East Africa, Nairobi, Kenya.

Judy N. Muthuri, Associate Professor, Corporate Social Responsibility, International Centre for Corporate Social Responsibility, Nottingham University Business School, Nottingham, United Kingdom.

Alice Nakagwa, Communications Consultant, Kampala, Uganda.

Cecilia Navarra, Policy Analyst, European Parliamentary Research Service, Brussels, Belgium.

Andrea Sottini, PhD Candidate, Università Cattolica del Sacro Cuore, Milan, Italy.

Rob van Tulder, Professor of International Business-Society Management, Rotterdam School of Management, Erasmus University, Rotterdam, the Netherlands.

Elena Vallino, Research Fellow, Department of Environment, Land and Infrastructure Engineering, Politecnico di Torino, Torino, Italy.

Part I
BOP markets

1 The Base of the Pyramid markets in Africa

Opportunities and challenges

Judy N. Muthuri and Mohamed Farhoud

Introduction: defining the "Base of the Pyramid" markets

The Base of the Pyramid (BOP) concept was first introduced in the business and management scholarship in 1998 by Prahalad and Lieberthal (1998). The BOP was later popularised by Prahalad and Hammond (2002) in their article published in the *Harvard Business Review* that identified the "missing market" or "the invisible poor", often ignored by international, multinational, and transnational corporations. An earlier reference to the term was by President Roosevelt of the United States of America (USA) who in 1932 spoke about "the forgotten, the unorganized but indispensable units of economic power . . . the forgotten man at the bottom of the economic pyramid" (quoted in Mason, Chakrabarti, & Singh, 2013, p. 402).

The main thesis of the BOP concept is that poverty can be eradicated through market transactions. The earlier proponents championed BOP as a market-based approach with the potential to unlock societal prosperity. BOP essentially involves an external commercial organisation "that either sells goods to, or sources products from, those at the Base of the Pyramid in a way that helps to improve the standard of living of the poor" (London, 2008, p. 1). Prahalad and Hammond (2002) urged multinational corporations (MNCs) to give market access to the low-income segment of society as consumers, and in return they would reap economic benefits whilst alleviating poverty. They opposed the idea of MNCs relying on philanthropic approaches to lift billions of people out of poverty in communities in which they operated. Since 2007, the concept has been researched widely with an increasing body of literature from diverse disciplinary fields including marketing, strategy, international business, general management, development studies, and information technology, to name but a few (Dembek, Sivasubramaniam, & Chmielewski et al., 2019; Kolk, Rivera-Santos, & Rufín, 2014; Follman, 2012). The concept has been adopted by for-profit enterprises, government bodies, and not-for-profit organisations and proved very popular, especially at a time when "market stagnation across the developed world was widespread" (Mason et al., 2013, p. 401).

The BOP concept has, therefore, become indispensable in modern discourse on tackling grand societal challenges through business and management research. There is no prescriptive academic definition of what constitutes a BOP population, but, broadly speaking, it defines a group of people who are ranked the lowest on the socioeconomic ladder of a country, region, or society. According to Kolk et al. (2014, pp. 351–352), measurement of poverty varies widely, with most published research defining the BOP population as those with per capita income at or below US$1,500 or US$2,000 per annum expressed in internationally comparable "purchasing power parity". Euromonitor defines the Africa BOP as those households with an annual disposable income of US$2,500 or less (Euromonitor, n.d.). Scholars define the term using a mix of incomes, buying power index, living standards, and levels of access to goods and services including education, healthcare, financial services, etc. The use of different poverty thresholds, dimensions, and target populations, and an agreed-upon definition of what constitutes a BOP venture in the BOP[1] literature has fuelled criticisms of BOP research for lacking rigour and for "creat[ing] confusion and hamper[ing] theory building and generalization" (Kolk et al., 2014, p. 353).

What we know is that the BOP concept has evolved from its original conceptualisation over the years. First, while it was originally conceptualised with MNCs[2] as the main players, the BOP business model is currently being used by small- and medium-sized enterprises (SMEs), cooperatives, social entrepreneurs, governments, and multi-stakeholder partnerships (Kolk et al., 2014). Second, the way that the "missing poor" are viewed – as consumers, producers, and/or entrepreneurs – has evolved (London, 2016). Prahalad and Hart (2002) introduced the first iteration, BOP 1.0, which conceived the role of the poor as consumers. The 1.0 approach was conceptualised around "selling to the poor and helping them improve their lives by producing and distributing products and services in culturally sensitive, environmentally sustainable, and economically profitable ways" (Prahalad & Hart 2002, p. 3). However, there was an ongoing criticism on how BOP 1.0 encouraged consumerist behaviour among the poor and made them spend their limited resources on unnecessary items instead of necessities (Karnani, 2007). As a consequence, BOP 2.0 was introduced to highlight the importance of co-creation in partnership with the poor – or to put it more concretely, "creating with the poor" (Simanis & Hart, 2008) – who are resilient entrepreneurs (Dembek et al., 2019). In both BOP 1.0 and BOP 2.0, products are introduced to the BOP markets (BOPM) where consumer education is limited and the marketplace is complex and highly volatile, resulting in very high mortality rates for BOP ventures (Dasgupta & Hart, 2017).

BOP 3.0 is the third iteration and builds on BOP 2.0 while integrating the socio-ecological perspective into BOP initiatives (Caneque & Hart, 2017). BOP 3.0 seeks "a greater conceptual shift, away from singular solutions of poverty alleviation to understanding how wider innovation ecosystems and engagement through cross-sector partnership networks can be developed" (Mason, Chakrabarti, & Singh, 2017, p. 267). BOP 3.0 recognises the importance of creating an entire ecosystem: technology suppliers, financiers, capacity builders, supply chain players, open innovation and drawing on the wisdom of the crowd, distributors to the last mile, cross-sector partnerships, and embracing the complexity of the BOPM. In other words, BOP 3.0 focuses on creating not only a wide and deep value proposition to the poor but also an ecosystem to deliver them.

Development challenges in Africa

The Financial Times and *The Economist* have in recent years defined Africa as "rising", a far cry from the "hopeless continent" headlines we read at the turn of the 21st century. The changing narratives on the continent can be attributed to the projected upward economic growth in sub-Saharan Africa that stood at 3.1% in 2018 from 2.6% in 2017, and which is estimated to rise towards 3.6% in 2019–2020 (World Bank, 2018). The Africa rising narrative is supported by the fact that a number of African countries' economies have grown significantly over the years, including Ethiopia, Kenya, Mozambique, and Ghana. However, in the recent past, some of Africa's largest economies, such as Nigeria and South Africa, have suffered slower economic growth reflected by global uncertainty and domestic macroeconomic instability (World Bank, 2018, pp. 141–148).

Despite the extraordinary progress made in reducing extreme poverty in Africa, the continent still faces a number of challenges, amongst them widespread poverty. In fact, Africa currently has the highest number of people in the world living in extreme poverty, measured as \$1.90/day. The World Data Lab[3] in October 2019 reported that there were about 428,205,433 people living in extreme poverty in Africa. This represents 33.9% of Africa's population of 1,262,273,527, and in the global context represents two-thirds of the world's poorest population (see also World Bank, 2018). Africa is the second largest and the second most populous continent. It is significantly diverse in many ways including the poverty realities across all its 55 countries. Table 1.1 presents a summary of African countries' poverty numbers drawn from data from the World Data Lab's real-time poverty estimates as calculated using the methodology of the World Poverty Clock, which monitors progress against the United Nations' Sustainable Development Goal of Ending Extreme Poverty (UN SDG1) for almost every country in Africa.

To compute the speed of poverty reduction in each country, poverty estimates have been calculated using publicly available data on income distribution, production, and consumption provided by various international organisations, such as the World Bank, International Monetary Fund, and the United Nations. We observe that while countries such as Ethiopia have made great progress to eradicate poverty, others like Nigeria, DR Congo, and South Sudan have the largest number of people living in poverty. Nigeria, for example, is experiencing a spike in numbers with about 87 million people living in extreme poverty. In 2018, it was overtaken by India, where the population was about 73 million, as the most populous country of people living in extreme poverty. Nigeria was followed closely by the DR Congo.

Table 1.1 Levels of poverty in African countries

Countries on-track for SDG Target	Countries off-track for SDG Target	Countries where poverty is rising	No extreme poverty
Mauritania – 135,224	Benin – 5,143,075	Angola – 5,019,538	Algeria – below 3%
Zimbabwe – 1,106,724	Botswana – 324,591	Burundi – 8,238,901	Equatorial Guinea – below 3%
Gambia – 178,365	Burkina Faso – 7,821,337	Chad – 5,418,171	Egypt – below 3%
	Cameroon – 4,861,036	Congo – 2,812,598	Gabon – below 3%
	Central African Republic – 3,764,491	Democratic Republic of the Congo – 60,134,227	Libya – below 3%
	Cote D'Ivoire – 4,557,684	Gabon – below 3%	Morocco – below 3%
	Djibouti – 147,839	Liberia – 2,411,987	Tunisia – below 3%
	Eritrea – 3,173,885	Madagascar – 20,185,795	Seychelles – below 3%
	Ethiopia – 25,072,176	Niger – 13,654,743	
	Ghana – 3,063,455	Nigeria – 94,487,874	
	Guinea – 2,401,359	South Africa – 13,325,299	
	Guinea Bissau – 1,001,509	South Sudan – 10,739,909	
	Kenya – 8,203,062 (subnational data)	Sudan – 12,164,001	
	Lesotho – 1,243,518	Zambia – 8,845,455	
	Malawi – 8,845,455		
	Mali – 7,408,618		
	Mozambique – 15,916,168		
	Namibia – 525,882		
	Rwanda – 6,356,993		
	Senegal – 4,567,372		
	Sierra Leone – 2,772,094		
	Somalia – 5,462,127		
	Swaziland – 534,920		
	Togo – 3,246,369		
	Uganda – 13,828,011		
	United Republic of Tanzania – 23,588,226		

Source: Authors' own.

The poverty reality in Africa was also confirmed by the World Resources Institute which, in their 2018 report, classified 486 million people in 22 African countries as BOP.[4] We know from the World Bank estimates that the number of people living in extreme poverty in Africa is set to grow. For example, 14 out of 18 countries in the world with increasing numbers of extreme poor are in Africa. This is a worrying trend as the increased economic growth in Africa remains insufficient to reduce poverty significantly (World Bank, 2018). Additionally, despite the fact that Africa receives the highest international aid per capita (Bewayo & Portes, 2016), the population continues to suffer from many social ills that need addressing (Kolo, Madichie, & Mbah, 2019). The fear of falling behind the global SDG1 targets (e.g. "No poverty: End poverty in all its forms everywhere") has contributed to the collective global development voice calling for the refocusing of energies on Africa if there is to be any meaningful progress towards ending global poverty (Bill & Melinda Gates Foundation, 2019). In the next section, we explore the approaches to poverty alleviation in Africa and focus on the BOP business model.

Approaches to poverty alleviation in Africa

The transformational vision of the 2030 Agenda for Sustainable Development and the Africa Vision 2063 calls on all stakeholders to work together to achieve a better world. The nagging question is how we might reverse the dire projections that Africa will account for nine-tenths of the world's extreme poor by 2030. How do we respond to figures that show that by 2030 the top ten poorest countries in the world will be from Africa? On October 17, 2018, the Brookings Institution in the USA declared "Africa: The last frontier for eradicating extreme poverty",[5] so what should we be doing differently to ensure we achieve SDG1?

To answer these questions, one might consider both development aid and market-based solutions. On one hand, although supply-based solutions such as development aid programmes have been the primary poverty alleviation approach for the last 50 years, they have not been sustainable and have been criticised for not improving the lives of the poor (Dembek et al., 2019; Easterly, 2006; London, 2016; London, 2008). On the other hand, market-based solutions such as the BOP have not been successful either, and in some cases they have resulted in more ill than good (Karnani, 2010). While much debate between supply-based and demand-based solutions has been ongoing (Banerjee & Duflo, 2011), we argue that poverty alleviation needs both approaches (Easterly, 2006; Prahalad & Gouillart, 2008; Sachs, 2005). Rwanda, for instance, is an example of the good that aid can do (Sachs, 2005), but it is also an example of self-reliance (Moyo, 2009). In fact, the poor might use the aid to kick-start and improve their lives and be prepared to catch up on existing opportunities that market-based solutions might provide. What is certain, however, is that some markets for the poor are missing, and the conditions to create markets that are accessible and affordable to the poor are absent (Banerjee & Duflo, 2011; Hart, 2017). This is an opportunity for the private sector to play a major role as a potential partner in the creation of the missed markets (Caneque & Hart, 2017).

Africa's local marketplace is often resource-poor with acute poverty levels, unstable, and highly influenced by ethnic group identity (Acquaah, 2007; Rivera-Santos, Holt, Littlewood, & Kolk, 2015). Thus, to ensure sustainability and scalability, the BOP venture must, first, follow a community-centric and social approach to gain trust and licence to operate amongst the local community, and second, stay commercially successful (London, 2016; Panum, Hansen, & Davy, 2018). The BOP business model's premises provide a distinctive approach that predicates on these principles and thus has the promise of servicing the poor at scale. BOP, in essence, brings solutions to eradicate poverty using the markets' disciplines and the private sector's organisational elements and resources (i.e. organisational capabilities, technological advances, and capacity to produce scalable and cost-effective solutions). BOP underpins the importance of co-creation and calls for convergence between different actors to collectively work on finding solutions to poverty (Prahalad & Gouillart, 2008).

To increase effectiveness of solutions, the BOP business model recognises the importance of keeping efforts locally focused. When designing solutions for the BOP population, they must be understood as they relate to and fit within the context of local communities in order to gain legitimacy and acceptance. In Africa, differences and variations (i.e. societal, political, institutional, historical, spatial, and temporal) between communities are enormous, and solutions cannot be designed uniformly. To circumvent these complexities, the BOP business model celebrates the importance of partnership – between and among the public sector, private sector, civil society, and local communities – as an integral part of any solution structure. Defining multiple layers of partners throughout the value chain provides possible solutions for the barriers, as defined by the BOP business model, viz. awareness, affordability, availability/accessibility, and acceptability (Prahalad, 2005). All in all, BOP ventures differ in comparison to other market-based poverty alleviation models. London (2008) identified six principles, namely: external participation, co-creation, connecting local with non-local, patient innovation, self-financed growth, and focusing on what is "right" at the BOP. Table 1.2 below illustrates the mechanism of each principle.

The BOP population faces severe constraints, as both consumers and producers, in sectors such as nutrition, education, healthcare, insurance, and credit. These constraints make BOPM the largest untapped market in the world. However, as hundreds of companies that operate in BOPM do not deliver as they hoped for, with the majority exiting the market (London, 2016), developing a sustainable and scalable business model in BOPM continues to be a challenge. In the next section, we explore these challenges, barriers, drivers, and the future of BOP in Africa with a group of experts.

Experts' views on the BOPMs in Africa

The BOPM in Africa is diverse and ever expanding. The 2016 Euromonitor International[6] statistics showed that Nigeria, Kenya, and South Africa were the three largest BOPMs in Africa in terms of the total expenditure by BOP households, accounting for over 16 million households with an annual disposable income of below US$2,500. It is estimated that BOP households

Table 1.2 Principles of BOP concept

Principle	Mechanism
External participation	The involvement of external partners like MNCs, domestic firms, NGOs, non-native entrepreneurs, etc. The diverse actors enable conditions to emerge for missing marketplaces.
Co-creation	Working in BOPM requires a social capital approach where customers, local companies, and entrepreneurs are stakeholders. The local knowledge facilitates operation and social legitimacy of the solution for the external actor. In many cases, innovation, skills, and co-discovery of opportunities flow down from the external company to local markets, and up from BOPM to affluent markets.
Connecting local with non-local	Facilitate access to inaccessible markets by either connecting non-local goods and services to BOPMs (BOP-as-consumer) or connecting BOP producers of goods and services to non-local markets (BOP-as-producer).
Patient innovation	Business model development at the BOP is a long innovative process which requires patient capital.
Self-financed growth	BOP ventures are scalable business models which synergise profits and poverty alleviation.
Focusing on what is "right" at the BOP	BOP initiatives do not push external solutions on the local marketplace but rather build bottom-up and develop from existing capabilities of the BOP community (pull). This is less likely to disrupt the existing informal sector and is welcomed by the local community (accessibility).

Source: Authors' own construction based on London (2008).

will reach 20.4 million by 2030 with a total spending of US$52.0 billion. To enrich our understanding of the nature of BOP initiatives and marketplaces in Africa, in autumn 2019 we interviewed three experts – Professor Cees van Beers, Niek van Diik, and Beryl Oyier – who have a wealth of knowledge and experience through their research and practical experience in developing and implementing market-based solutions to poverty alleviation in Africa. Their insights into different topics around BOPM in Africa are very illuminating and widen our understanding of the topic.

Cees van Beers

Cees van Beers is full professor of Innovation Management and Head of the section Economics of Technology and Innovations. He is also one of the co-leaders of the Leiden Delft Erasmus (LDE) Centre for Frugal Innovations in Africa. He holds a Doctorate in Economics (PhD) from the Free University Amsterdam. He worked at the University of Leiden as an assistant professor, the Institute for Research on Public Expenditure in the Hague as a senior researcher, and as Associate Professor of Innovation Economics at Delft University of Technology. He has also worked as consultant and expert for several international organisations, such as the OECD, FAO, and the World Bank.

Niek van Dijk

Fascinated and motivated by the crossroads of agribusiness development and food security, with a particular interest in making this work for consumers in low-income markets, Niek van Dijk has been working for BOP Innovation Center for close to seven years as a senior programme manager on different inclusive agribusiness projects, most notably the 2SCALE programme. Niek has a master's degree in International Relations from the University of Groningen, the Netherlands. Prior to joining BOP Innovation Center, he gained extensive experience working on agribusiness and food security in different policy positions at the Dutch Ministries of Agriculture and Foreign Affairs and CSR Netherlands.

Beryl Oyier

Beryl is the Managing Director for the East Africa office at BOP Innovation Center (Kenya). Her work entails guiding programmes and companies, both MNCs and SMEs, in inclusive business models working with inclusive innovation tools, inclusive business empowerment tools, and generating marketing and distribution strategies for low-income communities to spur entrepreneurship and empowerment. She has facilitated projects in agri-food, renewable energy, and WASH with a focus on gender transformative models. Beryl's experiences have been attained through a career spanning over ten years and gathering relevant experience in different low-income community environments including urban, peri-urban, and rural Kenya, and supporting activities in Zambia, Tanzania, Uganda, and Ethiopia. Beryl has both a Master of Arts and Bachelor of Arts in Anthropology from the University of Nairobi.

What are the main characteristics of BOPMs in the Africa context, in particular concerning innovation, business models, networks, challenges, etc.?

Cees van Beers: The BOP markets in Africa are characterised by severe resource constraints on both the producer and consumer sides of the market. The consumers, who are at the end of the value chain in the BOPM, often cannot afford a lot because they live on US$2 or less per day, unless there is some kind of a business model that takes that into account. On the producers' side, they have to perform their technical and economic activities in environments characterised by a lot of voids (i.e. technical, technological, and physical infrastructure) in many countries in sub-Saharan Africa. If one wants to innovate for markets like this, then one has to take into account these severe resource constraints in the design of products, services, or systems. To do this, the innovation process right from the beginning should define what the constraints in the outside world are, then adapt the design process to take these constraints into account. The business model must be sustainable right from the beginning because, if the product is designed in a very frugal way but the business model does not account for this, then the company's innovation will not be successful. Of course, it will remain a nice invention that demonstrates technological success, but it will never be an innovation if it lacks both technological and commercial success!

Niek van Dijk: One thing to bear in mind is that you cannot assess the continent as a whole: there are some differences in the maturity of BOPMs between Anglophone and Francophone countries. However, we can see a trend in the increase in support from incubators, accelerators, and initiatives that focus on enabling and encouraging more innovative products and services tailored to BOP markets across Africa, in particular in Kenya and Nigeria, but also in other countries. Africa witnesses a rise of start-ups and companies that provide truly needed products and services in, what I would call, "basic needs sectors", like agriculture, renewable energy, water and sanitation, and healthcare. What is also good is that there is a solid base of intermediary organisations that help foster innovations in these sectors. This could be further strengthened by the increased attention universities and vocational institutions give to studying BOPM. On the business model side, the main goal of a BOP business model or inclusive business model is to ultimately have a true and commercially sustainable impact by involving people at the BOP, whether they are producers, consumers, employees, or micro-entrepreneurs. For these business models to succeed, it is extremely important to collect data and insights on BOP consumers and producers so as to make a convincing case for companies to more actively target BOPM across Africa.

Beryl Oyier: The BOPM is a significant US$5 trillion market[7] of which US$215 billion is from sub-Saharan Africa. However, globally, 821 million BOP consumers are yet to be reached. This is a great business potential for products and services here in Africa. It is good, too, from a development perspective. But the big question remains: how might business interventions or ventures reach the BOPM? How do we work with micro-entrepreneurs and micro-enterprises to reach the BOPM? The BOPM is highly driven by market approaches which are driven by push rather than pull factors. We need to be innovating and developing new last-mile distribution models to reach the BOP population who naturally live in remote rural areas where infrastructure is poor. A viable business model is imperative, as the BOP population do not go into the mainstream markets to access products but rather buy from the little kiosks or shops that are available within the locales they can easily access.

Who do you consider as the main players in the BOPMs in Africa?

Cees van Beers: On the demand side are the local consumers and communities who are end users of new products and services. On the supply side are companies including local entrepreneurs, transnational, and multinational companies from all over the world, including those emerging from developing countries such as Tata Steel from India. I think MNCs can be very important as they know how to scale up innovations in the BOPMs. They are able to capture value as well as create value locally for the BOP community. The point is to come up with a business model that overcomes the tension between value capturing, which is profit for the MNC, and value creation for the local economy. SMEs are other important players who probably have a bigger advantage over MNCs as they are much more used to working in an environment where resource constraints are severe.

Perhaps the challenge SMEs have is that of scaling up innovations. In my opinion, MNCs, SMEs, and the BOP community have to work together. Innovation these days is not born in one company. Whereas innovation is done inside a company, information from outside is needed in order to make the innovation a reality. Obviously, MNCs need local knowledge that can be acquired from local entrepreneurs. MNCs need to involve local stakeholders in the whole innovation process right from the start. SMEs and local entrepreneurs provide the innovative company with relevant information that increases the chances of making the frugal innovation a success. They also distribute the innovation of the new products, services, or systems through their local outlets. For example, it is important to have these local companies and/or players on board to achieve last-mile delivery in remote rural areas.

Niek van Dijk: In publications, disproportionate attention is paid to what products and services MNCs provide to BOPMs, especially in the Fast-Moving Consumer Goods (FMCG) sector. Companies like Unilever, Procter & Gamble, Nestlé, and many others have dedicated strategies to reach BOPMs. However, the ultimate group of companies to reach BOPMs are, and will continue to be, local SMEs. Intermediary organisations and progressive financiers like Acumen, Root Capital, and others can play a big role in the development of this segment. There are also more and more philanthropic organisations that play an increasingly important role, like the Gates Foundation and Rockefeller Foundation. There are also a few progressive government donors (primarily the Dutch, British, German, Swiss, and Scandinavian) who do a lot in financing activities to help these local SMEs reach the consumer market. The role of (local) governments in the BOPM in Africa is a challenging one. I think one of their roles should be to prepare the grounds and ensure and proactively foster an equal playing field. For instance, we have been working with a dairy multinational with a partnership with local farmers in Nigeria, and the government does play a great role in building the infrastructure that is needed for the collection of this milk in rural areas. If governments play a role in laying the groundwork for companies to do their jobs, that would be great. But we also have to be realistic: how involved should local governments really be in driving the development of the private sector?

Beryl Oyier: I think for us at the BOP Innovation Center, the key player is the BOP consumer who is an aspiring consumer despite their very little and/ or stagnant income. If you are trying to innovate or come up with products for them, it is essential to develop necessary, not luxurious, products. BOP consumers do not have that extra income to buy things that they may not need. It is equally important to bring the BOP consumer to play a role and interact with the different players in the value chain. The other important players are MNCs, SMEs, and governments. By and large, local SMEs play a bigger role than MNCs because (1) they innovate products that usually resonate locally, and (2) they create not only products but also employment and an entrepreneurship ecosystem for many low-income markets in the community. The main challenge is that these actors sometimes try to push innovations into the BOPMs and then try to figure out how to bring in a pull mechanism in order for the intervention or the initiative to be sustainable. The main element that would influence the sustainability of the initiative or enterprise is a deep understanding of consumer behaviour.

What are the main drivers of BOPMs in Africa?

Cees van Beers: Searching for profit opportunities is a key driver, and this equally applies for MNCs, local SMEs, and entrepreneurs. Whereas capturing value through profit to shareholders is necessary, it is equally important to create social value in the local economic environment, otherwise the whole market might turn against the company and the value capture will go down the drain.

Niek van Dijk: I would say the ultimate driver of any market should be the consumer. At the same time, relatively little attention is paid to understanding BOP consumer markets in Africa. The lack of market intelligence is a major barrier for the further development of the BOPM. We must get a better understanding of BOP consumer preferences, trends in consumption of food products, etc. I also see the companies themselves as an interesting driver. Next to the huge segment of local SMEs, there are more and more multinational companies that consider the African BOPM as the next market for global business development. Unilever, for instance, is now making profits more and more from BOPM as their growth is stagnating in some western markets. This will continue to be the case, even though we should not necessarily overestimate the role that multinationals can play. Lastly, what would really drive further development of BOPM is when companies collaborate in public-private partnerships in such a way that they can approach these often remote and scattered BOPMs in an integrated way. For instance, in agriculture, an integrated approach would be when companies that work with actors across the value chain, from the field all the way up to the end consumer, are brought together to see how they can collectively better serve and develop the market, like we do in the 2SCALE programme.

Beryl Oyier: Companies exist in this market for both social and business objectives. However, the key driver is usually their business goals followed by the social impact. Companies try to join the social and environmental conversations in order to push behaviour change to create awareness around their products or services. Companies are motivated by (1) the need to develop innovative approaches that reach the most remote BOPMs with affordable products/services, (2) the economies of scale, (3) pricing, which is a critical element, and (4) the acceptability of the intervention. Of course, the demand is already there. Governments sometimes support the BOPM when the innovation aligns with their political agendas. In many cases, the projects will be allowed (pushed) to work with no clear legislation or even consumer demand. Governments may also provide different incentives: for instance, in Kenya, the manufacturers as well as the SMEs are supported to create products that are demanded locally in the market. Manufacturing is one item on the government's Big Four agenda. The other three are food security, affordable housing, and affordable healthcare for all.

What are the main barriers of BOPMs in Africa?

Cees van Beers: On the side of the innovators who have the potential to scale up, BOPMs are sometimes considered not a very important market because the prices of products and services are extremely low. A company will require a very efficient process of developing and producing innovations to be successful. Nonetheless, the gain from BOPM is the deep market penetration where companies' profits are based on the vast amount of sales as opposed to high prices or profit margins. For many MNCs, venturing into these BOPMs is a tricky adventure because the markets are very different from those in Europe or the USA. BOPMs in Africa are characterised by voids – for example, regulations may be limited or insufficiently enforced. Having said that, the barriers are both objective and subjective. A subjective barrier is that foreign companies are a bit scared of being perceived by the local communities and NGOs as the capitalist enemy. Similarly, western MNCs in particular face a lot of competition in Africa from those from India and China who have more experience in producing for the BOPMs. The objective barrier is that the BOPMs in Africa are not very visible because, often, the consumers or producers operate in the informal economy. People who are working in the informal sector have no bookkeeping or bank accounts, and so it is very hard to know with certainty where the potential is.

Niek van Dijk: Some of the enablers that we discussed earlier have their flip sides. For instance, the governments can definitely play a bigger role in organizing a conducive market environment for companies to grow the BOPM.

However, at the same time, their policies (e.g. about market entrance) often also form barriers. Secondly, reaching the BOP can be challenging due to the uniqueness of the market itself. Both the literal as well as relative remoteness of BOP consumers to markets can make it extremely difficult for companies to reach the BOPM segment, to bridge the metaphorical "last mile". In our work in Africa, the four As (i.e. Awareness, Affordability, Availability, and Acceptability) as defined by CK Prahalad remain the most appropriate pathways to look at how to overcome the main barriers to reach BOPM. Next to obvious barriers, such as purchasing power (affordability), I think lack of awareness is one of the most difficult barriers to overcome in the African BOPM. Finding a way in which companies together with other stakeholders will work on increasing awareness on a topic like nutrition, for instance, is very important. Lastly, as I mentioned earlier, the lack of really rigorous consumer market research is affecting market performance and growth.

Beryl Oyier: We need to conduct a credible needs assessment of this market. Sometimes companies assume that their innovations are relevant or needed, but they later discover that this is not the case or the innovations are not working properly. BOPM's penetration is always a challenge. Accessibility and affordability of these innovations are tricky to design for. Sometimes the innovation exists, but the finances to operationalise it are not available. Capacity building is another barrier; for example, financial inclusion for the population or financial empowerment for local SMEs is very limited.

How have the BOP initiatives contributed to the advancement of sustainability more generally, and to the sustainable development of Africa?

Cees van Beers: Frugal innovation in BOPMs is a recent phenomenon, around ten years old. BOPMs are generally a small part of visible economic activities in Africa. In order to see a significant effect on sustainability or advancement of the SDGs, there must be some successful innovations that are scaled up. Local NGOs and communities start projects that are very sustainable, but the scale at which they produce makes it very difficult to say they contribute to the SDGs.

Niek van Dijk: There must be a sustainable approach to BOPM and, of course, ultimately the companies should be in the driver's seat. The partnership approach where companies are trying to foster collaboration among companies, governments, NGOs, and knowledge institutions holds the greatest potential to contribute to how we can create more sustainable business models.

Beryl Oyier: Designing business models where the four As are achieved is a big contribution to the market-based approaches to sustainability. BOP ventures do not give aid but, rather, they are embedded in a local value chain. As a result, local entrepreneurship opportunities are enabled, especially micro-entrepreneurship. Creating an entrepreneurship ecosystem lowers unemployment and increases the prosperity of the BOP population.

What are the limits of BOP to sustainability, and to sustainable development of Africa?

Cees van Beers: The biggest challenge as far as I can see is the creation of business models that do not collapse at the slightest counter movements. Sustainable business models should allow scaling up of the use of innovations in low-income groups at the BOPMs. The question is: what kind of business model can be used that really fits into the preferences of the people in the BOP and that creates social and economic value, particularly in remote rural areas?

Niek van Dijk: We do know from experience that being involved in BOPM requires companies to strike a very delicate balance between business interests and development interests. A way for companies to better manage this delicate balance is to engage in partnerships, for instance with governments, NGOs, and knowledge institutions. An eye-opening lesson for us was when our organisation was involved in a project some time ago where we worked on horticultural development in East Africa with a number of Dutch companies. We witnessed on several occasions a conflict of interest between the type of business solution that was needed locally and the interest of the Dutch companies. True and sustainable solutions for reaching BOPMs can be found somewhere in the middle. Looking at the SDGs, BOPM can basically contribute to all SDGs. I follow most closely the developments in the Netherlands where the Dutch government is setting up more and more public-private partnership financing instruments that are specifically tailored around some of the SDGs, like SDG2 (zero hunger), SDG5 (gender equality), and others. This is an important approach that underpins the sustainable way of looking at the future. From the evaluations of these funding instruments, I know that striking a balance and marrying all these different interests in one approach is very difficult.

Beryl Oyier: The biggest limit is the access to finance to local SMEs in order to start a relevant innovation or even to replicate a successful one into another community. Financial inclusion of customers is also critical. The challenge is how to make profit from BOP consumers without earning the distrust of households; I would call this a safe profit. Another limit is literacy. When a radical innovation is introduced to BOPM, the different literacy levels become relevant. In this respect, how BOP consumers access different variations of the innovation becomes a challenge.

What needs to be done to mitigate the negative consequences of BOP initiatives or ventures in Africa?

Cees van Beers: The most important thing is that innovations should be done in a polycentric way. This means engaging local stakeholders, creating different scenarios, and considering what can be done in the design of new innovations and business models. Companies also need to take into account, when designing a product or service, the negative consequences of that innovation on the local community. It is also possible that you might have a product that fits the local preferences but that is not really ethical or sustainable. If companies do not consider all these issues in the innovation development process, the local people may reject the innovation. In case of a foreign Western company, the company might run into trouble because the Western customers might not like the innovation for moral reasons. Consequently, the company is most likely to lose in both markets. Additionally, the governments have a role to play and should definitely be on board. Local governments in Africa and their administrations are not very effective. In theory, governments should play a role, but in practice there is a big "but"!

Niek van Dijk: This is difficult to answer in a general manner, as potential negative consequences are often quite specific and so is the approach to mitigate them. For example, when working on the inclusion of small farmers in value chains, quite often middlemen are crowded out, and consequently, they lose their economic position. Inclusive business models need to have an answer to what role these middlemen can still play in a more inclusive model for agricultural value chains, for instance, as service providers to farmers. If I were to pick one more particular negative consequence related to the development of BOPM that, in my opinion, should be tackled more actively, it would be finding a solution to the increasing volumes of waste, especially plastic packaging. How can we help companies to better develop food products and at the same time create a system to minimise the use of packaging materials or find models to re-use or recycle them? While there are some early-stage initiatives that focus on this challenge, in my opinion, they are not sufficient. We need to see how we can grow the number of, often local, companies that do a great job in collecting and valorising this waste, and create new jobs while doing this. Also, bigger companies like Unilever need to further step up their game in countering waste. Recently, several coalitions of companies working on tackling the waste challenge emerged in countries like Nigeria and Kenya, and more of these should see the light.

Beryl Oyier: First, before we innovate we need to have clear market research in order to generate insights of what the market needs are and the nature of these needs. We should then pilot the innovation before its commercial launch to ensure that the innovation actually works. Recognising what works and what does not before going full-scale is important for the sustainability of the innovation and its replication in other communities. The pilot also gives a clear evaluation of the positive or negative impact on the consumers.

What is the future of BOPMs in Africa?

Cees van Beers: The potential is high both in the short and medium run. I think if BOP products or services become very successful, this will lead to more economic development and, in turn, the local people in the BOP will be able to migrate to the middle-class. The implications are that the BOPM might become a bit less important, but this will take a very long time to achieve.

Niek van Dijk: I would say that the future is bright. Of course, we should question and be very cautious and careful of some of the abovementioned negative consequences of BOPM and how to mitigate them. The growing class of local SMEs that are tapping into these BOPMs is a clear sign that the market holds great potential. For the multinationals, becoming active in BOPM is no longer a nice-to-have but really a must-have. Initiatives focused on further developing BOPMs can help in solving many societal problems and challenges across Africa. For instance, the demographic dividend in many African countries is seen by many as a problem; youth unemployment rates are huge and are causing migration. But this demographic dividend can also be seen as a great economic asset when companies can provide the opportunities for these youth to find employment and economic opportunities. The future is bright if we manage to develop BOPMs in such a way that they can tackle the social and also the environmental challenges in Africa.

Beryl Oyier: This US$5 trillion market is growing and open to new technologies. The BOP consumers are curious and ready to adopt new solutions and services. This challenges the assumption among many businesses that the BOPM is a traditional market that does not look at new technologies and new innovations. The BOP consumers are very aspiring and constitute a great business opportunity. On the one hand, if companies tap into BOPM with a sustainable business model which also addresses the local developmental problems, they will be able to harvest big profits. On the other hand, creating innovations to solve problems such as nutrition, women empowerment, entrepreneurship, and gender inclusion is very important to the future of the continent.

Concluding remarks

Africa is a great business opportunity for BOP ventures to emerge. However, it is a different context that is "highly personalized, it challenges our understanding of both market and non-market strategies" (Barnard, Cuervo-Cazurra, & Manning, 2017, p. 9). The environment is volatile, and resources are scarce (Arnould & Mohr, 2005). Given that the BOP initiatives are not homogeneous and vary across geography and communities (Kolk et al., 2014), African BOP ventures may be different not only from the implicit view of BOP initiatives prevalent in the literature, but also in that they vary significantly across the African contexts. The complex dynamism of the context across Africa offers a broader understanding of contextualising BOP and how to address complex problems like the lack of institutional support, corruption, inequality, and conflicts, which might uncover specific determinants, patterns, and implications for BOPM in other contexts.

To address these grand challenges, both market- and non-market-based solutions are privileged by different state and non-state actors in the BOPM. A partnership approach amongst different actors, i.e. MNCs, SMEs, governments, intermediary organisations, progressive financiers and philanthropic donors, BOP consumers, and local communities, ought to be forged to advance the BOP market. However, the pursuit of development (social and environmental) and business (profit) goals are sometimes viewed as incongruous and the opposite of one another. For example, social ventures seem to struggle to reconcile and successfully address both business and developments goals (Battilana & Lee, 2014). The BOP business model might provide a solution to this dilemma as an opportunity to create social value in BOPM, even if the explicit social mission is absent. Panum et al. (2018) showed how six social enterprises in Kenya overcame the BOPM pressures and demands by adapting a BOP approach in order to access resources. Subsequently, they improved their commercial performance and remained true to the social missions. The problem seems to arise in the assessment of the overall impact of BOP and reporting the created social and environmental value; as a consequence, studies have focused on the value as created to the business, which is usually "profit" (Mason et al., 2013), and ignored the impact on the BOP population.

The wide range of actors in the BOP space, the different definitions of what constitutes the BOP population in the literature, challenges of collecting data at the BOP, paucity of empirical verification of successes and failures, and lack of agreed-upon constructs have dwarfed theory development and advancement of the field. Studies of poverty alleviation that could invoke the BOP are cross-fertilised and pursued under the guise of different literatures, such as development economics, microfinance, subsistence marketplaces, inclusive business, and social entrepreneurship, which seems to be the outcrop; some of the BOP business models use social entrepreneurship frameworks and vice versa (Simanis & Hart, 2008; Panum et al., 2018). As a result, by and large, there is little known empirical evidence of the overall impact of BOP initiatives to either BOP ventures or BOP communities (Dembek et al., 2019). This scarcity of reporting on the economic, social, and environmental impact of BOP initiatives has contributed to the claims that BOP ventures do not deliver on the anticipated promise of alleviating poverty through profits. Hart (2015, p.1), who is one of the advocates of the BOP approach, argues that "most BOP ventures and corporate initiatives over the past decade have either failed outright or achieved only moderate success at great cost".

We are beginning to see BOP case studies emerging from the African continent; however, research on the BOP in Africa continues to be scarce. In a recent systematic review conducted by Dembek et al. (2019), the authors found that only 10% (i.e. 29 of 276) of the articles published between 2002 and 2016 focused exclusively on Africa, as compared to 60% (i.e. 178 of 276) of the articles focused on Asia. With the developmental challenges that Africa continues to face, it is important to explore how market-based solutions might contribute to the sustainable development of the continent. All in all, a number of avenues for further research have emerged to build knowledge about the BOP in Africa, for example: 1) evaluating the effectiveness of BOP initiatives to alleviate poverty; 2) the role of the BOP community as co-creators, mutual value creation, and cross-sector partnerships; 3) incorporating and assessing the triple-bottom-line impact including the negative consequences of BOP initiatives on communities; 4) describing and contextualising BOP initiatives; and 5) financial inclusion and empowerment for both BOP enterprises and the BOP population. The findings can be marshalled to enhance the BOP model and enrich scholarship of how BOP ventures can succeed in highly complex and underdeveloped marketplaces. We add our voices to those who have called for more studies that help us understand how BOP initiatives operate within and across the intricate African contexts (Dembek et al., 2019; Kolk et al., 2014).

Notes

1 For a working definition and more on this inconsistency, see London (2016).
2 Often-cited BOP studies include Hindustan Lever Ltd. in India (subsidiary of Unilever), Celtel in Africa, Hewlett-Packard in Africa, Avon in South Africa, Cemex in Mexico, and SC Johnson in Kenya. Other players include: Amul is a cooperative in India and Grameen Bank is a local bank in Bangladesh.
3 Data downloaded on October 9, 2019 from the World Data Lab (n.d.).
4 Downloaded on October 3, 2019 from the World Resources Institute (n.d.).
5 Downloaded on October 9, 2010 from Baier and Hamel (2018).
6 Downloaded on October 3, 2019 from Euromonitor (2019).
7 For more on this, see World Bank (2019). Also see Hammond, Traner, Katz, Tran and Walker (2007), de Soto (2000) and London (2016).

References

Acquaah, M. (2007). Managerial social capital, strategic orientation, and organizational performance in an emerging economy. *Strategic Management Journal, 28*(12), 1235–1255.
Arnould, E., & Mohr, J. (2005). Dynamic transformations for Base-of-the-Pyramid market clusters. *Journal of the Academy of Marketing Science, 33*(3), 254–274.
Baier, J., & Hamel, K. (2018). *Africa: The last frontier for eradicating extreme poverty.* Retrieved from Brookings Institute website: www.brookings.edu/blog/future-development/2018/10/17/africa-the-last-frontier-for-eradicating-extreme-poverty/
Banerjee, A., & Duflo, E. (2011). *Poor economics: A radical rethinking of the way to fight global poverty.* New York: PublicAffairs/Perseus Books Group.
Barnard, H., Cuervo-Cazurra, A., & Manning, S. (2017). Africa business research as a laboratory for theory-building: Extreme conditions, new phenomena, and alternative paradigms of social relationships. *Management and Organization Review, 13*(3), 467–495.
Battilana, J., & Lee, M. (2014). Advancing research on hybrid organizing – Insights from the study of social enterprises. *Academy of Management Annals, 8*(1), 397–441.
Bewayo, E., & Portes, L. (2016). Environmental factors for social entrepreneurship success: Comparing four regions. *American Journal of Management, 16*(4), 39–56.
Bill & Melinda Gates Foundation (2019). *The Goalkeepers report: Examining inequality 2019.* Retrieved from: www.gatesfoundation.org/goalkeepers/report/2019-report/
Caneque, F. C., & Hart, S. L. (2017). *Base of the Pyramid 3.0: Sustainable development through innovation and entrepreneurship.* New York: Routledge.

Dasgupta, P., & Hart, S. L. (2017). Creating an innovation ecosystem for inclusive and sustainable business. In F. C. Caneque & S. L. Hart (Eds.), *Base of the Pyramid 3.0: Sustainable development through innovation and entrepreneurship* (pp. 96–109). New York: Routledge.

Davies, I. A., & Torrents, A. (2017). Overcoming institutional voids in subsistence marketplaces: A Zimbabwean entrepreneurial case. *Journal of Macromarketing, 37*(3), 255–267.

Dembek, K., Sivasubramaniam, N., & Chmielewski, D. A. (2019). A systematic review of the Bottom/Base of the Pyramid literature: Cumulative evidence and future directions. *Journal of Business Ethics*, 1–18.

De Soto, H. (2000). *The mystery of capital: Why capitalism triumphs in the West and fails everywhere else.* New York: Basic Books.

Easterly, W. (2006). *The white man's burden: Why the West's efforts to aid the rest have done so much ill and so little good.* Oxford: Oxford University Press.

Euromonitor. (2019). Africa's three largest BOP markets. Retrieved from https://blog.euromonitor.com/three-largest-BOP-markets-africa/

Euromonitor. (n.d.). Euromonitor Blog. Retrieved from https://blog.euromonitor.com/

Follman, J. (2012). BOP at ten: Evolution and a new lens. *South Asian Journal of Global Business Research, 1*(2), 293–310.

Hammond, A. L., Kramer, W. J., Katz, R. S., Tran, J. T., & Walker, C. (2008). The next 4 billion: Characterizing BOP markets. *Development Outreach, 10*(2), 7–26.

Hart, S. L. (2015). BOP 2.0: The next generation of strategy for the Base of the Pyramid. In S. A. Mohrman, J. O'Toole, & E. E. Lawler III (Eds.), *Corporate stewardship: Achieving sustainable effectiveness* (pp. 190–204). Sheffield, UK: Greenleaf Publishing.

Hart, S. L. (2017). Prologue: Defining the path towards a BOP 3.0. In F. C. Caneque & S. L. Hart (Eds.), *Base of the Pyramid 3.0: Sustainable development through innovation and entrepreneurship* (pp. 1–4). New York: Routledge.

Karnani, A. (2007). The mirage of marketing to the Bottom of the Pyramid: How the private sector can help alleviate poverty. *California Management Review, 49*(4), 90–111.

Karnani, A. (2010). Failure of the libertarian approach to reducing poverty. *Asian Business & Management, 9*(1), 5–21.

Kolk, A., Rivera-Santos, M., & Rufin, C. (2014). Reviewing a decade of research on the "Base/ Bottom of the Pyramid" (BOP) concept. *Business & Society, 53*(3), 338–377.

Kolo, J., Madichie, N. O., & Mbah, C. H. (2019). Commonomics: Rhetoric and reality of the African growth tragedy. In V. Ratten, P. Jones, V. Braga, & C. S. Marques (Eds.), *Subsistence entrepreneurship: The interplay of collaborative innovation, sustainability and social goals* (pp. 17–32). Cham, Switzerland: Springer, Cham.

London, T. (2008, August). The Base-of-the-Pyramid perspective: A new approach to poverty alleviation. Paper presented at the Academy of Management Proceedings.

London, T. (2016). *The Base of the Pyramid promise: Building businesses with impact and scale.* Stanford, CA: Stanford Business Books, an imprint of Stanford University Press.

Mason, K., Chakrabarti, R., & Singh, R. (2013). What are Bottom of the Pyramid markets and why do they matter? *Marketing Theory, 13*(3), 401–404.

Mason, K., Chakrabarti, R., & Singh, R. (2017). Markets and marketing at the Bottom of the Pyramid. *Marketing Theory, 17*(3), 261–270.

Moyo, D. (2009). *Dead aid: Why aid is not working and how there is a better way for Africa.* New York: Farrar, Straus and Giroux.

Panum, K., Hansen, M. W., & Davy, E. (2018). The illusive nature of social enterprise at the Base of the Pyramid: Case studies of six Kenyan social enterprises. *Journal of Entrepreneurship in Emerging Economies, 10*(2), 249–276.

Prahalad, C. K. (2005). *The fortune at the Bottom of the Pyramid.* Upper Saddle River, NJ: Wharton School Pub.

Prahalad, C. K., & Gouillart, E. (2008). An interview with CK Prahalad. *Journal of International Affairs, 62*(1), 215–227.

Prahalad, C. K., & Hammond, A. (2002). Serving the world's poor, profitably. *Harvard Business Review, 80*(9), 48–59.

Prahalad, C. K., & Hart, S. L. (2002). Fortune at the Bottom of the Pyramid. *Strategy + Business, 26,* 2–14.

Prahalad, C. K., & Lieberthal, K. (1998). The end of corporate imperialism. *Harvard Business Review, 76*(4), 68–80.

Rivera-Santos, M., Holt, D., Littlewood, D., & Kolk, A. (2015). Social entrepreneurship in sub-Saharan Africa. *Academy of Management Perspectives, 29*(1), 72–91.

Sachs, J. (2005). *The end of poverty: How we can make it happen in our lifetime.* London: Penguin.

Simanis, E., & Hart, S. L. (2008). *The Base of the Pyramid protocol: Toward next generation BOP strategy (Version 2.0).* Ithaca, NY: Cornell University Press.

World Bank. (2018). Global economic prospects: The turning of the tide? Retrieved from the World Bank Group website: https://elibrary.worldbank.org/doi/abs/10.1596/978-1-4648-1257-6

World Bank. (2019). Global consumption database. Retrieved from http://datatopics.worldbank.org/consumption/

World Data Lab. (n.d.). Making everyone count. Retrieved from the World Data Lab website: https://worlddata.io/

World Resources Institute. (n.d.). BOP market by income segment: Africa – $429 billion. Retrieved from the World Resources Institute website: www.wri.org/resources/charts-graphs/BOP-market-income-segment-africa-429-billion

2 Why do firms choose to fight poverty?

The motivation behind inclusive business practices in Africa

Addisu A. Lashitew and Rob van Tulder

Introduction

Over one-third of the world's population lives in extreme poverty, out of which the share of Africa remains large and rising. In spite of decades of international efforts made through the Millennium Development Goals (MDGs) and subsequently the Sustainable Development Goals (SDGs), a world of zero poverty appears to be out of reach for decades to come (George, Howard-Grenville, Joshi, & Tihanyi, 2016). There is a growing realization that a successful effort to eradicate poverty globally takes more than governmental action and requires the active efforts of all societal actors, including civil society and business organizations. There is particular interest in leveraging the vast technological and organizational capabilities of businesses to devise market-based strategies that can help mitigate some of society's grand challenges (van Tulder, 2018).

The question of how businesses can align their strategies with developmental aspirations such as poverty alleviation is hence a highly relevant research domain. A growing body of research explores how businesses can create "shared" or "blended" value by pursuing strategies that advance competitive performance in a manner that reduces social issues, such as poverty, inequality, and environmental waste (Porter & Kramer, 2011; Prahalad, 2004). The potential for profitable ventures is especially likely to be bountiful in lower-income economies, also called Base of the Pyramid (BOP) countries, that experience widespread social issues including poverty and lack of public goods. *Inclusive businesses* are commercial businesses that seek to create profit by addressing social issues through their core operations by taking advantage of social problems that provide untapped business opportunities (Prahalad, 2004; London & Hart, 2004). As opposed to traditional corporate social responsibility (CSR) practices, which tend to decouple social issues from strategic considerations, inclusive businesses aim to improve the social wellbeing of BOP inhabitants as part of their core business strategy (Halme, Lindeman, & Linna, 2012).

Growing research in social entrepreneurship, BOP strategies, and business sustainability literatures has started to document the various challenges that inclusive businesses face, along with potential coping strategies. There is, however, relatively limited systematic research efforts to understand the underlying organizational motivations and processes of inclusive business practices, especially in lower-income economies (Kolk, Rivera-Santos, & Rufin, 2014). This is in part because of factors such as lack of data availability and shortage of time, resources, networks, and socio-cultural and institutional gaps (Mol, Stadler, & Ariño, 2017).

To help bridge this gap, this chapter looks into the motivational factors that drive businesses in Africa to take up poverty alleviation as part of their business strategy. Motivations for inclusiveness emanate from organizational culture and values, which in turn have roots in the value system of their senior managers and founders (Stevens, Moray, & Bruneel, 2015; van Tulder, 2018). Inclusive business practices can be inspired by intrinsic motives that attribute inherent value to social causes, or market-oriented extrinsic motives, or a mixture of these two (Mair & Naboa, 2006). Intrinsic motives are related to ethical standards, such as fairness and justice, or psychological cues related to sympathy and moral judgement (Patzelt & Shepherd, 2011). Extrinsic motives, also known as economic motives, are founded in rational views related to the interdependence between social and economic outcomes (Bansal & Roth, 2000; Miller, Grimes, McMullen, & Vogus, 2012). While intrinsically motivated firms are mainly driven by the desire to alleviate social issues, extrinsically motivated businesses tend to consider social issues as a means for achieving financial competitiveness through increased reputation, brand image, and market access. The relative significance of each of these motives, as well as their co-occurrence, will not only affect the mechanisms through which the firm seeks to create social value, but also influence its success in creating social impact (Lashitew, Bals, & van Tulder, 2018).

To understand how motivations affect strategic decision making in relation to inclusive business practices, this study develops a conceptual model that relates different motivation types to different inclusive business approaches and strategies. We subsequently generate hypotheses on how motivation types (intrinsic, extrinsic, mixed) are associated with the adoption of inclusiveness practices. We test our hypotheses using a survey dataset of 430 small- and medium-sized businesses that are frontrunners of inclusive business practices in seven sub-Saharan African countries. This dataset covers a purposefully selected sample of inclusive businesses that address social issues through their core operations. The empirical results show that intrinsic motivations are more important than extrinsic motivations in driving inclusiveness in various domains, including employee development, business ecosystem development, and other functional areas of inclusion. Among larger firms, however, we find that economically related extrinsic motives are paramount in certain domains of inclusive business practice. Finally, we find that extrinsic and intrinsic motives do not appear to reinforce each other, pointing to the limited incidence of mixed motives among frontrunner inclusive businesses in Africa.

The remaining parts of the chapter are organised as follows. Section 2 lays out our conceptual approach that relates motivation types to different inclusive business strategies. Section 3 builds on this framework to outline a set of our hypotheses. Section 4 describes our data collection procedures and outlines the operationalization of key constructs. Section 5 presents the results of the empirical analysis, and Section 6 concludes the chapter.

Conceptual framework

The motives for inclusive business practices

Research into prosocial organizational practices distinguishes between *intrinsic motives* that are altruistic in nature, and *extrinsic motives* that are underpinned by economic rewards (Mair & Noboa, 2006; Muller & Kolk, 2010). These motives are rooted in the value system of top managers and founders, which can have a profound effect on strategy making, especially among small and young firms where shorter hierarchies and limited institutional memories enable more direct managerial influence (Stevens et al., 2015; van Tulder, 2018). The dominant research paradigm in CSR underscores that social responsibility practices are primarily driven by the extrinsic, or more specifically economic, motive of advancing competitiveness and profitability (Muller & Kolk, 2010). A vast segment of the stakeholder management literature likewise views prosocial stakeholder strategies in light of their potential to improve competitiveness by enhancing legitimacy, lowering transaction and agency costs, and facilitating the exploitation of external opportunities (Laplume, Sonpar, & Litz, 2008).

Intrinsic motives that derive from the emotional and cognitive attributes of entrepreneurs or managers can also be important drivers of inclusiveness (Patzelt & Shepherd, 2011). Intrinsic motives are related to normative behavioural responses, such as sympathy, empathy, and a sense of moral obligation to "do the right thing" (Bansal & Roth, 2000; Miller et al., 2012). Mair and Noboa (2006) argue that emotional and cognitive factors, such as empathy and moral judgement (obligation), determine entrepreneurs' perceptions of the desirability of creating social enterprises. Bansal and Roth (2000) find that a sense of moral obligation to provide the "social good" was an important imperative for corporate sustainability initiatives. Businesses can also take up social causes out of a sense of duty of corporate citizenship and stewardship towards their stakeholders (Hahn, Pinkse, Preuss, & Figge, 2015). In smaller and younger firms, these values tend to be embodied by managers and founders, whereas in larger ones they can take the form of a shared sense of organizational purpose and culture (Hollensbe, Wookey, Hickey, George, & Nichols, 2014; Husted & Allen, 2007).

While economic and intrinsic motives constitute two different drivers of inclusive business practices, they are not mutually exclusive and indeed often occur together (Baron, 2009). Researchers have looked into the interplay between intrinsic and extrinsic motives in shaping social strategies and performance. Hahn, Pinkse, Preuss, and Figge (2016) argue that ambidextrously balancing between instrumental and normative prescriptions for social engagement can lead to greater social performance. Muller and Kolk (2010) document how extrinsic and intrinsic motivations reinforce each other to boost corporate social performance in emerging countries. Bansal and Roth (2000) report the presence of both pragmatic and ethical motives behind corporate sustainability initiatives. Recent calls towards greater business engagement with social issues, such as poverty alleviation and sustainability, are predicated upon the view that economic and normative motives can coexist and complement each other (Porter & Kramer, 2011; London & Hart, 2004).

How motives affect inclusiveness strategies

Understanding the motives for inclusiveness can shed light on firms' heterogeneous choices of inclusiveness strategies and, consequently, their different levels of success (van Tulder, 2018). Traditionally, corporate social responsibility has been associated with the use of social and environmental initiatives for improving brand image, although this view has started to give way to strategic approaches towards CSR that attribute greater strategic value to social initiatives (Baron, 2009). More recent research into BOP markets and sustainable business models considers more radical approaches that place social and environmental causes at the heart of strategic decision making (Porter & Kramer, 2011). These approaches emphasize the need to develop and exploit synergies between the intrinsic drive to improve social and environmental outcomes and the economic motivation of achieving sustainable value creation. These trends indicate a fundamental shift in the underlying motivations for prosocial organizing, which range from purely intrinsic to purely economic. Firms at a given time period are also likely to be driven by different combinations of motivations, leading to varying approaches and strategies and, consequently, differences in organizational performance. Figure 2.1 introduces a framework that captures the relationship between intrinsic and extrinsic motives on the one hand, and the choice of inclusive business strategies on the other. The figure identifies four inclusiveness strategies that vary depending on the level of the two motivational types.

A. Laissez faire (disengagement)

A large share of businesses can be characterized as disengaged from social issues, in part due to the absence of any form of motives for doing so. Firms that lack intrinsic and extrinsic motives thus remain disengaged from social issues, failing to recognize and act upon social issues even when they could have provided profitable business opportunities. If they address social issues at all, such firms do so through ad hoc philanthropic initiatives that are decoupled from their core business operations and, thus, are unlikely to be sustained or pursued with strategic focus.

B. Instrumental strategies

The dominant focus on economic outcomes in mainstream businesses means that corporate sustainability and social responsibility are seen as instrumental

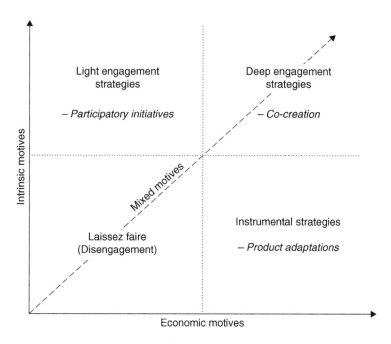

Figure 2.1 A framework relating motivational types with inclusive business strategies.
Source: The authors.

for advancing financial performance (Hahn et al., 2015). The instrumental view of stakeholder theory, for example, emphasizes proactively anticipating, managing, and responding to the demands of salient stakeholders to advance competitive advantage (Laplume et al., 2008). Strategic CSR likewise asserts the advantage of integrating a company's social practices with its business and corporate-level strategies to attract socially responsible customers (Baron, 2009). In BOP economies, instrumental strategies related to poverty allevi-ation include interventions in the firm's value chain to empower primary stakeholders (Garcia-Castro & Francoeur, 2016). This could involve innovating products and services that meet local needs or modifying the value chain to make (socially valuable) products affordable to the poor (Anderson & Markides, 2007; Prahalad, 2004). An example of instrumental strategies is the practice of contract farming, whereby agribusiness firms such as breweries try to support small-scale farmers that supply their raw materials (Reficco & Márquez, 2012).

Instrumental strategies are viewed favourably due to their win-win outcomes, which boost competitiveness while also creating social impact (Prahalad, 2004). The firm can gain intangible benefits, such as improved reputation and brand image, or economic advantages, such as market access, higher quality raw materials, and improved productivity in the value chain (Brugmann & Prahalad, 2007; Reficco & Márquez, 2012). Instrumental strategies, however, are likely to have limited potential to achieve transformative social change, which will require sustained effort to develop radically new capabilities (Dembek, Singh, & Bhakoo, 2016; Nahi, 2016). Lacking the intrinsic motive and the associated drive to radically adapt its internal strategies, the firm is likely to settle for piecemeal strategies such as superficial product adaptations. It thus fails to exploit the potential for reconfiguring its core activities to develop new capabilities that can advance social value. For example, instrumental strategies that emphasized "selling to the poor" at the BOP have been criticized for lack of genuine interest in addressing deeper social problems, such as poverty and low productivity (Anderson & Markides, 2007; Dembek et al., 2016).

C. Light engagement strategies

When intrinsic motives are dominant, the firm is likely to employ engagement strategies that address salient social issues but might not necessarily have a business case. The emphasis on social causes will lead to inclusiveness strategies that are primarily concerned with empowering social stakeholders, often regardless of their business relevance. Examples of light engagement strategies are participatory social initiatives that aim to empower disadvantaged and fringe stakeholders by giving them voice or building their capabilities (Nahi, 2016). Such participatory approaches are said to facilitate effective social action by enabling proper diagnosis of complex and multi-faceted social issues (Austin & Seitanidi, 2012).

Light engagement strategies will not have strategic significance due to their weak connection with the firm's core capabilities and strategic aims. As a result, managers will find it difficult to justify allocating significant time, resources, and attention to these initiatives. The provisional and short-term nature of the initiatives consequently inhibits learning and capability development, which require multiple loops of iterative adaptation. Since the involved stakeholders are also typically beneficiaries rather than business partners with their own resources, these initiatives fail to develop new capabilities through the integration of the firm's resources with those of its stakeholders. Their scope, therefore, will be limited to making one-off, incremental welfare changes to the targeted beneficiaries rather than achieving systemic and transformative social change (Husted & Allen, 2007). Partnerships between multinational corporations and NGOs at the BOP – for example, to preserve biodiversity and wildlife – can be characterized as asymmetric and having limited transformative potential because the involved multinationals lack sufficient economic motivation to commit attention and resources to develop meaningful solutions (Hahn & Gold, 2014).

D. Deep engagement strategies

Deep engagement strategies that involve significant engagement with social issues require strong alignment between the firm's economic motives and its intrinsic drive for creating impact (Porter & Kramer, 2011; Prahalad, 2004).

Deep engagement is often attended by fundamental appreciation of the interconnected nature of social challenges and the need for collaborative approaches to convert complex social issues into business opportunities (Rivera-Santos, Rufin, & Kolk, 2012). Such strategies leverage ideas and resources from internal and external sources to create unique business solutions that sustainably mitigate social issues (Austin & Seitanidi, 2012; Brugmann & Prahalad, 2007; Nahi, 2016). Compared to instrumental and light engagement strategies that involve transactional, piecemeal approaches for creating social value (Austin & Seitanidi, 2012), deep engagement involves intensive co-creation endeavours that integrate the distinct capabilities of diverse societal actors for achieving systemic change. Deep, intense, and sustained engagement with the right partners leads to mobilization of diverse resources and development of the requisite capabilities for achieving transformational change (Austin & Seitanidi, 2012). BOP firms that aim to create long-term impact thus require strong social ties with a diversity of organizations and institutions, which facilitates the emergence of "native capabilities" through the effective combination of local and global knowledge (Hart & London, 2005; Webb, Kistruck, Ireland, & Ketchen, 2010). Implementing deep engagement strategies could further necessitate structural integration of social and commercial goals through novel, purpose-driven organizational identities that balance between the two competing goals (Lashitew et al., 2018).

Successful deep engagement strategies among commercial businesses are rare, which testifies to the significant organizational and institutional constraints that inhibit the development of hybrid motives. In a study of an exceptionally successful case, Lashitew et al. (2018) document how the Kenyan telecom firm, Safaricom, developed a hybrid, mission-driven identity through a lengthy process of experimentation with inclusive business practices. Having built a brand image as a national champion, Safaricom had strong social ties with a broad set of stakeholders, which heightened the incentive to internalize social issues by engaging in inclusive business practices. Its social embeddedness also enhanced the pragmatic feasibility of inclusive business practices, as it facilitated collaborations with banks and regulatory bodies, which was crucial for implementing deep engagement strategies. An important outcome of such strategies was the mobile money innovation of M-Pesa, which has extended financial access to tens of millions of users in Kenya and beyond while providing a major revenue source for the company. This example illustrates that, while deep engagement strategies are lengthy and involve intensive co-creation exercises, they also have the potential to transform the company and its social environment.

Hypotheses

Intrinsic motives

For social and hybrid businesses, addressing social issues typically constitutes the rationale of their existence, driving them to give precedence to social impact over financial profit (Mair & Marti, 2009). They are, hence, primarily driven by intrinsic motives related to the ethical concerns or problem-solving desires of their founders and top managers (Hart, Sharma, & Halme, 2016). Many social enterprises are established and run by entrepreneurs who aspire to leverage their technical and business skills towards resolving key constraints that beset their environment (George, McGahan, & Prabhu, 2012). These drives are related to cognitive and affective attributes such as empathy (i.e. the emotional recognition of others' needs) and moral judgement (i.e. the desire to search for a common good) that create an intrinsic drive to set up social ventures (Mair & Naboa, 2006, 128). Intrinsically-driven entrepreneurs develop deep and sympathetic understanding of local needs, which can be an important capability in BOP economies where market information and knowhow is not readily available (Prahalad, 2004). Sustained managerial passion and commitment can also be an asset among enterprises that partake in implementing complex and multi-stakeholder inclusive business initiatives.

In contrast, inclusiveness practices among larger firms are more likely to be driven by economic motives. Some of these drivers have to do with external pressures that force established firms to carve out new sources of competitive advantage. For example, the importance of poverty alleviation strategies at the BOP was mainly motivated on the grounds that they give access to new markets with higher growth potential than stagnant markets in developed economies (Prahalad, 2004). Another exogenous change driving inclusive business practices in advanced economies is an ever-increasing public awareness of sustainability issues. Pressure from interconnected and informed customers is a major driver behind organizational soul-searching towards more sustainable and inclusive business practices, and this is compounded by the ever-increasing visibility of social enterprises that cater to the needs of socially-conscious customers (Fosfuri, Giarratana, & Roca, 2016; van Tulder, 2018). Finally, many large corporations seek to develop a brand image as a sustainable, cause-driven company that is seen as likeable by employees and external stakeholders, with a general aim of advancing long-term competitiveness.

Many of the external pressures that push sustainable and inclusive business practices in advanced economies are not predominant in BOP economies. As a result, the economic motivation of using social issues as a means for advancing competitiveness is unlikely to be compelling in African markets. For example, building brand image as a cause-driven or sustainable business is not likely to be a source of market differentiation in Africa and other BOP markets with limited market information and customer awareness. Likewise, the use of inclusive businesses to achieve differentiation is likely to be limited to multinationals and a select set of local firms that deal with a small segment of brand-sensitive customers. For the vast majority of African firms, on the other hand, competitiveness will hinge upon operational efficiency and the ability to provide affordable products to highly price-sensitive customers. Surveys show that African businesses identify the low purchasing power of consumers and their high price sensitivity to be important market challenges (Lashitew & van Tulder, 2017).

The strategic view of social responsibility as a means of advancing long-run competitiveness, therefore, is unlikely to be a key driver of inclusive business practices in African contexts.

It is, hence, more likely that intrinsic rather than economic motives will be major drivers of inclusive business practices among frontrunner inclusive businesses in Africa. The pervasiveness of extreme poverty in African markets is likely to attract businesses that share the normative and empathic consideration of alleviating human suffering. Budding research into entrepreneurship performance in subsistence markets suggests that the motives that drive managerial decision in these contexts tend to have significant normative elements (Viswanathan, Sridharan, & Ritchie, 2010). The significance of cultural norms vis-à-vis formal governance mechanisms is thus likely to create strong managerial emphasis on normative considerations involving the advancement of collective welfare, reciprocity, maintaining the status quo, and nurturing social relationships (Bruton, Ahlstrom, & Obloj, 2008). We thus expect that intrinsic (rather than economic) motives will be foundational in driving inclusive business practices in Africa and other similar BOP economies:

Hypothesis 1: Intrinsic motives are major drivers of inclusive business performance among frontrunner inclusive businesses in BOP economies.

Extrinsic (economic) motives

As indicated above, economic drivers of inclusiveness tend to be underpinned by external changes in the economic and institutional environment, and these drivers are more likely to be pronounced among large firms. For example, large firms that have successfully exploited their base market have greater incentive to be on the lookout for new growth and diversification opportunities through sustainable business practices. Initial interest in BOP strategies was, for instance, fuelled by the big appetite of large enterprise for new markets, which tended to see the poor as untapped (potential) consumers in high-growth emerging economies. Seen this way, inclusive business at the BOP provided multinationals with an opportunity for redeploying their technological and organizational capabilities to make inroads into new markets with significant growth potential (Halme et al., 2012; Hart & London, 2005).

The drive to use inclusive business practices for building brand image and rehabilitating a damaged reputation are also likely to be more compelling for large enterprises that have larger customer bases and garner significant media attention. Major crises that spawn pronounced reputational damage can trigger such firms to adopt sustainable and inclusive business practices. Their visibility also pushes large companies to devise proactive stakeholder management strategies, which can range from building employee motivation and loyalty to actively reaching out to fringe stakeholders to elicit their cooperation (van Tulder, 2018). Large companies actively seek out win-win approaches that have material or reputational benefits while also addressing social value, thus offering an authentic "virtue signal" for targeted audiences. For example, corporations actively work with partners in BOP economies to ensure a sustainable and efficient supply chain, as in the case of Starbucks' initiatives to empower small-holder coffee farmers (Perez-Aleman & Sandilands, 2008).

Extrinsic motives are thus likely to be more important drivers of inclusiveness among large, established businesses that aim to build their brand image, increase market access, and find new growth opportunities. In comparison, inclusive business practices in small and young businesses are more likely to be driven by the commitment of their founders towards specific social causes. This leads to the following hypothesis:

Hypothesis 2: Extrinsic motives are important drivers of inclusive business performance among larger businesses.

Mixed motives

The conceptual diagram presented in Figure 2.1 suggests deep engagement approaches for inclusiveness are likely to be adopted when intrinsic and extrinsic motives coexist. Deep engagement strategies are unique for their capacity to create transformative impact, both in terms of social change and competitive advantages. The presence of a balanced mixed of intrinsic and extrinsic motives is crucial for facilitating the development of capabilities needed for implementing deep engagement strategies. Unfortunately, developing the right mix of motivations is likely to be tenuous, in part because of the difficulty to develop new organizational identities (van Tulder, 2018).

Most inclusive businesses tend to be driven either by a social cause, as in the case of social enterprises, or by the need to advance strategic advantages, as in the case of multinationals at the BOP. The identification with a single cause, as opposed to a hybrid cause that straddles intrinsic and economic motives, could stem from external pressures that reward institutional conformity. Hybrid firms for example, could struggle to meet certain institutionalized expectations, which reduces their regulative legitimacy (Battilana & Lee, 2014). An example is the failure of many social enterprises to enjoy the tax exemption advantages offered to civil society organizations, even when they provide similar services. Hybrids also tend to lack cognitive legitimacy as they do not fall neatly into pre-established mental templates, which reduces their ability to gain support from market and non-market actors (Mair & Marti, 2009). Since legitimacy is the mechanism through which value is recognized and resources are allocated, businesses could be forced to give primacy to either social or commercial goals to avoid clashes with institutions that confer access to financial, market, and relational resources.

Research into social enterprises highlights that even enterprises that consciously choose to develop mixed motives fall prey to internal conflicts and instabilities, especially when competing goals are perceived to be central but incompatible with each other (Battilana & Lee, 2014; Besharov & Smith, 2014). The challenging task of balancing between hybrid goals could easily collapse, for example, among social enterprises that experience mission drift towards financial goals in the face of intense market pressure (Yunus, Moingeon, & Lehmann-Ortega, 2010). In businesses where extrinsic motives are dominant, a marked shift towards intrinsic motives is unlikely to occur due to the difficulty of developing new hybrid identities. Developing a hybrid identity that balances between the two motives would involve significantly reframing the organization's goal and mission as well as adapting its capabilities and internal processes (Lashitew et al., 2018). This also explains why civil society organizations and social enterprises tend to continue to give explicit priority to social causes over commercial profit (Yunus et al., 2010), even when doing so limits their ability to fully exploit market opportunities (Kolk et al., 2014).

Given the difficulty of developing hybrid identities that draw on the right balance of the two motivational types, we anticipate that there will be few such firms among frontrunner inclusive businesses in Africa. The absence of a balanced mix of motives will consequently constrain deep engagement strategies that can have transformative social and commercial impact. We thus expect that intrinsic or extrinsic motives will not co-occur, and/or will not successfully reinforce each other in advancing inclusiveness performance in Africa and other BOP economies.

Hypothesis 3: Extrinsic and intrinsic motives will not reinforce each other in advancing inclusiveness among frontrunner inclusive businesses in BOP economies.

Methodology

Sampling and empirical framework

We use a survey dataset of frontrunner inclusive businesses in Africa to test the hypotheses developed in the previous section. The authors collected the data through fieldwork and an online survey covering questions related to the motives for engaging in inclusive business practices and performance in various domains of inclusiveness in 2015. The data collection yielded valid responses for 430 small- and medium-sized enterprises in seven sub-Saharan African countries – 108 of which came from the fieldwork, and 322 from the online survey. The largest number of observations came from Kenya (37% of sample), followed by Tanzania (18%), Uganda (16%), Ethiopia (12%), Nigeria (8%), Mozambique (4%), and Rwanda (4%).

Given the goal of our research, the survey purposefully targeted a subset of frontrunner businesses that actively pursued inclusive business practices. We selected firms that follow active inclusive business approaches, either from their business models (e.g. microfinance banks), from the social impact they created (as reported in their annual reports), or their strategies (e.g. agribusiness firms that integrate subsistence farmers in their supply chains). We framed all the survey questions in such a way that they indicated consciously chosen inclusive business practices rather than merely desired goals or inadvertently achieved outcomes. In both kinds of surveys, we made efforts to collect data from owners or senior managers with a minimum of two years of work experience. To reduce extreme heterogeneity in our data, we exclusively targeted privately owned small- and medium-sized enterprises, thus excluding microenterprises (with fewer than five workers) and large corporations (with 1,000 or more workers). This reduces the risk of including very large multinational firms or public enterprises that have significantly different motivations towards inclusiveness compared to the majority of small- and medium-sized private firms.

We use the following empirical specification to test our hypotheses:

$$Inclusiveness_{ijc} = \alpha(Int_{ijc}) + \beta(Ext_{ijc}) + \gamma(X_{ijc}) + \delta(D_j) + \theta(D_c) + (\varepsilon_{ijc}),$$

where i denotes the firm, j its industry, and c the country of location. The dependent variable, *inclusiveness*, includes a set of outcome variables that measure inclusive business performance in various domains. The independent variables of interest are *Int* and *Ext*, which measure intrinsic and extrinsic motives for inclusive business practices, respectively. X is a vector of firm-level control variables including measures of financial performance, firm size, age, foreign ownership, and self-identification as a social-enterprise. The inclusion of these variables ensures that we keep constant potentially confounding structural differences in age, size, and ownership while testing our hypotheses. Finally, D_j and D_c are sets of country and industry dummies that are included to capture institutional and economic variations across countries and other market-related structural differences across industries.

To test Hypothesis 1, we estimate the above equation, while its variations are estimated to test the other two hypotheses. Specifically, an interaction between *Ext* and *firm size* is included to test Hypothesis 2, and an interaction between *Ext* and *Int* is included to test Hypothesis 3.

Measurement of variables

Inclusive business performance. Inclusive businesses address social issues by catering for the social and economic needs of different "beneficiaries" through various "inclusiveness practices" (Mair, Battilana, & Cardenas, 2012). The beneficiaries can reside within the firm (e.g. employees), the value chain (e.g. suppliers), or outside the business ecosystem (e.g. women customers). Given the broad range of inclusive business practices and the multiplicity of the loci where social impact is created (Porter & Kramer, 2011), it is very difficult to capture inclusiveness through universally applicable and objective performance metrics. Our analysis is thus based on self-reported levels of performance in different domains of inclusive business practices. To capture the broad nature of inclusive business practices, we measure inclusive business performance in three different domains.

- **Human development**, covering three inclusive business practices that aim to advance human development through gender equality, employment creation, and employment quality.
- **Functional inclusion**, focusing on three inclusive business practices in selected economic functions that are pertinent to BOP markets, namely education and skills training, agricultural development, and financial access.
- **Ecosystem development**, including three inclusive business practices related to business ecosystem development by supporting microenterprises, small and medium enterprises (SMEs), and value chain partners.

All of the indicators of inclusiveness performance are measured using Likert-type perceptual response items with seven scales. Table 2.1 reports the specific questions that were asked for soliciting responses for these variables.

Intrinsic and extrinsic motives. We developed indicators of intrinsic and extrinsic motives by drawing on prior research on the drivers of corporate social and sustainability performance (Bansal & Roth, 2000; Mair & Noboa, 2006; Miller et al., 2012). To measure intrinsic motives, the survey included questions on the extent to which inclusive business practices were motivated by moral judgement ("doing the right thing") and altruistic behaviours such as sympathy. To measure economic motives, questions were included that assessed the extent to which inclusive business practices were motivated by goals such as improving brand image, reputation, and differentiation (see Table 2.1). For our analysis, we take the average values of four individual elements of intrinsic and extrinsic motives, respectively. The overall Cronbach's alpha amongst the respective indicators of the two motivation types was greater than 0.8, indicating strong internal consistency and reliability.

Control variables. As indicated in the regression framework, our analysis requires data on a number of control variables and financial performance. We measure financial performance using average performance based on five self-reported performance indicators: sales growth, profitability, return on capital, market share, and productivity. Further, we include firm size, age, foreign ownership, and self-identification as a social enterprise. The measurement of these variables is summarized in Table 2.1.

Results

Descriptive results

Table 2.2 reports descriptive statistics for the nine indicators of inclusive business performance. Since inclusiveness performance is likely to be heterogeneous across indicators, we conduct the analysis using each individual measure of performance rather than using group averages. Table 2.2 shows that all three elements in the human development category have average values of at least five, indicating relatively high performance in this domain of inclusive business

Table 2.1 Description of variable measurement

Inclusiveness performance

Indicate the extent to which your organization's core operations contribute towards addressing the following social issues [1 = *Extremely low* . . . 7 = *Extremely high*]

Human development
- Gender equality
- Job creation
- Employee development, equity, and diversity

Business ecosystem development
- Supporting informal and microenterprises
- Supporting small and medium businesses
- Developing other businesses in the value chain (e.g. suppliers and distributors)

Functional inclusion
- Education and skills training
- Agricultural development
- Access to financial services

Intrinsic motives

Indicate to what extent the following reasons explain your organization's motivation to increase its social performance or to create social impact [1 = *Extremely low* . . . 7 = *Extremely high*]
- Because we believe in giving back to our society
- Because we want to make good use of our knowledge and skills
- Because it gives purpose to our lives and those of our employees
- Because we are passionate about addressing social issues

Extrinsic motives

Indicate to what extent the following reasons explain your organization's motivation to increase its social performance or to create social impact [1 = *Extremely low* . . . 7 = *Extremely high*]
- Because it improves our image in the market
- Because it builds brand awareness among customers
- Because it can limit reputational damage
- Because it differentiates us from our competitors

Financial performance

Please assess your organization's performance compared to similar organizations in your industry using the criteria below [1= *Extremely low* . . . 7 = *Extremely high*]
- Sales growth
- Profitability
- Return on capital invested
- Market share
- Productivity

Control variables
- *Firm size* is measured using employment categories that range between one and seven.
- *Firm age* is measured using age cohorts that range between one and four.
- *Social enterprise* is a dummy variable with a value of one for firms that self-identify as social enterprises.
- *Foreign ownership* is a dummy variable with a value of one when the firm is (partially) foreign-owned.

Note: section heads indicated in the table were not included in the original questionnaires to avoid introducing bias in responses.

Source: the authors.

Table 2.2 Descriptive statistics of indicators of inclusiveness performance

	Obs	Mean	SD	Min	Max
Human development					
Gender equality	413	5.27	1.36	1	7
Employment creation	418	5.46	1.28	1	7
Employee development, equity, and diversity	422	5.28	1.31	1	7
Business ecosystem development					
Supporting informal businesses and microenterprises	379	5.12	1.59	1	7
Supporting small and medium businesses	388	5.31	1.51	1	7
Developing other businesses in the value chain	408	5.29	1.42	1	7
Functional inclusion					
Education and skills training	412	5.47	1.31	1	7
Agricultural development	357	4.68	1.85	1	7
Access to financial services	382	4.80	1.75	1	7

Note: all indicators are measured using Likert-type responses with a scale of seven (see Table 2.1).
Source: authors' calculations.

practices. The three measures of inclusiveness performance under the business ecosystem development category also have average responses of at least five. There is greater performance variation across indicators in the last category – i.e. functional inclusion. The average response to education and skills training is the highest among all the nine indicators, whereas agricultural development and financial access have relatively lower average values. In addition, the latter two responses have relatively high standard deviations, suggesting less universal adoption of inclusiveness in these domains.

Table 2.3 provides pairwise correlations for the nine indicators of inclusiveness performance and the two motivation types. Intrinsic and extrinsic motivation are positively and significantly correlated with each other (coefficient = 0.39). Moreover, both types of motivation have positive and significant correlations with nearly all of the nine indicators of inclusiveness performance, which are in turn positively correlated with one another. The strong correlation between the two motivation types, and their similar association with inclusiveness performance, suggest a potential challenge in isolating the effect of one from another through regression analysis. The correlation coefficients, however, are much larger for intrinsic than for extrinsic motives, indicating that the two motivation types have unequal associations with inclusiveness performance.

Before proceeding to the regression results, Table 2.4 reports the correlations between the two motivation types and other control variables. Both intrinsic and extrinsic motives have a positive and significant correlation with financial performance, suggesting that more competitive firms also have greater motivation to engage in inclusive business practices. The negative and significant correlation between intrinsic motives and firm size and age indicates that intrinsic motives are greater among younger and smaller firms. Extrinsic

Table 2.3 Correlation among motivation types and inclusiveness performance

	1	2	3	4	5	6	7	8	9	10	11
1	Intrinsic motives	1										
2	Extrinsic motives	0.39 0	1									
3	Gender equality	0.36 0	0.12 0.01	1								
4	Employment creation	0.35 0	0.27 0	0.40 0	1							
5	Employee development	0.46 0	0.20 0	0.46 0	0.48 0	1						
6	Agricultural development	0.24 0	0.09 0.11	0.36 0	0.28 0	0.28 0	1					
7	Financial access	0.24 0	0.22 0	0.27 0	0.37 0	0.31 0	0.40 0	1				
8	Education and training	0.41 0	0.18 0.00	0.42 0	0.40 0	0.48 0	0.30 0	0.33 0	1			
9	Supporting microenterprises	0.41 0	0.20 0.00	0.31 0	0.37 0	0.43 0	0.47 0	0.46 0	0.38 0	1		
10	Supporting SMES	0.34 0	0.26 0	0.33 0	0.50 0	0.39 0	0.40 0	0.53 0	0.40 0	0.71 0	1	
11	Supporting value chain actors	0.38 0	0.25 0	0.33 0	0.45 0	0.55 0	0.41 0	0.39 0	0.36 0	0.47 0	0.51 0	1

Note: for each variable on the first column, the figures on the same row indicate Pearson correlation coefficients, and the values in the cells below indicate their statistical significance (*p*-value).

Source: authors' calculations.

Table 2.4 Correlation among motivation types and firm characteristics

	1. Intrinsic	2. Extrinsic	3. Finance	4. Size	5. Age	6. Foreign	7. SE
1. Intrinsic motives	1						
2. Extrinsic motives	0.39	1					
	0						
3. Financial performance	0.21	0.19	1				
	0	0					
4. Firm size	−0.11	0.07	0.25	1			
	0.03	0.16	0				
5. Firm age	−0.12	0.08	0.18	0.52	1		
	0.01	0.10	0	0			
6. Foreign ownership	0.01	−0.10	0.09	0.32	0.11	1	
	0.79	0.04	0.06	0	0.02		
7. Social enterprise (SE)	0.04	−0.17	−0.11	−0.18	−0.16	0.01	1
	0.42	0	0.03	0	0	0.87	

Source: authors' calculations.

motivation is not significantly correlated with firm size, while it has a weakly significant positive correlation with age ($p = 0.098$). Intrinsic motives are not significantly correlated with the probability of being foreign-owned or being a social enterprise, while extrinsic motives are negatively correlated with both. The different correlation patterns between the two motivation types and firm characteristics suggest that the underlying motives that drive inclusive business practices generally differ across firms.

Regression results

Table 2.5 reports the ordinary least squares estimates for our baseline regression model that includes indicators of intrinsic and extrinsic motives as independent variables. The bottom row reveals that between 20% and 30% of the total variation in the dependent variables is explained by the explanatory variables, which is a decent amount for micro-level data that tend to exhibit significant heterogeneity.

Table 2.5 reveals that intrinsic motives are dominant explanators for all measures of inclusive business performance. In contrast, extrinsic motives are strongly significant only for two measures of inclusiveness, namely employment creation and supporting SMEs in the value chain. Extrinsic motives also have a weakly significant effect on supporting other businesses in the value chain

Table 2.5 The effect of different motivation types on inclusiveness performance

	(1)	(2)	(3)	(4)	(5)	(6)	(7)	(8)	(9)
	Human development			*Ecosystem development*			*Functional inclusion*		
	Gender equality	*Employment creation*	*Employee development*	*Support microenterprises*	*Support SMEs*	*Support value chain*	*Education and training*	*Agric'l develop't*	*Financial access*
Intrinsic motives	0.436★★★	0.344★★★	0.540★★★	0.501★★★	0.345★★★	0.418★★★	0.443★★★	0.320★★	0.331★★
	(0.065)	(0.075)	(0.031)	(0.073)	(0.067)	(0.047)	(0.051)	(0.126)	(0.097)
Extrinsic motives	−0.039	0.124★★★	−0.005	0.059	0.180★★★	0.113★	0.037	0.042	0.096
	(0.035)	(0.026)	(0.018)	(0.087)	(0.047)	(0.055)	(0.052)	(0.084)	(0.049)
Financial perf.	0.125	0.170★★	0.156	0.277★★★	0.203★★	0.116★★	0.163★	0.215★	0.282★★
	(0.071)	(0.063)	(0.085)	(0.048)	(0.065)	(0.046)	(0.078)	(0.088)	(0.092)
Firm size	0.055	0.092★	0.049	0.020	−0.022	−0.003	−0.028	0.010	0.125★★★
	(0.042)	(0.042)	(0.094)	(0.048)	(0.061)	(0.059)	(0.038)	(0.056)	(0.031)
Firm age	0.003	−0.089	0.008	−0.100	−0.034	0.029	−0.063	−0.083	0.101
	(0.062)	(0.071)	(0.114)	(0.093)	(0.087)	(0.044)	(0.087)	(0.148)	(0.056)
Foreign ownership	−0.104	−0.128	−0.071	0.021	0.112	0.068	−0.011	−0.451★	0.158
	(0.243)	(0.098)	(0.146)	(0.060)	(0.130)	(0.188)	(0.217)	(0.213)	(0.155)
Social enterprise	0.514★★★	0.168	0.064	0.188	0.363★★	−0.078	0.200★	0.408★	0.496★
	(0.083)	(0.094)	(0.090)	(0.217)	(0.107)	(0.160)	(0.083)	(0.178)	(0.250)
Constant	2.485★★★	1.867★★	1.314★★★	1.181★	1.808★	1.560★★★	2.019★★★	2.205	1.597★★★
	(0.546)	(0.556)	(0.296)	(0.528)	(0.788)	(0.408)	(0.456)	(1.331)	(0.314)
Observations	393	398	403	363	371	389	394	337	367
R-squared	0.199	0.212	0.254	0.259	0.218	0.215	0.216	0.299	0.311

Note: regression analysis was conducted using the ordinary least squares method. The reported standard errors are corrected for clustering within countries.

Source: authors' calculations.

($p = 0.08$). Extrinsic motives have no significant effect on the remaining measures of inclusiveness, while intrinsic motives have consistently positive and strongly significant effects. These results thus support Hypothesis 1, which argued that normative and cognitive–emotive factors are more likely to be major performance drivers among frontrunner inclusive businesses in Africa. The consistency and strong significance of intrinsic motives along different areas of inclusiveness provide compelling support for Hypothesis 1. Considering the positive and significant correlation between our measures of intrinsic and extrinsic motives (see Table 2.2), the consistency of these results also indicates the presence of sufficient variation between the two types of motives – confirming the discriminant validity of the measures for the two types of motives.

Among the control variables, financial performance is positively correlated with inclusiveness performance for most measures of inclusiveness. This confirms that performance along commercial and social dimensions goes hand-in-hand. This result is also supportive of the slack-resource view of social performance, which suggests that firms become inclusive when they have a sufficient surplus of financial resources for social investments. Not surprisingly, firms that self-identify as social enterprises exhibit significantly greater performance in many areas of inclusive business practices. The remaining control variables do not seem to have a discernible, consistent effect on inclusive business performance.

Table 2.6 reports the regressions results for an extended version of the model in Equation (1), in which an interaction term between firm size and extrinsic motives is included to test Hypothesis 2. The interaction term is strongly significant for two measures of inclusiveness performance (gender equality and agricultural development) and weakly significant for another (education and training). In these specific areas of inclusive business practice, therefore, the effect of extrinsic motives on inclusiveness performance increases with firm size. Note that, for these three inclusive business practices, the direct effect of extrinsic motives was not significant in Table 2.5. The results, therefore, suggest that, while extrinsic motives may appear not to have a positive direct effect on inclusiveness performance in some domains, they tend to have a larger and significant effect among relatively larger firms. The results thus provide partial support for Hypothesis 2, confirming that extrinsic motives are important enablers of inclusiveness among large firms, although this is likely to be restricted to certain inclusiveness practices.

Finally, we run regressions by including an interaction term of intrinsic and extrinsic motives to test whether or not the two motives reinforce each other. The conceptual diagram (see Figure 2.1) suggests that when intrinsic and extrinsic motives coexist, firms are likely to adopt deep engagement strategies that have the potential for transformative outcomes in terms of social impact as well as competitiveness. In Hypothesis 3, we argued that various internal and external factors will inhibit the emergence of such mixed motives, and firms will rely on either predominantly normative (intrinsic) or economic motives to guide their inclusiveness practice. As a result, there will be a limited chance that frontrunner inclusive businesses will pursue strategies that reinforce

Table 2.6 Interaction between extrinsic motives and size

	(1)	(2)	(3)	(4)	(5)	(6)	(7)	(8)	(9)
	Human development			Ecosystem development			Functional inclusion		
	Gender equality	Employment creation	Employee development	Supporting microenterprises	Supporting SMES	Supporting value chain	Education and training	Agricultural develop't	Financial access
Firm size x Extrinsic motive	0.078**	0.019	0.021	0.041	0.032	0.054	0.064*	0.104***	0.031
	(0.025)	(0.031)	(0.041)	(0.023)	(0.034)	(0.034)	(0.026)	(0.014)	(0.036)
Intrinsic motives	0.429***	0.341***	0.538***	0.497***	0.343***	0.415***	0.434***	0.310*	0.328**
	(0.059)	(0.072)	(0.034)	(0.074)	(0.069)	(0.047)	(0.052)	(0.130)	(0.100)
Extrinsic motives	-0.248**	0.076	-0.059	-0.050	0.095	-0.027	-0.128**	-0.224*	0.012
	(0.075)	(0.086)	(0.098)	(0.132)	(0.119)	(0.060)	(0.035)	(0.101)	(0.108)
Financial perf.	0.112	0.167**	0.152	0.271***	0.199**	0.107*	0.152	0.200*	0.277**
	(0.072)	(0.064)	(0.081)	(0.048)	(0.066)	(0.048)	(0.079)	(0.089)	(0.089)
Firm size	-0.365**	-0.008	-0.064	-0.203	-0.196	-0.293	-0.370**	-0.543***	-0.039
	(0.137)	(0.194)	(0.205)	(0.109)	(0.192)	(0.206)	(0.142)	(0.051)	(0.217)
Firm age	0.009	-0.088	0.009	-0.097	-0.033	0.030	-0.062	-0.088	0.101
	(0.067)	(0.071)	(0.112)	(0.093)	(0.087)	(0.045)	(0.084)	(0.151)	(0.054)
Foreign ownership	-0.147	-0.137	-0.083	-0.002	0.091	0.032	-0.043	-0.518**	0.138
	(0.242)	(0.098)	(0.131)	(0.048)	(0.124)	(0.169)	(0.218)	(0.200)	(0.145)
Social enterprise	0.507***	0.164	0.058	0.176	0.355***	-0.095	0.188**	0.375	0.494
	(0.096)	(0.090)	(0.092)	(0.204)	(0.095)	(0.170)	(0.075)	(0.200)	(0.263)
Constant	3.686***	2.155**	1.632*	1.817**	2.297*	2.381**	3.009***	3.776**	2.083**
	(0.575)	(0.616)	(0.739)	(0.710)	(1.017)	(0.669)	(0.616)	(1.365)	(0.753)
Observations	393	398	403	363	371	389	394	337	367
R-squared	0.211	0.213	0.255	0.261	0.219	0.220	0.225	0.312	0.313

Note: regression analysis was conducted using the ordinary least squares method. The reported standard errors are corrected for clustering within countries.

Source: authors' calculations.

economic and intrinsic motives advancing inclusiveness performance. In terms of regression analysis, we would expect that the interaction between intrinsic and extrinsic motives will not be positive and significant.

This indeed is what transpires from the regression results in Table 2.7. The interaction term of intrinsic and extrinsic motives is for the most part insignificant, and it in fact becomes negative and significant for two inclusiveness practices (employment creation and financial access). The negative coefficient in these results suggests that when the two motives co-develop, they are likely to undermine inclusiveness performance in certain domains. This is in line with the view that the presence of a significant commitment towards hybrid (economic and social) goals could lead to internal conflict and instability when these goals are perceived to be equally important but incompatible with each other (Battilana & Lee, 2014; Besharov & Smith, 2014). The insignificant interaction term for most inclusiveness practices indicates that the two motives mostly fail to reinforce each other in advancing inclusiveness performance, which is in line with Hypothesis 3.

Table 2.7 shows that the direct effect of intrinsic motives on inclusiveness performance remains almost always positive and significant even when an interaction term is included. Intrinsic motives thus increase inclusiveness notwithstanding the level of extrinsic motives or the mixture thereof, highlighting the lack of complementarity between the two motives. As indicated in Figure 2.1, inclusiveness strategies that are driven only by intrinsic motives are likely to constitute "light engagement strategies" that have stronger social impact but relatively limited strategic value. This suggests that limited interest in the economic aspects of inclusive business practices in Africa is likely to lower social impact as well as the financial gains of involved firms.

Conclusion

There is currently a limited research effort to unpack the underlying organizational and managerial rationales that drive poverty alleviation strategies (Bruton et al., 2008). This has limited our understanding of the entrepreneurial and organizational mechanisms that create, sustain, and reinforce business practices that address social issues. This research has sought to improve our understanding of the motivational drivers of inclusive business practices in Africa by looking into the relationship between motivations, inclusiveness strategies, and performance levels.

Our analysis has revealed that the nature of motivations that inspire inclusiveness is associated with different levels of inclusiveness performance. We find that intrinsic motives are the most important driving forces among frontrunner inclusive businesses in Africa. This suggests that normative or emotive-cognitive factors are comparatively more prominent in driving inclusiveness performance compared to economic considerations. However, economically-oriented extrinsic motives tend to be more important among larger firms, although this is limited to certain domains of inclusive business practices. Finally, we find

Table 2.7 Interaction between extrinsic and intrinsic motives

	(1)	(2)	(3)	(4)	(5)	(6)	(7)	(8)	(9)
	Human development			*Ecosystem development*			*Functional inclusion*		
	Gender equality	*Employment creation*	*Employee development*	*Supporting microenterprises*	*Supporting SMES*	*Supporting value chain*	*Education and training*	*Agricultural develop't*	*Financial access*
Intrinsic X Extrinsic	0.042	−0.091**	−0.064	−0.064	−0.015	−0.066	−0.079	0.017	−0.154***
	(0.078)	(0.030)	(0.061)	(0.055)	(0.031)	(0.061)	(0.063)	(0.078)	(0.031)
Intrinsic motives	0.236	0.773***	0.844**	0.796**	0.417*	0.729*	0.814**	0.243	1.045***
	(0.406)	(0.199)	(0.276)	(0.251)	(0.179)	(0.309)	(0.274)	(0.380)	(0.131)
Extrinsic motives	−0.294	0.666**	0.378	0.440	0.273	0.506	0.507	−0.057	1.024***
	(0.476)	(0.184)	(0.366)	(0.329)	(0.164)	(0.377)	(0.426)	(0.513)	(0.193)
Financial perf.	0.129	0.165**	0.151*	0.274***	0.202**	0.110**	0.158*	0.216**	0.275**
	(0.069)	(0.057)	(0.078)	(0.046)	(0.066)	(0.045)	(0.072)	(0.088)	(0.080)
Firm size	0.054	0.093*	0.048	0.019	−0.022	−0.003	−0.027	0.010	0.129***
	(0.043)	(0.043)	(0.092)	(0.045)	(0.061)	(0.059)	(0.039)	(0.056)	(0.026)
Firm age	0.001	−0.084	0.013	−0.097	−0.033	0.032	−0.059	−0.084	0.101
	(0.059)	(0.074)	(0.111)	(0.089)	(0.087)	(0.045)	(0.087)	(0.144)	(0.052)
Foreign ownership	−0.100	−0.129	−0.073	0.018	0.111	0.064	−0.012	−0.450*	0.149
	(0.242)	(0.100)	(0.143)	(0.055)	(0.130)	(0.185)	(0.220)	(0.213)	(0.135)
Social enterprise	0.521***	0.151	0.051	0.175	0.359**	−0.094	0.186*	0.412*	0.465
	(0.088)	(0.104)	(0.102)	(0.230)	(0.107)	(0.176)	(0.091)	(0.180)	(0.245)
Constant	3.655	−0.642	−0.460	−0.558	1.387	−0.244	−0.145	2.660	−2.626***
	(2.574)	(1.244)	(1.730)	(1.172)	(1.060)	(1.877)	(1.850)	(2.630)	(0.673)
Observations	393	398	403	363	371	389	394	337	367
R-squared	0.201	0.222	0.259	0.262	0.218	0.219	0.223	0.299	0.327

Note: regression analysis was conducted using the ordinary least squares method. The reported standard errors are corrected for clustering within countries.

Source: authors' calculations.

that intrinsic and extrinsic motives do not reinforce each other, suggesting the limited development of mixed motives. This offers a potential explanation for the rarity of highly successful inclusive businesses, even in areas where addressing social issues appears to provide significant commercial benefit. This suggests that the absence of the right mix of motivations could be a factor that inhibits inclusiveness performance.

Our results also point to a number of useful areas for future research. An important theme is why mixed motives fail to emerge, or why intrinsic and extrinsic motives fail to co-develop in such a way that they reinforce each other among inclusive businesses. As highlighted in our conceptual framework (see Figure 2.1), this could reveal the reasons for the scarcity of transformative deep engagement strategies that are both intrinsically inspired and economically competitive. Previous research has suggested that motives do not remain fixed, as firms adapt their value system and organizational mission in response to demands of internal and external stakeholders (Lashitew et al., 2018). The motivations for inclusive business practices can transition gradually from reactive to active and then proactive strategies when companies internalize the importance of social and environmental issues and develop intrinsic motives (van Tulder, 2018). Future research, therefore, can explore how internal incidents, or external market or institutional changes, induce the emergence of mission-driven, hybrid identities.

The factors that inhibit transitioning towards hybrid business models might not be universal across firms. Large and established businesses can be constrained by an "adaptation trap" and cultural inertia that limits their ability to cultivate a new set of intrinsic motives and the associated capabilities. Small firms, on the other hand, can face financial, managerial, and technological handicaps that limit their ability to develop new capabilities or organizational identities. Multinational firms could have inadequate knowledge of local stakeholders and their market needs, which reduces their ability to strike the right balance of social and economic end goals (Hart et al., 2016). Future research can shed light on the specific conditions that inhibit the emergence of mixed motives in African and other developing markets.

References

Anderson, J., & Markides, C. (2007). Strategic innovation at the Base of the Pyramid. *MIT Sloan Management Review, 49*(1), 83.

Austin, J. E., & Seitanidi, M. M. (2012). Collaborative value creation: A review of partnering between non-profits and businesses: Part I. Value creation spectrum and collaboration stages. *Non-profit and Voluntary Sector Quarterly, 41*, 726–758.

Bansal, P., & Roth, K. (2000). Why companies go green: A model of ecological responsiveness. *Academy of Management Journal, 43*(4), 717–736.

Baron, D. P. (2009). A positive theory of moral management, social pressure, and corporate social performance. *Journal of Economics & Management Strategy, 18*(1), 7–43.

Battilana, J., & Lee, M. (2014). Advancing research on hybrid organizing–Insights from the study of social enterprises. *Academy of Management Annals, 8*(1), 397–441.

Besharov, M. L., & Smith, W. K. (2014). Multiple institutional logics in organizations: Explaining their varied nature and implications. *Academy of Management Review*, *39*(3), 364–381.

Brugmann, J., & Prahalad, C. K. (2007). Cocreating business's new social compact. *Harvard Business Review*, *85*(2), 80.

Bruton, G. D., Ahlstrom, D., & Obloj, K. (2008). Entrepreneurship in emerging economies: Where are we today and where should the research go in the future. *Entrepreneurship Theory and Practice*, *32*(1), 1–14.

Dembek, K., Singh, P., & Bhakoo, V. (2016). Literature review of shared value: a theoretical concept or a management buzzword? *Journal of Business Ethics*, *137*(2), 231–267.

Fosfuri, A., Giarratana, M. S., & Roca, E. (2016). Social business hybrids: Demand externalities, competitive advantage, and growth through diversification. *Organization Science*, *27*(5), 1275–1289.

Garcia-Castro, R., & Francoeur, C. (2016). When more is not better: Complementarities, costs and contingencies in stakeholder management. *Strategic Management Journal*, *37*(2), 406–424.

George, G., Howard-Grenville, J., Joshi, A., & Tihanyi, L. (2016). Understanding and tackling societal grand challenges through management research. *Academy of Management Journal*, *59*(6), 1880–1895.

George, G., McGahan, A. M., & Prabhu, J. (2012). Innovation for inclusive growth: Towards a theoretical framework and a research agenda. *Journal of Management Studies*, *49*(4), 661–683.

Hahn, R., & Gold, S. (2014). Resources and governance in "Base of the Pyramid"-partnerships: Assessing collaborations between businesses and non-business actors. *Journal of Business Research*, *67*(7), 1321–1333.

Hahn, T., Pinkse, J., Preuss, L., & Figge, F. (2015). Tensions in corporate sustainability: Towards an integrative framework. *Journal of Business Ethics*, *127*(2), 297–316.

Hahn, T., Pinkse, J., Preuss, L., & Figge, F. (2016). Ambidexterity for corporate social performance. *Organization Studies*, *37*(2), 213–235.

Halme, M., Lindeman, S., & Linna, P. (2012). Innovation for inclusive business: Entrepreneurial bricolage in multinational corporations. *Journal of Management Studies*, *49*(4), 743–784.

Hart, S. L., & London, T. (2005). Developing native capability. *Stanford Social Innovation Review*, *3*(2), 28–33.

Hart, S., Sharma, S., & Halme, M. (2016). Poverty, business strategy, and sustainable development. *Organization & Environment*, *29*(4), 401–415

Hollensbe, E., Wookey, C., Hickey, L., George, G., & Nichols, C. V. (2014). Organizations with purpose. *Academy of Management Journal*, *57*(5), 1227–1234.

Husted, B. W., & Allen, D. B. (2007). Corporate social strategy in multinational enterprises: Antecedents and value creation. *Journal of Business Ethics*, 345–361.

Kolk, A., Rivera-Santos, M., & Rufín, C. (2014). Reviewing a decade of research on the "Base/Bottom of the pyramid" (BOP) concept. *Business & Society*, *53*(3), 338–377.

Laplume, A. O., Sonpar, K., & Litz, R. A. (2008). Stakeholder theory: Reviewing a theory that moves us. *Journal of Management*, *34*(6), 1152–1189.

Lashitew, A. A., Bals, L., & van Tulder, R. (2018). Inclusive business at the Base of the Pyramid: The role of embeddedness for enabling social innovations. *Journal of Business Ethics*, 1–28.

Lashitew, A. A., & van Tulder, R. (2017). Inclusive business in Africa: Priorities, strategies and challenges. In C. U. Uche (Ed.), *African Entrepreneurship Dynamics* (71–94). Leiden: Brill Publishers.

London, T., & Hart, S. L. (2004). Reinventing strategies for emerging markets: beyond the transnational model. *Journal of International Business Studies, 35*(5), 350–370.

Mair, J., Battilana, J., & Cardenas, J. (2012). Organizing for society: A typology of social entrepreneuring models. *Journal of Business Ethics, 111*(3), 353–373.

Mair, J., & Marti, I. (2009). Entrepreneurship in and around institutional voids: A case study from Bangladesh. *Journal of Business Venturing, 24*(5), 419–435.

Mair, J., & Noboa, E. (2006). Social entrepreneurship: How intentions to create a social venture are formed. In J. Mair, J. Robinson, & K. Hockerts (Eds.), *Social Entrepreneurship* (pp. 121–135). London: Palgrave Macmillan.

Miller, T. L., Grimes, M. G., McMullen, J. S., & Vogus, T. J. (2012). Venturing for others with heart and head: How compassion encourages social entrepreneurship. *Academy of Management Review, 37*(4), 616–640.

Mol, M. J., Stadler, C., & Ariño, A. (2017). Africa: The new frontier for global strategy scholars. *Global Strategy Journal, 7*(1), 3–9.

Muller, A., & Kolk, A. (2010). Extrinsic and intrinsic drivers of corporate social performance: Evidence from foreign and domestic firms in Mexico. *Journal of Management Studies, 47*(1), 1–26.

Nahi, T. (2016). Cocreation at the Base of the Pyramid: Reviewing and organizing the diverse conceptualizations. *Organization & Environment, 29*(4), 416–437.

Patzelt, H., & Shepherd, D. A. (2011). Recognizing opportunities for sustainable development. *Entrepreneurship Theory and Practice, 35*(4), 631–652.

Perez-Aleman, P., & Sandilands, M. (2008). Building value at the top and the bottom of the global supply chain: MNC-NGO partnerships. *California Management Review, 51*(1), 24–49.

Porter, M. E., & Kramer, M. R. (2011). Creating shared value: Redefining capitalism and the role of the corporation in society. *Harvard Business Review, 89*(1/2), 62–77.

Prahalad, C. K. (2004). *The Fortune at the Bottom of the Pyramid: Eradicating poverty through profits.* Upper Saddle River, NJ: Wharton School Publishing.

Reficco, E., & Márquez, P. (2012). Inclusive networks for building BOP markets. *Business & Society, 51*(3), 512–556.

Rivera-Santos, M., Rufin, C., & Kolk, A. (2012). Bridging the institutional divide: Partnerships in subsistence markets. *Journal of Business Research, 65*(12), 1721–1727.

Stevens, R., Moray, N., & Bruneel, J. (2015). The social and economic mission of social enterprises: Dimensions, measurement, validation, and relation. *Entrepreneurship Theory and Practice, 39*(5), 1051–1082.

van Tulder, R. (2018). *Getting all the motives right: Driving international corporate responsibility (ICR) to the next level.* Rotterdam, Netherlands: SMO.

Viswanathan, M., Sridharan, S., & Ritchie, R. (2010). Understanding consumption and entrepreneurship in subsistence marketplaces. *Journal of Business Research, 63*(6), 570–581.

Webb, J. W., Kistruck, G. M., Ireland, R. D., & Ketchen Jr, D. J. (2010). The entrepreneurship process in base of the pyramid markets: The case of multinational enterprise/nongovernment organization alliances. *Entrepreneurship Theory and Practice, 34*(3), 555–581.

Yunus, M., Moingeon, B., & Lehmann-Ortega, L. (2010). Building social business models: Lessons from the Grameen experience. *Long Range Planning, 43*(2–3), 308–325.

Part II

Drivers and barriers of BOP markets

3 Juxtaposing supply- and demand-side drivers and barriers of technology adoption at the Base of the Pyramid markets in Uganda

Jimmy Ebong, Giacomo Ciambotti, Abel Kinoti, Alice Nakagwa, and Ogechi Adeola

Background

Several studies (Bhavnani, Chiu, Janakiram, & Silarszky, 2008[7]; Carmody, 2012; Diga, 2007; Sife, Kiondo, & Lyimo-Macha, 2010; Smith, Spence, & Rashid, 2011) document how rural communities benefit from mobile telephone technology and services and impacts that such services have on rural livelihoods. These studies assert that technology can contribute to poverty reduction, especially when people living at the Base of the Pyramid (BOP) adopt and use technological products and services. Mobile phone usage contributes to poverty reduction and improvement of rural livelihoods by expanding and strengthening social networks (Sife et al., 2010), increasing people's ability to deal with emergencies (Bhavnani et al., 2008; Sife et al., 2010), increasing temporal accessibility, reducing costs of doing business (Bhavnani et al., 2008), increasing productivity by helping rural traders and farmers to secure better markets and prices, and promptly communicating business-related information (Sife et al., 2010).

According to Subhan and Khattak (2016), BOP is a term used to classify the populations of the world by their abilities to earn and, from such earnings, afford an acceptable standard of living. Based on this description, one side of the world is made up of a few privileged and affluent people who are more than able to afford a decent living. The other side of the world makes up the majority of the global population; these are people who cannot afford a decent living. A majority of the BOP population is located in developing countries where the standard of living is low (Lashitew, Bals, & van Tulder, 2018). Poverty is most prevalent among the lowest segment of the BOPs, with 10% of the world population living in extreme poverty on less than $1.90 per day (Beltekian & Ortiz-Ospina, 2018). Targeting BOP countries as markets for goods and services (Bharti, Agrawal & Sharma, 2014; Sy-Changco, Pornpitakpan, Singh, & Bonilla, 2011; Smit, Sheombar, & Silvius, 2009) and as providers of labour (Cooney & Shanks, 2010) can potentially reduce poverty by providing them with livelihoods and income in a sustainable way.

There are multiple determinants of poverty. There is also a bi-directional link between poverty and technology adoption. Much as the adoption of technology may reduce poverty, Mitropoulos and Tatum (2000) posit that levels of income affect technology adoption. Technology adoption and usage potentially reduce poverty if BOPs adopt and use technology to increase their efficiency and productivity. The solutions that mobile technology provide are related or geared towards increasing efficiency by reducing the time farmers spend looking for inputs as well as reducing information asymmetry and increasing transparency (Foster & Rosenzweig, 1995) in sourcing inputs, reducing costs, and making inputs affordable. Usage of inputs is likely to increase productivity and, consequently, incomes.

Mobile phone-related technology innovations have been advanced to provide solutions to the challenges faced by BOPs. These innovations include technology for providing extension services (Akpabio, Okon, & Inyang, 2007) and technology for disseminating market information (Kiiza & Pederson, 2012). Technology adoption can reduce poverty, but there is also a possibility that low income, associated with poverty, inhibits adoption of technology (Foster & Rosenzweig, 2010). Whereas some theories attribute failures to adopt innovation to intervention approaches (e.g. donations as opposed to market-driven approaches), uptake and usage of innovation have been attributed to supply- and demand-side drivers and barriers. Factors from the supply side, which can hinder or drive usage of innovation, include design features and costs.

The objective of this study is to compare uptake and usage of EzyAgric, a mobile and web-based application for linking farmers to farm services, by two organizations, Bugiri Agribusiness Institutions Development Association (BAIDA) and Zirobwe Agali Awamu Agribusiness Training Association (ZAABTA). Consequently, the study draws insights from supply- and demand-side drivers and barriers of technology adoption and usage among farmers who are the target beneficiaries and who are at the Base of the Pyramid in order to assess their usage of mobile and web-based platforms to improve their incomes and livelihood. This study investigates supply- and demand-side triggers of the uptake of technology, which are necessary to enhance sustained adoption and usage and to eventually lead to poverty reduction. The next section provides a brief description of the case companies and describes how EzyAgric works.

Bugiri Agribusiness Institutions Development Association (BAIDA)

BAIDA was established in 2004 and became officially registered in 2007; it is a higher-level farmers' organization constituting 64 groups of smallholder farmers. These groups are spread across five sub-counties in Bugiri District, namely: Nankoma, Bulidha, Buwunga, Nabukalu, and Iwemba. BAIDA constitutes a total of 2,325 farmers; of these, 1,104 are males and 1,221 are females. There are 675 and 537 male and female youths, respectively. BAIDA's

Table 3.1 Summary of the number of BAIDA farmers who are using the mobile platform

Use of the platform	Number of farmers per use category
Sourcing inputs	392
Accessing market	103
Accessing financial services	490
Accessing advisory/extension services	730

Source: Key Informant Interview and secondary data.

mission is to improve the standards of farmers by providing access to agribusiness services, capacity building, enterprise development, production, processing value addition, and collective bulking and marketing.

The association's objectives are to increase members' access to agricultural production and productivity, improve the post-harvest handling of members' products, access better markets for members' products, add value to members' products, and to build the capacity of members. BAIDA undertakes activities that are aligned to its mission and objectives. These include the providing market information and access to better markets, facilitating access to improved inputs, facilitating linkages to financial services, facilitating access to post-harvest handling technologies, and facilitating value addition. BAIDA members grow maize, beans, and soybeans, targeting the local commodity markets.

BAIDA started utilizing the mobile platform, EzyAgric in 2018. Initially, the organization received training from MobiPay Agrosys Limited, a home-grown company that provides technology solutions with the aim of improving people's lives in order to drive the provision of financial services to the agriculture sector. BAIDA employed the services of MobiPay Agrosys Limited to profile its farmers. The company also installed an application for the mobile platform on the organization's computers. BAIDA uses the mobile application to facilitate members' access to market information, access to mobile payments, ordering of inputs, and to access general agricultural extension information. Table 3.1 summarises BAIDA's usage of the platform.

Zirobwe Agali Awamu Agribusiness Training Association (ZAABTA)

ZAABTA is also a higher-level farmers' organization that was registered in 2004 as a company limited by guarantee. It is one of the Government's Model Projects under the Ministry of Agriculture, Animal Industry and Fisheries (MAAIF) for improvement of post-harvest handling and agro-processing through farmers and farmer organizations. ZAABTA bridges the gap by providing backward and forward linkages and assisting smallholder farmers to access agricultural credit facilities from financial institutions to boost production, support seed lending through the seed bank project, train and assist in the basic agronomic practices, train and

Table 3.2 Summary of the number of ZAABTA farmers using the EzyAgric platform

Use of the platform	Number of farmers per use category
Sourcing inputs	214
Accessing market	351
Accessing financial services	123
Accessing advisory/extension services	606

Source: Key Informant Interview and secondary data.

support the post-harvest handling and agro-processing, and at the same time help farmers access profitable markets for their value-added products. Currently, ZAABTA has 4,632 members; most of them are registered smallholder farmers who make up 162 groups of farmers in six sub-counties (Zirobwe, Kikyusa, Kalagala, Katikamu, Kamira, and Bamunanika) and are spread across six districts (Luweero, Mukono, Kayunga, Wakiso, Nakasongola, and Nakaseke). ZAABTA offices are located in Zirobwe Town Council, Luwero District.

ZAABTA is focused on agribusiness training, grain production and processing, seed and stock multiplication, inputs, and outputs market linkages. ZAABTA manages an integrated agricultural value chain for rice, soybeans, beans, maize grains, and horticulture with operations from procurement, bulking, cleaning, packaging, storage, and marketing from smallholder farmers to profitable markets. ZAABTA started using the EzyAgric mobile platform in 2015, through participating in a project supported by the United States Agency for International Development (USAID) Feed the Future Program. The project was called Commodity Production and Marketing Activity (CPMA). Table 3.2 summarises ZAABTA's adoption and usage of the platform.

BAIDA and ZAABTA were linked by CPMA in 2015 to use the EzyAgric digital platform. The USAID project incubated Akorion Company Limited, an AgTech private limited company seeking to provide digital solutions and services through EzyAgric. EzyAgric provides an array of agricultural services, which include digital farmer profiling, garden mapping, extension services, and agrishop – a platform for buying inputs, market linkages, and digital records. EzyAgric has been in use since 2014 by village agents to render services to farmers. BAIDA and ZAABTA use EzyAgric to aggregate demand for inputs and also provide extension services to farmers.

The EzyAgric mobile platform

EzyAgric is a one-stop-shop, a digital supermarket for crop and animal production, designed to track farm records and farmer's digital footprints. From such footprints, users are able to leverage other services such as credit, thereby enhancing data-driven agriculture. When a farmer enrols to use EzyAgric, their profile is generated. The profile captures various information about the farmer, including farm size. Profiling enables accurate measurement of farm size because it is done digitally using satellite technology linked to a smartphone. At later stages, farm size is used to estimate inputs required and expected yields, hence it is useful for planning operations. Financial institutions are also able to use farmers' profiles when assessing their eligibility for credit using alternative credit scoring algorithms. EzyAgric is used to link farmers to inputs and professional farm services such as labour. Product buyers also access information on the availability and quantity of products through EzyAgric. Extension services are also provided through the same platform. Users of EzyAgric download and install the application on their smartphones and are able to navigate the various functionalities once online.

Figure 3.1 shows that there are two models through which farmers access the mobile platform of EzyAgric, namely: village agents and smartphone farmer models. In the village agent model, farmers order fertilisers, pesticides, insecticides, herbicides, and farm implements, as well as access markets for farm products and extension services through the agent. The agent is a member of the same community in which the farmers live. Some agents are members of the farmer organization. In some cases, agents also serve as community-based extension service providers, providing the first line of extension services. The village agent aggregates orders for farm inputs and submits such orders to the farmer organization, also known as the master agent.

The farmer organization compiles and sends orders to an input company, negotiates for discounts on bulk purchases with the input supplier, and sets up

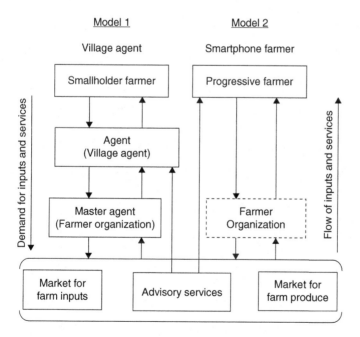

Figure 3.1 An illustration of how the mobile platform works.
Source: authors' own.

a commission structure to remunerate the village agent. Savings made from discounts are shared between the farmer organization, the village agent, and the farmer. This is done such that the farmer still gets to pay a lower price for the input as compared to the price being offered on the open market. In the case of extension services, farmers report suspected crop infections to the village agent. The village agent uses the smartphone to identify possible causes of and treatments for the infection. In extreme cases, and where the smartphone does not provide solutions to the observable symptoms of crop infection, the village agent refers the case to experienced government extension staff. In the case of ZAABTA, suspected crop infection is referred to an agriculture research institute.

Access to the market is also communicated through the smartphone. The first model works best for smallholder farmers who may not be able to afford smartphones and may also be illiterate, including digitally illiterate farmers. In the second model, farmers can afford the cost of smartphones, are literate and can use the smartphones, and can afford to buy inputs in larger quantities. However, such farmers are still members of the farmer organization.

As a result of using EzyAgric, farmers attain an improved quality of products that attracts high prices in the market. Also, aggregation of orders for inputs is made more efficient and transparent. Before the advent of EzyAgric, farmers physically travelled long distances to the office of the farmer organizations to obtain updates on markets for their products, and to access extension services in a timely manner was burdensome. Currently, farmers use the agent and the platform to access market information and extension. As a result of this access, farmers look for the appropriate varieties of crops to grow. These varieties are ones that the market needs and for which it can potentially attract higher prices. In addition, farmers are able to access financial services as a result of their usage of the platform. Farmers obtain higher yields through the usage of inputs and prompt access to extension; in the case of BAIDA, they also have a transparent payment system using MobiPay. In addition, farmers also access inputs at lower prices when they buy from the organizations compared to when they buy from the open markets. Village agents obtain commission pegged on the volume of inputs that farmers demand. This means they have to mobilise more farmers to buy and use inputs if they would like to have more money. The farmer group also derives some amount of income from commissions obtainable from the bulk purchase of inputs.

The linkage between technology adoption and poverty, as well as the introduction to the two cases, are presented in section 1 above. This section presents a review of relevant literature, as well as the theoretical and conceptual underpinnings of this research. The methodology of the study, discussion of findings, and conclusions are presented.

Literature review

Three theoretical perspectives are useful for the discussion of drivers and barriers of adoption of technology, which is the subject of this study. This study leans on the technology diffusion theory (Rogers, 1995; Surry, 1997), technology acceptance theories (Venkatesh, Thong, & Xu, 2016; Venkatesh, Thong, & Xu, 2012), and theories and principles related to market facilitation (Ripley & Nippard, 2014).

The diffusion theory is relevant and can be applied to explain factors underpinning the supply-side triggers of technology adoption. According to Surry (1997), diffusion is the "process by which an innovation is adopted and gains acceptance by members of a certain community" (p. 1). Rogers (1995) provides four major factors that can influence the process of diffusion, including the features of the innovation, the mode of information communication, time, and the nature of the social system where the innovation is being introduced.

According to Surry (1997) and Rogers (1995, 2002, 2004), within the broader diffusion theory, sub-theories that are widely used include the innovation-decision process, individual innovativeness, rate of adoption, and perceived attributes of a technology. According to the innovation-decision process (Rogers, 1995), potential adopters of an innovation must learn about the innovation, be persuaded as to the merits of the innovation, decide to adopt, implement the innovation, and confirm the decision to adopt the innovation. This theory postulates the role of the supplier of technology as instrumental in enhancing the learning of the potential users and convincing them of the merits of the technology. The individual innovativeness theory (Rogers, 1995, 2002, 2004) postulates that individuals who are predisposed to being innovative will adopt an innovation earlier than those who are less predisposed to this quality. The theory views potential users of technology along a continuum of innovators and laggards. Innovators adopt easily, and laggards take time to be convinced before they later adopt a technology. This theory reveals the role of early adopters in driving the overall adoption. Suppliers of technology can drive adoption by targeting early adopters and using them to demonstrate the merits of the technology.

The theory of the rate of adoption (Rogers, 1995, 2002, 2004) postulates the role of time in enhancing adoption. Rate of adoption theorises that innovations go through a period of slow, gradual growth before experiencing a period of dramatic and rapid growth, followed by a later slowdown. This theory proposes that the supplier of technology should deliver communications that persuade users to adopt the technology at the earlier stages of the innovation and progressively intensify such communications in order to sustain usage and enhance further adoption of the technology. The theory of perceived attributes (Rogers, 1995, 2002, 2004) stipulates that potential adopters would judge an innovation based on their perceptions of five attributes of a technology, namely: trialability, observability, relative advantage, complexity, and compatibility. Innovation will undergo an increased rate of diffusion if adopters perceive that the innovation can be tried, offers observable results, has merit over other innovations or the status quo, is not complex, and is compatible with existing values and practices. The theory of perceived attributes, therefore, places emphasis on a presentation that focuses on unravelling the advantages of a technology, especially to create a good first impression on the potential users of such a technology.

Technology acceptance theory (Venkatesh et al., 2016;Venkatesh et al., 2012) is relevant and is hence applied to explain adoption and usage of technology. Teo (2011) applied the theory to develop a model to study the intention to use technology. Teo (2011) modelled five variables as factors that drive the intention to use technology: perceived usefulness (performance expectancy), perceived ease of use (effort expectancy), subjective norms (social influence), facilitating conditions, and attitude towards use. Perceived usefulness describes intending users' assessments of the usefulness of the application. It is a state of aligning the use of the application to the needs of the intending users. In other words, a user will adopt a technological innovation when there is a perception of usefulness to the individual's needs and that the technology will meet the targeted expectation. Perceived ease of use describes the ability to use an application effortlessly. It is assumed that when an application is easy to use, there will likely be a high rate of adoption among users. Subjective norms relate to the extent to which an individual will adopt and use technology because others in the same society or others within their vicinity have adopted and are using the same technology and the society is likely to criticise them if they do not follow suit.

Perceived ease of use and perceived usefulness are the two tenets of the technology acceptance model. The theory has thus been extended to include subjective norms, which has been tested in the work of Lee and Wan (2010) and Beldad and Hegner (2018). Subjective norms are embedded in the broad scope of social norms, which has two dimensions known as the injunctive norm and the descriptive norm. According to Beldad and Hegner (2018), a generic interpretative meaning of social norms is an individual's actions that are influenced by beliefs and social interactions. It is also referred to as an individual's behaviour that is influenced by friends, colleagues, and other relatives. For present purposes, an individual's choice of technology adoption is influenced by its usage and approval of others. Specifically, a social norm is injunctive when an individual adopts or does what most people typically approve or disapprove of; a descriptive social norm refers to an adoption based on observation of what most people do or are engaged in.

Past studies have revealed that subjective social norms influenced people's adoption of technology in the form of instant messaging (Lu, Zhou, & Wang, 2009), mobile payment services (Yang, Lu, Gupta, Cao, & Zhang, 2012), and anti-spy software (Lee & Kozar, 2008). With the use of the technology acceptance model, the subjective norm constitutes key assumptions about the social norms and explains why and how farmers will adopt technological innovations. Within the context of this argument, the farmers will not adopt a technological innovation if the majority of their members do not approve of it or do not use it, or if it does not appeal to their social beliefs.

Another relevant theory or approach that explains drivers and barriers of technology is market facilitation. According to Cunningham and Jenal (2016), the roots of market facilitation approaches that address development constraints from a systemic perspective are traceable in evolutionary economics, new institutional economics, and complexity theory. A collection of bodies of knowledge from these sources and the ways they affect economic development are often referred to as new economic thinking. Market facilitation approaches (i.e. Ripley & Nippard, 2014; Kessler, 2014) addressed the root causes of why markets most times do not meet the needs of the poor. Market facilitation approaches are based on the principles that market interventions should deal with the underlying causes of market failures, rather than just the superficial symptoms, as aid funding can have a powerful yet temporary influence.

Market facilitation theories are relevant in explaining the linkages between market systems, particularly the linkage between markets for technology such as EzyAgric and other farm-related technologies. They are also useful in understanding markets for farm inputs (e.g. fertilisers, pesticides and insecticides, extension services, finance), as well as markets for farm products (e.g. cereals, legumes, etc.). A market system constitutes a network of buyers and sellers who come together for the purpose of selling a given product or providing services (Redmond, 2018). There are different stakeholders in the market system which include direct market players (buyers and consumers who push economic activities), suppliers of goods and needed services, and the business environment regulatory agencies and infrastructure providers. Market facilitation theories address systemic constraints affecting how markets function. This is attained by in-depth analysis and understanding of systemic constraints affecting the functioning of a whole market and its interconnected systems and thereafter designing interventions that address specific constraints that hinder smooth functioning of the entire market.

The consequential conceptual framework of the study is presented in Figure 3.2. This represents the drivers and supply assumptions of technology adoption at the Bottom of the Pyramid for farmers.

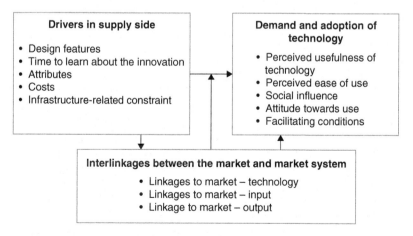

Figure 3.2 Conceptual framework.
Source: authors' own.

Figure 3.2 shows that there are factors that drive adoption and usage of technology. These factors include design features, ease of learning and time it takes to learn, attributes of a technology (Rogers, 1995, 2002, 2004; Surry, 1997;), costs (Mitropoulos & Tatum, 2000), and infrastructure-related constraints (Akpabio et al., 2007) such as electricity. According to Akpabio et al. (2007), constraints to technology adoption may include inadequate Information and Communications Technology (ICT) infrastructure, interconnectivity, and electricity supply problems. From a demand side, acceptance and use of technology is driven by many factors, such as perceived usefulness of a technology, perceived ease of use, social influence and attitudes towards use (Venkatesh et al., 2012), pleasurable appearance, price value, and habit (Venkatesh et al., 2012), as well as factors related to trust and perceived risk (Pavlou, 2003). The works of Legris et al. (2003) and Lee, Hsieh, and Hsu (2011) postulate that perceived ease of use of the technology and perceived usefulness of the technology may also drive adoption and usage of the application. For increased adoption and usage of web-based and mobile technology in agriculture, farmers need to be linked to markets for their inputs and to services (Aleke, Ojiako, & Wainwright, 2011) that enable them to access inputs. The strength of linkage to services and the market for their products is likely to mediate the adoption of technology. Web-based and mobile technology is only relevant in as much as it facilitates linkages and leads to efficiency in sourcing inputs and accessing markets (Sife et al., 2010).

The following section presents a review of the empirical literature on innovation in agrarian contexts, use of mobile devices for agricultural markets, technology adoption and how it relates to risk and the risk-bearing capacity of farmers, as well as wealth and income constraints to adoption of technology.

Adoption of agricultural innovation in developing economies

A majority of inhabitants in less developed countries derive their livelihood from agriculture (Feder, Just, & Zilberman, 1985). As new technologies that offer opportunities that will yield an increase in agricultural products emerge, it is expected that the income, quality, and quantity of agricultural products in these nations will increase. This will have an economic effect on a nation's Gross Domestic Product (GDP) and the standard of living of the people. However, adopting and utilizing new technologies among farmers in these nations has been an issue of concern. The rate of adoption of these technologies has met partial success (Feder et al., 1985). Previously, the assumptions regarding lack of adoption were limited access to information, inadequate farm size, aversion to risk, and lack of human capital and supply of inputs (e.g. seed, chemicals, and water). In addition, poor transportation was documented as a reason for the failure of technological adoption in agricultural activities (Feder et al., 1985). Subsequently, measures were put in place to control these challenges. However, the status quo remains the same in terms of farmers' adoption of technological innovations. Essentially, the adoption of technological tools for farming activities is still limited.

Most farmers of BAIDA and ZAABTA fit into the BOP market as they face similar constraints associated with these markets. Consumers at the bottom of the pyramid constitute the largest market, with more than 4 billion people living on incomes below \$2 per day (Prahalad, 2012). They are mostly engaged in the informal sector and contribute vastly to a nation's economic activities. Farmers in BOP markets will likely be constrained in their demand for and adoption of technology.

According to Foster and Rosenzweig (1995), inadequate knowledge of farmers about seeds and technological innovations serve as a barrier to effective adoption. However, this barrier decreases as they become more accustomed to adopting technologies. The findings show that knowledge on how to use new varieties is a barrier to its adoption and effectiveness. Drechsel, Olaleye, Adeoti, Thiombiano, Barry, and Vohland (2005) advocate that knowledge sharing on technology can be facilitated through communication infrastructure, media access, and having a functional network of continuously updated agents.

It is important to encourage the adoption of technological innovation amongst farmers who are mostly engaged in the informal sector and contribute immensely to a nation's economic activities. Farming is one of the indigenous occupations in developing nations, and this should be of interest to the global community to understand why farmers will not adopt technological innovations for the success of their farming business. Based on the assumptions of the Technology Adoption Model (TAM), despite the enormous benefits of the utilisation of technological innovation for their operational activities, the ease of usage of the technology can be a challenge to its adoption. There is a high rate of illiteracy at the BOP, which ultimately affects the usage and adoption of technology. Technological innovations may require a high level of technicality, which can be understood with a level of exposure and literacy that is not possessed by the farmers within this market.

Another factor that can influence technological adoption is the cost of adopting technological innovation. Most of the farmers within this market are poor, and it is difficult for them to purchase the technological equipment that will facilitate their farming business. Particularly in Africa, it may be challenging for them to raise sufficient funds to invest in the technology due to lack of capital, limited access to credit, or cash flow problems (Drechsel et al., 2005).

There are two opposing views regarding the argument that farmers are innovation averse. Some studies document that farmers' perceptions and values have an impact on technology adoption (Drechsel et al., 2005). Due to taboos, customs, cultural norms, values (Drechsel et al., 2005), and high levels of illiteracy, their perception of its usefulness may be biased. They would mostly prefer indigenous methods, which they trust and are familiar with. This would likely affect their attitude towards technological innovation and their perception of its social influence. One of the unique characteristics of consumers at the bottom of the pyramid is that they are conservative and do not have an impulsive reaction to goods and services. They hold their beliefs and culture in high esteem, making them resistant to innovation. Essentially, farmers at the bottom of the pyramid are least likely to adopt technological innovations because of their high level of illiteracy, the cost of technology adoption, and their cultural and ideological stance. The technology adoption model can, therefore, be used to predict farmers' adoption of technology.

However, studies such as those conducted by Fafchamps (2003) and de Janvry and Sadoulet (2002) challenge the argument and belief that poor farmers are innovation averse. According to Fafchamps (2003), smallholder farmers in developing countries need and are able to use new technology to escape poverty. According to de Janvry and Sadoulet (2002), technology relevant to agriculture has the potential to reduce poverty by enhancing gains to those who adopt the technology and gains derived when others in the vicinity adopt the technology.

Mobile-based market and agricultural interaction

In a technology-driven world, ICT is finding its way into agricultural practices through mobile applications, as it encourages and supports market interaction among stakeholders. Apart from enhancing trading opportunities, it also provides information on prices. For instance, the impact of mobile phone usage on fishermen in India and Senegal has been validated in research where mobile phones were found to reduce waste caused by price dispersion by enhancing the spread of information. The availability of information through the application brought benefits to suppliers and consumers alike. Mittal, Gandhi, and Tripathi (2010) and Brugger (2011) observed that fishermen used mobile applications to keep themselves informed of price dynamics and make a timely decision to increase their profits. Aker (2008), as cited in Brugger (2011), averred that the greater availability of phones would impact price dispersion in Uganda. In essence, the adoption of technology will enhance agricultural benefits for farmers, fishermen, and other agricultural units.

Attitudes towards risk-taking among farmers

Moscardi and de Janvry (1977) researched the link between the risk evident in farmers' decision making and adoption of technological innovation. They asserted that attitude towards risk is a determinant of adoption of technologies among farmers. In the study, it was found that older farmers take fewer risks than their younger counterparts. Also, their study revealed that having a higher level of education is associated with positive risk-taking. Furthermore, farmers with a large family were found to have an aversion to risk-taking because of the fear associated with the effects of uncertain outcomes on family survival. A larger family provides family labour, thereby making a case against technological adoption in operational services on the farm. Moscardi and de Janvry (1977) further attributed family size, education status, and age as factors that determine attitude to risk and technological adoption by farmers in developing nations. The likelihood of farmer household characteristics affecting the adoption of technology in Uganda cannot be overlooked.

Wealth and income constraints to adoption

Bonjean (2017, 2019); Miyata and Sawada (2007); Maertens and Barrett (2012); and Bonjean, Platteau, and Verardi (2017) investigated the relationship between wealth and income and adoption of technology and innovations. Bonjean et al. (2017) investigated the role that income can play in reducing the pace of adoption of innovation. They found that income constraints affect adoption, but to a limited extent. Instead, they revealed, trust and familiarity are stronger drivers of technology adoption than are income or affordability of the technology. Bonjean et al. (2017) postulated that when trust is built as a result of familiarity between the technology supplier or seller and the user, households are likely to adopt costly technology and innovations. It can be predicted that adoption is likely to be higher in the two cases where village agents are involved. This is because farmers are familiar with the village agents. The authors investigated how price of products affects adoption of technology and demonstrated the extent to which conditions within a segmented market lead to diverse reward expectations, consequently affecting the motivation for adoption. Bonjean et al. (2017) revealed that price of farm output is not necessarily related to technology adoption. Similar findings were reported in a study on prices and incentives to adopt technology (Bonjean, 2019). Maertens and Barrett (2012) disputed the link between incomes or wealth and technology adoption, saying the assumption of such links is too simplistic. They documented that individual characteristics, social networks, and social interaction affect adoption more than wealth or income do.

The study by Miyata and Sawada (2007) adds another perspective to the discussion of the relationship between income and technology adoption. These scholars examined technology adoption related to the use of a floating net in aquaculture among Indonesian households. They compared three factors: "social learning, risk attitudes, and credit accessibility" (p. 1) in panel data gathered over 16 years. Miyata and Sawada (2007) revealed that access to credit influences the rate of investment in new technology. This is because access to credit reduces risk perception and the extent of exposure.

Foster and Rosenzweig (2010) conducted a review of studies on technology adoption and examined the processes influencing usage of technology. Their study was generally premised on the argument that technology adoption increases incomes. They assert that adoption and use of technology is part and parcel of development. A study by Suri (2011) found that the decision to adopt technology is a rational one and that there is a heterogeneous net benefit of technology adoption. From the literature reviewed above, it can be concluded that, indeed, there is a bi-directional relationship between wealth, income, and adoption of technology.

Methodology

Case studies are used in constructivist enquiry to compare the two cases of uptake and usage of mobile and web-based platforms for linking farmers to farm services, markets, and extension services. In-depth interviews (Eisenhardt, 1989; Saldana, 2011), focus group discussions (Gill, Stewart, Treasure, & Chadwick, 2008), and literature reviews were used to collect the data.

According to Saldana (2011), an in-depth interview is the most common and effective method of data collection used in qualitative research. Likewise, Gill et al. (2008) argue that focus group discussions (FGDs) give depth and insight to the data collection process and to the resultant data collected. Since theory is an instrument that guides research (Ribes-Iñesta, 2018), reviews of technology acceptance and innovation diffusion theories, as well as theories related to market facilitation, informed the development of the research tools and interview checklist. The researchers held four key informant interviews (KIIs) and six FGDs. KIIs were held with the management of the farmer organizations under study, a facilitator of CPMA, and with the leadership of the two farmer groups. FGDs were held with representatives of the two farmer organizations and village agents serving farmers in those organizations. In all, 39 respondents were involved through KII and FGD. Further details are provided in Table 3.3.

Saldana (2011) documents varying opinions concerning the necessary sample size in qualitative research. The sample size of 39 respondents adequately ensured saturation. The 39 respondents represented relevant categories of actors engaged in the provision and usage of mobile platforms. Respondents represented the management of farmer institutions, providers of technology, facilitators of the linkage between farmers and technology providers, as well

Table 3.3 Data collection approaches applied

Data collection approaches	BAIDA	ZAABTA
Key Informant Interviews (KIIs)	• 2 KIIs (with Manager of BAIDA and ZAABTA) • 2 KIIs (with warehouse managers of BAIDA and ZAABTA) • 1 KII held with the manager of Akorion • 1 KII with management of CPM	• 2 KIIs (with Manager of BAIDA and ZAABTA) • 2 KIIs (with warehouse managers of BAIDA and ZAABTA) • 1 KII held with the manager of Akorion • 1 KII with management of CPM
Focus Group Discussions (FGDs)	• 2 FGDs held with farmers representatives. Each FGDs was attended by 6 farmers • 1 FGD held with 4 village agents at BAIDA	• 2 FGDs held with farmers representatives. Each FGDs was attended by 6 farmers • 1 FGD held with 5village agents at ZAABTA

as farmers, themselves, who are users of the technology. Drawing respondents from diverse yet relevant categories of actors provided situational diversity (Saldana, 2011), which is adequate for identifying thematic patterns regarding demand- and supply-side barriers of the BOP markets, thereby ensuring trustworthiness and quality of the study. Purposive and criterion-based sampling techniques (Eisenhardt, 1989; Tekel & Karadağ, 2017) were adopted to identify the farmer groups and respective respondents. Purposive selection ensures that adequate samples of cases are selected, hence ensuring theoretical saturation. Criterion-based sampling ensures adequate evidence as well as adequate variety in the kind of evidence relating to demand- and supply-side drivers of BOP markets in Uganda. The researchers obtained the consent of respondents from the farmer organizations (ZAABTA and BAIDA), as a way to ensure integrity and to ensure that the study fulfilled ethical (Fischhoff, 2000) and legal (Katvan & Shnoor, 2017) requirements. Consent was obtained from the leadership of the farmer organizations and from the individuals who participated in the interviews and FGDs prior to the respective conversations.

Secondary data were obtained from literature regarding the farmer institutions; the CPMA project, which facilitated linkage of the two farmer groups to technology; and stock books and sales records of the two farmer organizations. Records of products available at the warehouses of the two farmer groups were also reviewed. Volume of purchases and sales of inputs were obtained from stock records. Volume of sales was obtained from records available at the warehouses.

Saldana (2011) suggested different "styles of qualitative research documentation and presentation" (p. 146), including descriptive, analytic, formal, confessional, impressionistic, interpretive, literary, critical, and writing collaboratively. The researchers adhered to writing and presentation styles that are acceptable for qualitative research. Verbatim quotations from the KIIs and FGDs are used to provide "evidentiary support" (Saldana, 2011, p. 143), consequently building the credibility of this study.

Findings and discussions

Findings indicate various supply- and demand-side drivers and barriers regarding how people living at the BOP adopt and use technology. Table 3.4 summarises findings categorised under three subheadings, namely: drivers and barriers from the supply side of adoption and usage of a digital platform, demand-side drivers of adoption and usage of digital platforms, and market linkages. Under each subheading, similarities and differences in the two cases are presented. A discussion of findings follows after the comparison of the cases.

Supply-side drivers and barriers of adoption

Drivers and barriers from the supply side, which affect the adoption and usage of digital platforms in both farmer organizations relate to service failure, cost

Table 3.4 Summary of key findings of the study

Key findings	BAIDA	ZAABTA
Supply-side drivers and barriers of adoption and usage of digital platform	*Similarities* • **Barrier; Service failure** – occasionally systems fail, making services inaccessible. Also, infrequent update of online information occasionally makes information inaccurate. • **Barrier; Cost** – The cost of smartphones is higher relative to farmers' incomes and expenditure streams. *Differences* • Two digital platforms are used: MobiPay and Akorion's EzyAgric mobile and digital platform. • **Barrier; Infrastructure** – Power failure occurs frequently at BAIDA, causing network failure and making users unable to charge phones.	• Only EzyAgric mobile and digital platform are currently being used. • **Driver; Infrastructure** – Power (electricity) failure occurs less frequently at ZAABTA.
Demand-side drivers and barriers of adoption and usage of digital platform	*Similarities* • **Barrier; Perceived ease of use of smartphones** – arise from illiteracy and inadequate digital literacy. • **Driver; Village agents** – play significant roles in helping farmers who are digitally illiterate to put in orders for inputs and to access extension services. • **Barrier; Attitudes towards use** – Reduced costs of inputs to farmers lead to increased affordability and usage of farm inputs. Also, efficiency and convenience of finding extension advice on the platform improve attitudes towards use. *Differences* • **Driver; Additional functionality of EzyAgric** has increased its adoption. For example, the application has been used for farmer mobilization. • **Driver; Social influence** – Village agents becoming popular and taking up leadership positions.	• **Driver; linkage** to a youth group (Nokia Farmers) that provides labour services. • **Driver; ZAABTA** has also linked government extension workers to use EzyAgric platform to support farmers.
Market linkages (linkages to markets of technology, inputs, and outputs)	*Similarities* • Adoption and usage of the platform is dependent on demand for inputs and extension services. • Effective demand for inputs and extension services is also dependent on the perceived prices of farm outputs and cost of accessing services on the platform. • Fluctuations in the prices of farm products affect adoption and usage of EzyAgric. *Difference* • BAIDA continues to rely on a volatile external market for the products of its members.	• ZAABTA is also processing and adding value to its grain products, hence providing an internal market for its members.

Source: authors' own.

of a smartphone, and inadequate infrastructure. A previous study (Feder, Just, & Zilberman, 1985) attributed low technology adoption to limited access to information, inadequate farm size, aversion to risk, lack of human capital, supply of inputs (e.g. seeds, chemicals, and water), and poor transportation. This study adds new perspectives and insights to the consideration of drivers of technology adoption. The role of the supplier of technology in enhancing adoption is mentioned in the technology diffusion theory (Surry, 1997). In this study, managing service failure and regularly updating information on the platform is the role of Akorion, the supplier of technology. Service failure is reported in FGDs with village agents in both groups, as quoted below.

> *We often face challenges when the platform is not accessible and when the symptoms farmers report are not described in the platform.*
>
> (Village agents, ZAABTA)

> *Sometimes the system is down, and the platform is not accessible.*
>
> (Village agents, BAIDA)

Service failure is caused by the lack of regular updates to the online platform. Irregular updating causes online content at certain times to be inaccurate. Ensuring that Akorion regularly updates the extension information is instrumental in the continuous uptake and usage of the mobile and web-based platform.

A previous study (Mitropoulos & Tatum, 2000) reported costs of the technology as a hindrance to adoption. In this study, the cost of smartphones varies depending on the type and origin, but generally, the price for the cheapest smartphone was about 200,000 Uganda shillings (US$50); this is relatively high in relation to farmers' incomes. This study corroborates the study by Mitropoulos and Tatum (2000) and reaffirms that, indeed, the relatively high cost of smartphones affects adoption and usage of the mobile and web-based platform. This is reported by the management of both farmer groups, as quoted below.

> *Most of the farmers we serve cannot afford smartphones. Only village agents have smartphones, and so farmers request services from the village agents.*
>
> (Management of ZAABTA and BAIDA)

Aker (2008) predicted that adoption of mobile phone-based technology will enhance agricultural benefits for farmers. Brugger (2011) observed that farmers can use mobile phones to keep themselves informed. In the case of BAIDA, two digital platforms, MobiPay and Akorion's EzyAgric mobile and digital platform, are currently being used. MobiPay is designed to be compatible with mobile phones and uses Unstructured Supplementary Service Data (USSD) applications, which work well in feature phones. Feature phones are generally cheaper and more affordable. The MobiPay platform is mainly used to send payments for grains, as reported by village agents in an FGD held at BAIDA.

> *We only use MobiPay to effect payments. We use the EzyAgric platform for sourcing inputs and for accessing extension services.*

> (Village agents, BAIDA)

Infrastructural constraints were cited in a study by Akpabio et al., (2007). In this study, infrastructural constraints took the form of power or electricity failure. Electricity is needed to enable farmers and village agents to charge their phones. In addition, the platform is internet-based, and because of this, unstable connectivity affects its stability. Infrastructural constraints are a significant challenge to BAIDA, partly because BAIDA is located upcountry, where coverage of public services is often inadequate. ZAABTA does not regularly encounter power outages, and this could be because of its proximity to Kampala, the main city. Electricity problems were reported by village agents at BAIDA:

> *We often face challenges with electricity. Supply of electricity is not consistent. When there is a power cut, we cannot charge our phones. When the phones are not charged, it is not possible to have access to the platform.*

> (Village agents, BAIDA)

Demand-side drivers and barriers to adoption

Demand-side drivers of adoption and usage of digital platforms relate to perceived ease of use of smartphones, illiteracy and digital illiteracy, attitudes towards use, and the reduced price of inputs arising from bulk purchase. Perceived ease of use of smartphones and attitudes towards use of technology was mentioned in an earlier study by Teo (2011).

Illiteracy and inadequate digital literacy affect how farmers perceive ease of use of technology. Village agents play significant roles in linking and enabling farmers who are illiterate to indirectly use the platform. In the case of sourcing inputs, farmers go to the village agents to make a demand for services, then the village agents aggregate and deliver orders from the various farmers to the leadership of the groups. The leadership of the two farmer groups then place orders for the inputs, hence obtaining discounts due to bulk purchasing. Similarly, in the case of accessing extension services, illiterate farmers approach village agents for help. The roles of village agents in driving adoption as well as in navigating perceptions about ease of use of the technology was mentioned by the management of Akorion, ZAABTA and BAIDA:

> *The village agents play an important role to support farmers who cannot read and write to request for inputs and also access extension services (KII, Akorion).*
> *The support of village agents is important to make farmers more willing to use the platform.*

> (Management of ZAABTA)

Agents aggregate needs for input from farmers, then pass the needs to us. We then negotiate the price and make orders from the input dealers. Inputs are delivered here, and we distribute to the respective farmers.

(Management of BAIDA)

ZAABTA mainly uses the EzyAgric mobile and digital platform. ZAABTA uses also uses the EzyAgric platform, but for two primary reasons: extension service provision and aggregating demand for inputs. Enhancing capacity to provide relevant extension services and driving usage of the platform is reported by the management of ZAABTA in a verbatim quotation:

We narrowed down usage of the platform to extension and purchase of inputs. In the case of extension, we realised that our agents have limitations, so we linked them to government extension service providers and to the nearby research institute.

(Management, ZAABTA)

Due to the limited knowledge and expertise of the village agents in providing extension services, ZAABTA has linked government extension workers and staff from a nearby research institute to use the EzyAgric platform to support farmers. Selected contacts of government extension workers are shared through the platform, and farmers are able to call such government extension staff for additional consultation and advice.

Incentives are relevant in enhancing adoption. Clear incentives and benefits from adoption of a technology improve attitudes towards use, which was postulated in technology acceptance theory (Venkatesh et al., 2016; Venkatesh et al., 2012) and in a study of intention to use technology (Teo, 2011). Incentives are related to reduced costs of inputs to farmers, increased affordability of farm inputs, and efficiency and convenience of finding extension advice on the platform. The incentive for the village agent and management of the farmer organizations to drive usage is commission obtainable from the bulk purchase of inputs.

A study by Foster and Rosenzweig (1995) postulated the role of adoption in enhancing transparency. Adoption of technology leads to transparency in the input market, hence addressing information asymmetry (Foster & Rosenzweig, 1995). Transparency is relevant in building trust. In both farmer groups, trust has emerged between farmers and village agents. The platform enhanced trust-building by encouraging transparency in dealings between the village agents, farmer organizations, and the farmers.

At BAIDA, the additional functionality of the application has increased its adoption. For instance, the application has been used for farmer mobilization purposes and to reach out to farmers easily by way of sending messages to farmers' mobile numbers. In addition, village agents are deriving increased value and incentives from their roles. Some village agents become popular among the farmers they serve and take up leadership and political positions in their communities. ZAABTA has integrated a linkage to a youth group (Nokia Farmers) that provides labour services to the platform. Where farmers need labour services for various purposes on the farm, they are able to contact the youth group that provides such labour services through the platform. The use of the platform for farmer mobilisation is described by the management of BAIDA as follows:

> *We have expanded usage of the platform. We use the additional functions to mobilise farmers when we are calling them for a meeting. We have also seen some of our village agents become popular among farmers, and their roles change. Some have become voted into leadership positions.*
>
> (Management of BAIDA)

Market linkages (linkages to markets of technology, inputs, and outputs)

Linkages to the markets of outputs or farm products are necessary to drive adoption and usage of the platform. In addition, price fluctuations that occur in the market for farm products also affect adoption and usage of the platform. When prices for farm products are low, farmers are not motivated to use inputs because the value of doing so is lower. Yields arising from using inputs may increase, but gains arising from such yields may not be adequate to cover the high prices of inputs, thereby causing a reduction in input usage and, ultimately, a reduction in usage of the platform to purchase inputs. Appropriate linkages are essential to drive usage. Linkages to markets of farmers' products are as important as linkages to the farm inputs. In both cases, the two farmer groups play significant roles in enhancing these linkages. ZAABTA is also processing and adding value to its grain products, hence providing a stable internal market for its members. BAIDA continues to rely on a volatile external market for farm products. Relating linkages in the market for products and inputs to adoption are key factors as reflected in these verbatim quotes:

> *When the price of maize was low in one season, usage of fertilizer goes down in the season that follows. So, a stable market for maize will allow for usage of fertilisers.*
>
> (Village Agents BAIDA)

> *We have the capacity to buy, stock, and process maize and sell maize flour. This has enabled us to stabilize prices for our farmers. We have seen fewer fluctuations in the usage of inputs.*
>
> (Management, ZAABTA)

Conclusions and recommendations

In this section, we present key conclusions and recommendations. First, in this study, we revealed significant similarities in the demand- and supply-side drivers and barriers in the two cases. Service failure, cost of a smartphone, and inadequate infrastructure constitute key drivers and barriers from the supply side that affect the adoption and usage of the digital platform. In addition, perceived ease of use of smartphones, which is influenced by illiteracy and digital illiteracy, attitudes towards use, and reduced price for inputs arising from bulk purchases constitute key demand-side drivers of adoption and usage of the digital platform. The two cases and the adoption and usage of digital platforms provide new and transparent models of market linkage to inputs and services and markets for products built around the farmer organizations and village agents. The farmer organization is the watchdog, mediating and building trust between agents and farmers.

Furthermore, we revealed ample evidence to demonstrate that the sustainable usage of digital platforms, such as EzyAgric, is reliant upon incentives that all concerned parties derive as well as the level of institutional development. In the two cases, the strength and cohesion of the farmer groups are instrumental to enhancing the usage of the platform. Mitigating service failure is an additional aspect of inculcating market sustainability. Service failure reduces users' faith and trust in the service and eventually reduces their interest in and support for using the service.

Also, there are inter-linkages between the adoption of technology, market for inputs, as well as markets for farm products. Essentially, adoption of technology only makes sense if the adoption leads to gains in the form of better prices of products and lower prices of farm inputs. It can be concluded that demand for technology is derived from the demand of markets for products and inputs.

Different recommendations are advanced for different stakeholders to undertake initiatives that will enable overcoming barriers to technology adoption. Improving access to infrastructure such as electricity is necessary to support the usage of digital services. This is because farmers and farmer groups need electricity to charge their phones, and in so doing, they are able to access the internet. It is recommended that governments increase investment in infrastructure and ensure efficient distribution of electricity.

In addition, private sector providers of mobile telephone services (mobile network operators) need to ensure network stability in order for farmers to be able to profitably utilize EzyAgric. This calls for increased private sector investments in improving network coverage. It is also recommended that providers of agricultural inputs invest in developing markets for their products. The implication is that these should provide inputs to invest in trials with farmers to demonstrate advantages of inputs' usage. Such companies also need to invest in training farmers to use inputs. Also, discounts arising from bulk purchases will enhance increased purchases and adoption of usage of inputs and the platform. Since farmer groups such as BAIDA and ZAABTA also benefit from commissions arising from the usage of the platform, then farmer groups should continuously promote usage of inputs and the platform. In addition, farmer groups should proactively facilitate linkages of farmers to inputs and markets for their products.

Limitations and suggestions for further studies

Despite the interesting contribution, the study has some limitations. This study has not, to a large extent, explored the role of linkages in strengthening supply and demand of services. As a result, further studies should explore the role of linkages of farmers to input sources and also linkages to markets of farm products in enhancing adoption and usage of ICT. Finally, this paper contributes to the understanding of the barriers to uptake of technology, however, further studies may investigate strategies to overcome these particular barriers in order to contribute to the success of social enterprises in the BOP context.

References

Aker, J. C. (2008). *Does digital divide or provide? The impact of cell phones on grain markets in Niger.* London: Center for Global Development.

Akpabio, I. A., Okon, D. P., & Inyang, E. B. (2007). Constraints affecting ICT utilization by agricultural extension officers in the Niger Delta, Nigeria. *Journal of Agricultural Education and Extension, 13*(4), 263–272.

Aleke, B., Ojiako, U., & Wainwright, D. W. (2011). ICT adoption in developing countries: Perspectives from small-scale agribusinesses. *Journal of Enterprise Information Management, 24*(1), 68–84.

Beldad, A. D., & Hegner, S. M. (2018). Expanding the technology acceptance model with the inclusion of trust, social influence, and health valuation to determine the predictors of German users' willingness to continue using a fitness app: A structural equation modeling approach. *International Journal of Human–Computer Interaction, 34*(9), 882–893

Bharti, K., Agrawal, R., & Sharma, V. (2014). What drives the customer of world's largest market to participate in value co-creation? *Marketing Intelligence & Planning, 32*(4), 413–435.

Bhavnani, A., Chiu, R. W. W., Janakiram, S. and Silarszky, P. (2008). *The role of mobile phones in sustainable rural poverty reduction.* Washington, DC: World Bank.

Bonjean, I. (2017, August-September). Heterogeneous gains from agricultural innovation adoption: The role of the price effect in Peru. Towards sustainable agri-food systems: Balancing between markets and society. Paper presented at the XV EAAE Congress, Parma, Italy. Retrieved from https://ageconsearch.umn.edu/record/260891/files/Heterogeneous%20Gains%20From%20Agricultural%20Innovation%20Adoption%3A%20The%20Role%20Of%20The%20Price%20Effect%20In%20Peru.pdf

Bonjean, I. (2019). Heterogeneous incentives for innovation adoption: The price effect on segmented markets. *Food Policy, 87,* 101741.

Bonjean, I., Platteau, J. P., & Verardi, V. (2017). Innovation Adoption and Liquidity Constraints in the Presence of Grassroots Extension Agents: Evidence from the Peruvian Highlands (No. 12263), CEPR Discussion Papers, CEPR.

Brugger, F. (2011). Mobile applications in agriculture. *Syngenta Foundation,* 1–38.

Carmody, P. (2012). The informationalization of poverty in Africa? Mobile phones and economic structure. *Information Technologies & International Development, 8*(3), 1–17.

Cooney, K., & Williams Shanks, T. R. (2010). New approaches to old problems: Market-based strategies for poverty alleviation. *Social Service Review, 84*(1), 29–55.

Cunningham, S. & Jenal, M. (2016). *Rethinking systemic change: Economic evolution and institution* (working paper). Retrieved from: https://beamexchange.org/uploads/filer_public/2e/76/2e76ef48-f317-4f20-9459-991f6d21b191/systemic_change_technical02.pdf

De Janvry, A., & Sadoulet, E. (2002). World poverty and the role of agricultural technology: direct and indirect effects. *Journal of Development Studies, 38*(4), 1–26.

Diga, K. (2007). *Mobile cell phones and poverty reduction: technology spending patterns and poverty level change among households in Uganda* (Master's thesis, University of KwaZulu-Natal Durban). Retrieved from https://idl-bnc-idrc.dspacedirect.org/bitstream/handle/10625/44374/130806.pdf?sequence=1

Drechsel, P., Olaleye, A., Adeoti, A., Thiombiano, L., Barry, B., & Vohland, K. (2005). *Adoption driver and constraints of resource conservation technologies in sub-Saharan Africa.* Berlin: FAO, IWMI, Humboldt Universitaet.

Eisenhardt, K. M. (1989). Building theories from case study research. *Academy of Management Review, 14*(4), 532–550.

Fafchamps, M. (2003). *Rural poverty, risk and development.* Cheltenham, UK: Edward Elgar Publishing.

Feder, G., Just, R. E., & Zilberman, D. (1985). Adoption of agricultural innovations in developing countries: A survey. *Economic Development and Cultural Change, 33*(2), 255–298.

Fischhoff, B. (2000). Informed consent for eliciting environmental values. *Environmental Science & Technology, 34*(8), 1439–1444.

Foster, A. D., & Rosenzweig, M. R. (1995). Learning by doing and learning from others: Human capital and technical change in agriculture. *Journal of Political Economy, 103*(6), 1176–1209.

Foster, A. D., & Rosenzweig, M. R. (2010). Microeconomics of technology adoption. *Annual Review of Economics, 2*(1), 395–424.

Gill, P., Stewart, K., Treasure, E., & Chadwick, B. (2008). Methods of data collection in qualitative research: interviews and focus groups. *British Dental Journal, 204*(6), 291–295.

Katvan, E., & Shnoor, B. (2017). Informed consent to legal treatment – lessons from medical informed consent. *International Journal of the Legal Profession, 24*(2), 125–144.

Kessler, A. (2014). *Assessing systemic change implementation guidelines for the DCED standard.* Retrieved from Beam Exchange website: https://beamexchange.org/uploads/filer_public/c1/f0/c1f0aa93-6bca-4f88-9bc4-758567bd3821/dcedsystemicchange.pdf

Kiiza, B., & Pederson, G. (2012). ICT-based market information and adoption of agricultural seed technologies: Insights from Uganda. *Telecommunications Policy, 36*(4), 253–259.

Lashitew, A. A., Bals, L., & van Tulder, R. (2018). Inclusive business at the base of the pyramid: The role of embeddedness for enabling social innovations. *Journal of Business Ethics, 162*(1), 1–28.

Legris, P., Ingham, J., & Collerette, P. (2003). Why do people use information technology? A critical review of the technology acceptance model. *Information & Management, 40*(3), 191–204.

Lee, Y. H., Hsieh, Y. C., & Hsu, C. N. (2011). Adding innovation diffusion theory to the technology acceptance model: Supporting employees' intentions to use e-learning systems. *Journal of Educational Technology & Society, 14*(4), 124–137.

Lee, Y., & Kozar, K. A. (2008). An empirical investigation of anti-spyware software adoption: A multitheoretical perspective. *Information & Management, 45*(2), 109–119.

Lee, C., & Wan, G. (2010). Including subjective norm and technology trust in the technology acceptance model: A case of e-ticketing in China. *ACM SIGMIS Database: The DATABASE for Advances in Information Systems, 41*(4), 40–51.

Lu, Y., Zhou, T., & Wang, B. (2009). Exploring Chinese users' acceptance of instant messaging using the theory of planned behavior, the technology acceptance model, and the flow theory. *Computers in Human Behavior, 25,* 29–39.

Maertens, A., & Barrett, C. B. (2012). Measuring social networks' effects on agricultural technology adoption. *American Journal of Agricultural Economics, 95*(2), 353–359.

Mitropoulos, P., & Tatum, C. B. (2000). Forces driving adoption of new information technologies. *Journal of Construction Engineering and Management, 126*(5), 340–348.

Mittal, S., Gandhi, S., & Tripathi, G. (2010). Socio-economic impact of mobile phones on Indian agriculture (Working Paper No. 246). New Delhi, India: Indian Council for Research on International Economic Relations (ICRIER).

Miyata, S., & Sawada, Y. (2007). Learning, risk, and credit in households' new technology investments: The case of aquaculture in rural Indonesia (unpublished manuscript). *IFPRI.*

Moscardi, E., & de Janvry, A. (1977). Attitudes toward risk among peasants: An econometric approach. *American Journal of Agricultural Economics, 59*(4), 710–716.

Ortiz-Ospina, E., Beltekian, D., & Roser, M. (2018). Trade and globalization. Retrieved from the Our World in Data website: https://ourworldindata.org/trade-and-globalization.

Pavlou, P. A. (2003). Consumer acceptance of electronic commerce: Integrating trust and risk with the technology acceptance model. *International Journal of Electronic Commerce, 7*(3), 101–134.

Prahalad, C. K. (2012). Bottom of the Pyramid as a source of breakthrough innovations. *Journal of Product Innovation Management, 29*(1), 6–12.

Redmond, W. (2018). Marketing systems and market failure: A macromarketing appraisal. *Journal of Macromarketing, 38*(4), 415–424.

Ribes-Iñesta, E. (2018). J. R. Kantor: Theory as the basic research instrument. *Psychological Record, 68*(2), 267–272.

Ripley, M., & Nippard, D. (2014). Making sense of "messiness." Monitoring and measuring change in market systems: A practitioner's perspective. Retrieved from the Beam Exchange website: https://beamexchange.org/uploads/filer_public/c9/bb/c9bb16e6-c5ff-43ac-8a5f-d6fcc1106f20/makingsensemessiness2014.pdf

Rogers, E. M. (1995). *Diffusion of Innovations* (4th ed.). New York: Free Press.

Rogers, E. M. (2002). Diffusion of preventive innovations. *Addictive Behaviors, 27*(6), 989–993.

Rogers, E. M. (2004). A prospective and retrospective look at the diffusion model. *Journal of Health Communication, 9*(1), 13–19.

Saldana, J. (2011). *Fundamentals of qualitative research.* New York: Oxford University Press.

Sife, A. S., Kiondo, E., & Lyimo-Macha, J. G. (2010). Contribution of mobile phones to rural livelihoods and poverty reduction in Morogoro region, Tanzania. *The Electronic Journal of Information Systems in Developing Countries, 42*(1), 1–15.

Smit, J., Sheombar, A., & Silvius, A. J. (2009). Cooperation issues in developing the BOP market. *Proceedings from AMCIS 2009: The 15th Americas Conference on Information Systems*. San Francisco, CA: DBLP.

Smith, M. L., Spence, R., & Rashid, A. T. (2011). Mobile phones and expanding human capabilities. *Information Technologies & International Development*, 7(3), 77–88.

Subhan, F., & Khattak, A. (2016). What constitutes the Bottom of the Pyramid (BOP) market? Paper presented at the Institute of Business Administration International Conference on Marketing (IBA-ICM), Kuala Lumpur.

Suri, T. (2011). Selection and comparative advantage in technology adoption. *Econometrica*, 79(1), 159–209.

Surry, D. W. (1997, February). Diffusion theory and instructional technology. Paper presented at the Annual Conference of the Association for Educational Communications and Technology, Albuquerque, New Mexico.

Sy-Changco, J. A., Pornpitakpan, C., Singh, R., & Bonilla, C. M. (2011). Managerial insights into sachet marketing strategies and popularity in the Philippines. *Asia Pacific Journal of Marketing and Logistics*, 23(5), 755–772.

Tekel, E., & Karadağ, E. (2017). A Qualitative study on the moral dilemmas of elementary and high school principals. *Turkish Journal of Business Ethics*, 10(1), 87–98.

Teo, T. (2011). Factors influencing teachers' intention to use technology: Model development and test. *Computers & Education*, 57(4), 2432–2440.

Venkatesh, V., Thong, J. Y., & Xu, X. (2012). Consumer acceptance and use of information technology: extending the unified theory of acceptance and use of technology. *MIS Quarterly*, 36(1), 157–178.

Venkatesh, V., Thong, J. Y., & Xu, X. (2016). Unified theory of acceptance and use of technology: A synthesis and the road ahead. *Journal of the Association for Information Systems*, 17(5), 328–376.

Yang, S., Lu, Y., Gupta, S., Cao, Y., & Zhang, R. (2012). Mobile payment services adoption across time: An empirical study of the effects of behavioral beliefs, social influences, and personal traits. *Computers in Human Behavior*, 28, 129–142.

4 Risk and social value creation in volatile BOP markets

A case study from Somalia

*Ahmad Arslan, Ismail Gölgeci, Minnie Kontkanen,
and Tiina Leposky*

Introduction

The Base of the Pyramid (BOP) markets represent the single most substantial portion of customers on the planet, but for a long time, these markets were neglected due to the low income levels of the individuals inhabiting them (Prahalad, 2006). Several studies have addressed issues like frugal innovation, social enterprise development, technology and its use by local entrepreneurs, and innovative services and product marketing strategies in BOP markets in Africa, Asia, and Latin America (e.g. Cieslik, 2016; Waibel, 2017). Taking a viewpoint that the aggregated buying power of BOP markets represents viable business opportunities and that the exceptional market conditions due to poverty are conducive for the introduction of innovative products and services, BOP research suggests that business ventures can be helpful in social value creation (Sinkovics, Sinkovics, & Yamin, 2014). However, a literature review reveals that there is a dearth of studies taking an international business (IB) approach to study market entry in volatile BOP markets, even though the success rate of international firms entering BOP markets has been relatively low (e.g. Rohatynskyj, 2011). Thus, we have a limited understanding of whether the entry and operation decision criteria are the same for foreign firms entering BOP markets compared to more traditional markets (e.g. Schuster and Holtbrugge, 2012). Moreover, what is also unknown is how the potential for social value creation influences these decisions.

It should be further noted that product and service marketing strategy analysis in BOP markets is increasingly gaining the attention of academic researchers (e.g. Payaud, 2014; Leposky, Arslan, & Dikova, 2019). A review of extant literature shows that the focus of such studies has primarily been on either local firms and their customer service strategies or western (developed market) multinational enterprises (MNEs) and their product or service marketing strategies in BOP markets (e.g. Kolk, Rivera-Santos, & Rufin, 2014; Leposky et al., 2019). However, the operations of emerging market (EM) small- and medium-sized enterprises (SMEs) in the BOP context are relatively under-researched so far. Firms from an EM background, specifically from Turkey and China, have entered the volatile market of Somalia despite the risk of civil war, violence, and political unrest. This interest by the foreign firms is understandable, as the international political economy literature has established that, in areas where states fail to provide services, external actors (e.g. foreign firms) tend to fill the gap (e.g. Hönke & Thauer, 2014). However, this attention by foreign firms to a country that is ravaged by instability and civil war goes against the conventional view of risk behaviour where firm managers are rational actors who tend to avoid entering such risky markets.

The current chapter challenges this generalised perception of risk behaviour. First, we argue for risk to be perceived at the firm-specific level instead of based at the country level in contexts of institutional voids. Our argument relies on prior work done in unstable and volatile contexts, including Africa (e.g. Frynas & Mellahi, 2003; Jensen & Young, 2008). In this context, it has been referred that "risk should be constructed as being primarily a firm-specific or project-specific value assessment rather than country risk, as it depends on the goal and resources of a firm or project" (Frynas & Mellahi, 2003, p. 546). Likewise, the concept of risk is double-edged, particularly in the construction sector, as its negative aspects in high-risk contexts are coupled with opportunities stemming from reconstruction efforts amid or in the aftermath of civil wars or conflicts (e.g. Reilly, 1950; Ganson & Wennmann, 2018). Moreover, in many BOP markets, especially in Africa, infrastructure is in bad condition due to years of negligence or other political problems (Calderón, 2009). At the same time, due to the importance of infrastructure and the construction industry in day-to-day life, there is a significant demand for such services, even in conflict-hit economies (Collier, 2003). This gives a firm operating in the construction sector an opportunity to serve the local needs and potentially create social value.

The current study aims to address the dynamics of risk and social value creation by a Turkish origin firm operating in the under-researched volatile BOP context of Somalia. The case firm is a construction enterprise with past and present operations spanning several developing countries where it has served BOP consumers as well. It entails rather unique motives for operating in Somalia, including social value creation for BOP consumers. Our chapter contributes to the extant literature by increasing the understanding of both international market entry and operations of EM firms in a volatile BOP context representing high risk. By doing so, we extend the discussion on entry and operation mode choice in the BOP market context by exploring the role of risk perception and home country image while entering volatile markets. We also increase understanding of how EM SMEs with limited resources manage their international business operations under extreme risk and uncertainty. Moreover, we highlight how foreign firms can create value for BOP consumers in the construction sector. Some prior studies have highlighted that foreign firms can potentially create social value by serving a niche product or service market which was previously inaccessible (e.g. Sinkovics et al., 2014; Leposky et al., 2019). Therefore, our study contributes to the literature stream on social value creation in BOP markets and highlights the dynamics of social value creation by a foreign construction firm in the volatile context of Somalia.

The rest of the chapter is organized as follows. The next section offers a discussion on theoretical background followed by a presentation of the study's methodology and empirical findings. The chapter concludes with a presentation of implications, limitations, and future research directions.

Literature review and research context

Foreign firm entry and operations in volatile markets

The IB literature has established that decision criteria for market entry and operation modes range from minimising costs and risks to maximising profits, getting access to resources, and dealing with institutional dynamics (e.g. Dunning, 2000; Arslan, 2011). Country risk has been seen as an essential factor that influences the choice of entry of foreign firms in a market (e.g. Henisz, Mansfield, & von Glinow, 2010; Mullner, 2016). The influence of risks on market entry and operations have been addressed using a range of theoretical lenses (e.g. transaction-cost based approach, real options theory, eclectic framework) and empirical methodologies in the IB literature (e.g. Mullner, 2016). Risks associated with a country stem mostly from the political environment. Historically, we have seen such risks manifest themselves in the form of nationalisation of industries (e.g. Cuba and Iran), restrictions on the repatriation of capital (e.g. Argentina and Malaysia), or political violence and war (e.g. Somalia, Sierra Leone, Democratic Republic of the Congo, Liberia, and other African countries; see, for example, Jensen & Young, 2008). Therefore, any firm interested in entering a relatively risky market needs to evaluate risks associated with breach of contract, restrictions on financial transfers, and risk of large-scale violence affecting ownership and operations (i.e. violence risk; Jensen & Young, 2008; Henisz et al., 2010) over the potential benefits.

Attractive benefits associated with operations of foreign firms in violence-hit markets include less competition and long-term growth prospects (e.g. Guidolin & La Ferrera, 2007; Dai, Eden, & Beamish, 2017). It was mentioned earlier that risk should not only be viewed generally, but also in the context of a specific firm and its goals (Fyrnas & Mellahi, 2003). This argument is supported by the foreign direct investment (FDI) literature, where findings show that violence does not necessarily reduce investment flows (e.g. Biglaiser & DeRouen, 2007; Li & Vaschilko, 2010). Even more interesting are the studies where the authors found a positive relationship between FDI and conflict or violence in specific industries (e.g. Biglaiser & DeRouen, 2006; Asiedu & Lien, 2011). Therefore, the operations of foreign firms in a violence-hit economy like Somalia are not unusual even though they may appear to go against the convention logic of risk aversion followed by most firms.

Construction sector in volatile markets and specificities of the Somalian context

Construction is a broad-based sector responsible for a range of activities that include material production, design, finance, planning, construction, operation, maintenance, and possibly demolition (Finkel, 2015). There are different categories of construction, including housing, commercial buildings, industrial construction, airports, train networks, roads and highways, telecommunication, energy, and electricity infrastructure (e.g. Finkel, 2015). The construction industry involves – directly or indirectly – many players, such as investment firms, financial institutions, contractors, material manufacturers and suppliers, labour sub-contracting firms, local authorities, and public agencies (Hillebrandt, 2000; Grosso, Jankowska, & Gonzales, 2008). As a result, its economic impact has been found to significantly increase if spillover effects are considered (e.g. Hillebrandt, 2000; Finkel, 2015).

Construction has increasingly become a global industry with many firms operating in different countries (e.g. Ofori, 2008). However, global construction markets have many possible risks that influence entry, operations, and project implementation by foreign firms (Grosso et al., 2008; Xiaopeng & Pheng, 2013). Despite these risks, returns on investment in construction sectors are relatively high, and they increase even further when the firm is operating in a volatile context, where the competition is relatively low (Edwards & Edwards, 1995). It should be further noted that risk propensity of EM firms is different from western MNEs, as they have experience dealing with political upheavals and institutional voids in their home countries (Ramamurti, 2012). Therefore, it can be argued that EM firms are more equipped to enter and operate successfully in volatile markets.

Prior research suggests that historical, cultural, and religious linkages between countries make operations easier for foreign firms from those specific markets (e.g. Basuil & Datta, 2015). Somalia and Turkey share historical and religious relations spanning over centuries (e.g. Ozkan, 2017). The Ottoman Empire, which was formed and predominantly governed by Turks, was one of the largest trading partners and military allies of different ruling dynasties in Somalia until the 19th century (Njoku, 2013). In recent years, political and economic relationships have strengthened based on geostrategic considerations of the Turkish government (e.g. Ozkan, 2017). As a result, Turkish firms tend to receive favourable treatment, such as greater access to public tenders in Somalia, which potentially offsets risks associated with entry and operations in such a volatile context. Therefore, despite the risks, Somalia is an attractive market for Turkish firms, especially in vital sectors like construction.

Construction industry, BOP markets, and value creation

The construction industry has the potential to promote significant economic activity that can uplift people from extreme poverty, especially in violence-hit economies (e.g. McCutcheon, 1995; Del Castillo, 2008). Therefore, the discussion on the construction industry as a social enterprise (e.g. Loosemore & Higgon, 2015) has been increasing in the academic discourse. Social enterprises are businesses with a social mandate that can vary from purely charitable to profit-driven with social implications. It has been argued in this context that social actions need not be stated, and firms can create social value, even out of profit-seeking motives (Acs, Boardman, & McNeely, 2013). To explore this phenomenon, it is necessary to understand what is meant by social value, conceptually, and how it relates to firms. Social value has been used as an umbrella term to cover all activities that can be construed as socially motivated rather than profit- or business-driven. There have been some attempts to create instruments to measure social value creation (e.g. Kuratko, McMullen, Hornsby, & Jackson, 2017). However, they have not been rigorously tested and agreed upon by scholars.

To differentiate between general organizational attitudes and visibility efforts, and real, ground-level activities that positively influence locals, the term strategic corporate social responsibility (CSR) was coined to join the profit and social aims of firms (Visser, 2011). Strategic CSR incorporates a value creation aspect, which requires engagement and working together with local actors (Yin & Jamali, 2016). It is important because otherwise foreign firms can end up missing their mark and disengaging and isolating locals from projects ostensibly aimed at them (Newenham-Kahindi, 2011). While strategic CSR conceptually relates to value creation with network actors, it merely deepens an existing concept. Much scholarly debate has been raised by an article by Porter and Kramer (2011) which specifically suggested moving towards creating shared value. They define shared value as "policies and operating practices that enhance the competitiveness of a company while simultaneously advancing the economic and social conditions in the communities in which it operates" (Porter & Kramer, 2011, 66). This concept explicitly recognises the business aims of an organization, whilst being incorporated in its core purpose and subsequently informing its activities (Porter & Kramer, 2014). This approach to business requires firms to juggle these dual goals simultaneously.

An interesting example in this concern is of Grameen Dannon, which offers highly nutritious but affordably priced yoghurt cups in rural areas of Bangladesh. This example shows that not meeting financial goals can force firms to redefine their distribution, pricing, and business logic, which in this situation led to establishing an urban sales arm for the product to offset losses in the original rural target market (Kuratko et al., 2017). Such strategies are necessary even in firms with primarily a social mandate, implying that ultimately, value creation comes with costs as well as benefits (Dembek, Singh, & Bhakoo, 2016). Based on these conceptualisations of social value that profit-seeking firms can provide, we argue that construction firms can take an active role in promoting societal well-being as they operate in a sector that addresses the basic human need of housing. Yet, social value creation does not occur in a vacuum, and it is influenced by the environment and institutions surrounding it. In contexts where institutions are weak with large BOP population segments, firms seeking to create social value must opt for a long-term orientation and engage with local actors and stakeholders to understand how their business model supports the community (Sinkovics et al., 2014; Barraket & Loosemore, 2018). In this way, they can develop an offering that targets BOP consumers' needs, rather than creating solutions based on their operations in different contexts. Also, this approach to value creation can help foreign construction firms to mitigate risk by engagement with key stakeholders while creating value for BOP consumers.

Research methodology

Research method choice and the case firm

There is scarce literature on why and how EM firms enter and operate in a specific type of volatile BOP market with high risk and how they can create social value in those markets. We undertook an explorative single case study (Yin, 2009) to increase the understanding of the phenomenon of social value creation by foreign firms in volatile BOP markets. We see context as necessary to understanding firm behaviour and strategies. This phenomenon-driven research justifies the choice of explorative study design so that we can approach the topic with flexibility and an open mind (Eisenhardt & Graebner, 2007). Further justification of the case study design is based on the complexity of the studied phenomenon, caused by the opposing forces of risks versus benefits and dynamics of social value creation while ensuring profitability in a volatile context.

The case firm is a middle-sized Turkish construction enterprise with operations spanning across several countries, including Ukraine, Russia, Kazakhstan, Congo, and Morocco, where it had dealt with the BOP population segment. However, the case firm had to grapple with the political fallout between Turkey and Russia after the shooting of a Russian jet by Turkish jets near the Syria–Turkey border on November 24, 2015. The firm faced immediate closure of its construction activities in its main foreign market of Russia following the incident and had to find a quick alternative market to ensure its existence. While in search of new markets for the firm's construction business, the CEO of the case firm met a Somalian professional who was in Turkey for educational purposes during 2015–2016. The Somalian professional's (who is currently the country head for the joint venture in Somalia) business prowess and convincing pitch about the potential of Somalia for construction business convinced the CEO of the case firm to enter Somalia. The first entry of the firm to the market was as a result of responding to a business offer on a specific construction project in 2016. Currently, the firm builds houses and residential blocks on its own and undertakes tenders for construction auctions in the public sector. The case Turkish firm established a joint venture and has operated it in a partnership with a local country head in Somalia since 2016. It should be noted that the case firm has 14 full-time employees in Turkey, while eight people work full time in different managerial positions for the case firm in Somalia. There are also several contractual workers associated with the case firm in Somalia, and their numbers vary according to the construction projects being undertaken.

Data collection and analysis

The case was selected based on the following criteria: activity and market presence in Somalia, operating in an industry (housing construction) that serves BOP consumers, and availability of respondents who can offer first-hand insights to the Somalian context and BOP consumers there. Housing is a vital BOP need and corresponds to the essential need of sheltering that is met through the construction industry. The choice of context and industry is in line with the extant research that examines affordable housing in BOP markets (Ferguson, Smets, & Mason, 2014).

Data collection was primarily done via semi-structured interviews following thematic style interviews conducted with the Turkish CEO of the case firm as well as the Somalian country head of the joint venture. The interviewees were selected based on their knowledge of the target areas and the development of the business relationships. By interviewing parties from both Turkey and Somalia, we have been able to acquire a dyadic view of how the case has developed and the forces that have influenced it. In addition to interviews, other secondary data resources, such as non-public corporate reports and context-specific documents on Somalia, were used to enhance the understanding of the studied phenomenon.

Given the size of the firm and our access to key informants (i.e. the CEO and the country head), two interviews were conducted. They were deemed sufficient for the purpose of the study, as there was no possibility to gain significant new information relevant to our purpose through further interviews (e.g. Gligor, Esmark, & Golgeci, 2016). The interview with the Turkish CEO was conducted in Turkish and has been translated by a bilingual native Turkish academic who has significant research and publishing experience in such cross-cultural qualitative settings. The interview with the Somalian country head was conducted in English. Both interviews took place in December 2018 and lasted approximately 2 hours. The interview with the Turkish CEO was carried out face-to-face, while the interview with the Somalian country head was carried out via Skype. Keeping in view our discussion in the literature review, the uniqueness of context, and the lack of specific prior research, the interviews followed these main themes: "BOP and case firm's perception", "Market entry in Somalia: Risk perception", "Operations in Somalia and home country influences", "Dealing with institutional voids", and "Social value creation for BOP consumers in Somalia". It is important to highlight that both interviewees were clearly aware of these terms and understood associated dynamics well. Interviewees discussed these mentioned themes in an open-ended manner. Open-ended discussions (interviews) in qualitative research are considered as being very useful, as this method does not restrict interviewees' explanations of the contextual topic, thereby increasing validity and reliability (Bell, Bryman, & Harley, 2018).

All interviews were recorded and properly transcribed, resulting in nine Microsoft Word pages. After transcribing the interviews, we undertook a content analysis, as recommended by Patton (2002). We identified categories in the data based on the themes mentioned above to present the findings clearly. Specifically, we first formed interim categories and identified first-order codes. Then, we integrated first-order codes and generated conceptual categories that eventually led to combining critical dimensions of our findings that are explicated below. We adopted the suggestions by Marvasti and Silverman (2008) to maintain rigour and ascertain the trustworthiness of the data. First, we treated data comprehensively and systematically. We then methodically analysed the data to enhance the interpretability based on the individual characteristics of both participants. Then, we searched for refutability by diligently looking for cues where our findings were inconsistent and suggestive of systematic differences. Furthermore, we adopted an iterative process to syndicate the interview findings with the extant theory on the critical issue we examined. We also made sure that both the researchers and informants were active participants in the research process to enhance participant validation; guarantee participants' anonymity; and uphold a professional and pleasant interview climate to enhance trustworthiness.

Findings

Base of the Pyramid and case firm's perceptions

Interviews revealed that the Turkish CEO, as well as the Somalian country head of the joint venture, are aware of the core premise of the BOP concept and understand the critical role construction firms can play in this context. The case firm's Turkish CEO mentions explicitly that a crucial reason for market entry in Somalia was public service by offering affordable, good-quality housing and ensuring some profitability for the firm as well. This is also a form of social value creation while serving BOP markets. The Turkish CEO has been in business for the last 42 years running his own firm. Over the years, his perceptions have developed, and he increasingly considers supporting his employees and serving consumers with less affordability as the primary motivation. As such, the CEO stated:

> *I have been in business for a very long time, and I am at the stage now that supporting my children* [employees] *is more important for me than earning money.*

The precarious economic and health conditions the local populace face in the country have recently solidified his conviction towards helping Somalian people by employing and offering above-market employment conditions. Currently eight people work full time for the case firm in managerial positions in Somalia. However, the number increases significantly if the contractual construction workers are added. It should be noted that the number of such workers varies according to construction projects being undertaken. Still both kinds of workers are benefiting from better pay conditions as well as possibilities for skills development. This prosocial motive is in line with the spiritual motives of Turkish firms originating specifically from the Anatolian region (e.g. Karakas & Sarigollu, 2019). This aspect has not been highlighted much in prior studies but can have significant implications for the extant research on CSR and BOP in other contexts as well. We expect that firms operating in BOP markets may have social motives beyond economic motives, and it would be interesting to see results of such research in other contexts.

Market entry in Somalia: risk perception

The Turkish CEO specifically highlighted that he had no in-depth information about the Somalian market at the time of entry. Nonetheless, he made his decision to enter the market based on the discussion with the Somalian country head who was a graduate student in Turkey at the time. Market entry was mainly down to the risk-taking propensity of the firm at the time of severe business disruption in the previous primary market, as mentioned above. In other words, once the firm had to abruptly exit Russia, its previous primary market, as a result of political fallout between Turkey and Russia, the risk of operating in Somalia became of secondary importance in the face of the threat to survival that the firm faced due to a considerable market loss. Furthermore, the country head's presentation of subtle business opportunities in Somalia amid threats and uncertainties made a convincing business case to the CEO, who already has had a propensity to take risks due to his background. The country head stated:

> *When I met him* [the CEO]*, I knew he would be a father figure to me. He would take the journey in Somalia with me in order to serve my country while doing business there.*

We first found that the risk propensity of the case firm is high, and such propensity plays a positive role in entering the Somalian market. In this vein, the CEO stated:

> *"I have done business in so many different dangerous countries that it would be even difficult for you to imagine. I know first-hand what real risks are in such countries, and I know what it takes to deal with them."*

As such, our findings are in line with the earlier research where risk propensity has been found to vary across cultures in prior studies (e.g. Mata, Josef, & Hertwig, 2016), influencing businesses in a variety of ways. In our case, prior experience in risky countries has positively affected the CEO's acceptance of the risks involved in doing business in Somalia. Moreover, Turkish firms originating from the Anatolian region (where the case firm also originates) tend to have higher risk propensity, as they emerged in the business scene under harsh and restrictive environments and learned to deal with these aspects over time (Haksöz, 2016).

Operation mode in Somalia and home country influences

The country head for the joint venture in Somalia states that the main benefit of having a joint venture in Somalia is that two partners in the joint venture function as a check-and-balance toward each other. The country head stated:

> We are like each other's "safety fuse". My boss's business acumen is combined with my first-hand experience of the country. So, we ensure that our ideas do not go unchecked.

The different experiences and mind-sets of the Turkish and Somalian partners are utilised to validate each point and complement different perspectives in serving the Somalian market. Such partnerships prevent blind spots and eliminate potential biases of each party in the joint venture. It also widens the perspectives through which opportunities and threats are assessed and products are developed within the joint venture. Secondly, the joint venture also helps support local businesses in their network regarding improving professionalism and structured management in the local context. The case firm further fosters these capabilities of the local micro-businesses that are part of its value chain. Hence, inculcation of the professionalisation of local value chain partners is also an aspect that creates value in that context.

The home country image played a significant role in operations and operation mode of the case firm in the eyes of both interviewees. The country head stated:

> Turkey is like a big brother to us. Turks work for our welfare without immediate expectations. So, we Somalians have affinity to them.

Turkish businesses and Turkish state-private sector ties are viewed positively by many in Somalia as a challenge to the Chinese dominance in the region that built up over the years. Turkish firms are somewhat late to the game, as they just recently discovered the region, while Chinese influence is rooted deeper. Turkish firms just recently are trying to be more active and present in the East African region, including in Somalia.

The interviews further revealed that the involvement of the Turkish government in developing and training Somalian security forces and the provision of other services helped the case firm's operations. The Turkish government's positive image in the eyes of most Somalian people, as well as historical linkages, were referred to as a positive factor for the case firm. This is further evidence of the notion that, while businesses in other African countries prioritise financial motives when doing business with Turkish firms, Somalians combine such motives with more personal ones, such as their close ties to and positive perception of Turkey. Therefore, Somalian consumers tend to prefer Turkish product or service offerings in many cases. This finding further supports the argument presented above that historical, cultural, and religious links can make operations of a firm relatively easier despite high risk and uncertainty (Casson & da Silva Lopes, 2003; Basuil & Datta, 2015).

Dealing with institutional voids

According to both interviewees, institutional voids are very visible in the Somalian context and, in turn, influence business strategies and the overall conductivity of the business environment. The CEO specifically stated:

> *You could easily say there is no state in Somalia. There are no clear rules to follow. Instead, everything revolves around clans. But we are learning how to operate around those realities.*

One of the main challenges for the case firm is the lack of project management as well as business planning and urban planning strategies by the local government. In such conditions of institutional voids, connections with local "clan leaders", who are influential political players in the country, are the primary source of the ability to enter a local market and continue to operate there.

As mentioned earlier, the case firm has experience operating and serving BOP consumers in Congo and Morocco. The CEO and country head both view Somalia as significantly riskier than other markets, with the CEO explicitly mentioning that "a person should be ready to die at any moment". This statement reflects both recognition of the nature and extent of risks involved in operating in Somalia and the spiritual background of the interviewee (i.e. their religious and spiritual conviction is of the type that accepts death as a natural and welcomed outcome of one's life on earth). However, beyond the spiritual motives of operating in such a risky context with a common religion, such overwhelming risks and challenges are balanced with attractive current and future market opportunities and significantly less competition.

Religious and cultural similarity appeared to be a source of legitimacy for the case firm, making Somalia an attractive place despite institutional voids and other associated risks. Legitimacy has been defined as "a recognised perception or assumption that the actions of an entity are desirable, proper, or appropriate within some socially constructed system of norms, values, beliefs, and definitions" (Suchman, 1995, p. 574). The case firm utilises this legitimacy to overcome problematic issues in a way a Western or otherwise unconnected firm would not be able to do. Being perceived as a legitimate social actor affords the case firm a greater position of power (Bouquet & Birkinshaw, 2008), which can be used to build trusting relationships and thus mitigate the institutional voids in an unstable context.

Social value creation for BOP consumers in Somalia

The case firm is aware of the importance of value creation in the Somalian context. According to the CEO, one aspect of value creation is hiring, training, and developing Somali employees as well as contractual workers, while paying them above-average salaries. The case firm is focusing on developing project management skills in managerial staff, while quality construction skills are being developed in contractual workers. This approach has been found to be very useful in prior studies, as it inculcates lifelong employability skills in those employees with the potential to become entrepreneurs themselves (e.g. Raditloaneng & Chawawa, 2015). Moreover, developing affordable housing is the critical value creation activity of the case firm in Somalia. The main goal of this value proposition is to provide affordable living spaces to customers in Somalia while maintaining higher levels of quality than their Chinese competitors. The CEO stated:

> *Our goal in Somalia is very clear: to build proper living spaces for people as much as we can. We believe it is essential for human dignity, and we try our best to provide that, relying on our previous experience.*

This is an essential point, as Chinese firms are also entering high-risk markets in Africa, including Somalia (Gu, Zhang, Vaz, & Mukwereza, 2016). However, the quality aspect of the service offering priced at reasonable (competitive) levels is the main competitive strength of the case firm.

Interviews revealed that there is a lack of benchmark examples and established quality standards of housing in the country. This emerged as a further opportunity for the case firm to create social value, as it set the quality benchmark in construction as well as the development of employees' skills as discussed above. Demonstration of quality-built houses priced at affordable rates increased the demand for the services of the case firm. Hence, it is expanding to other cities in Somalia after achieving success in Mogadishu. The main findings related to case firm's operations and value creation in the Somalian context are summarised in Figure 4.1.

Discussion and conclusions

The current chapter analysed operations of an EM origin firm in an underresearched BOP context. Based on a single case study of a Turkish construction firm operating in Somalia via joint venture operation mode, our study offers several implications. First, the market entry decision criteria used by the case firm for the volatile Somalian BOP market differed from the criteria often used by large MNEs in entering the traditional and relatively stable markets. Although the potential for profitable business operations was considered, the importance of prosocial motives to entering the markets was emphasised. Additionally, the risk of volatility and institutional voids did not deter the case firm, supporting the notion referred to in some studies that market risk is firm-specific rather than country-specific in many cases (e.g. Frynas & Mellahi, 2003). We also found support for arguments presented in some prior studies that firms originating from home countries representing a high risk or institutional voids

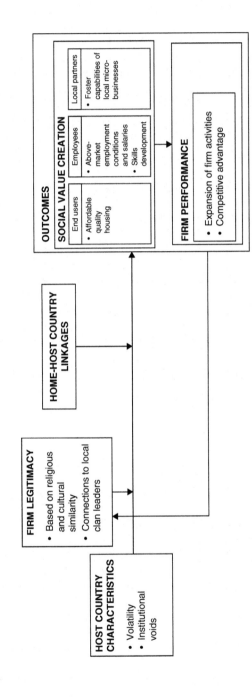

Figure 4.1 Summary of the study findings.
Source: authors' own illustration.

(Turkey, in the current case) are better at surviving in high-risk environments (e.g. Ramamurti, 2012). Hence, the case firm could operate relatively successfully in the volatile Somalian context.

Second, in terms of operation mode choice, several organizational benefits were identified, which led to the choice of the joint venture as an operation mode in the BOP markets. Some of the benefits of joint venture choice by case firm were quite like the ones found in prior studies focused on operation mode choice in traditional markets (Arslan, Larimo, & Dikova, 2019). However, the joint venture decision was also guided by the benefits that could be offered to local partners and employees, specifically. Therefore, social value creation appeared to be an important element influencing operations of firms in BOP markets.

Third, the findings increased understanding of how EM origin SMEs with limited resources manage their international operations under extreme risk and uncertainty and how this is linked to social value creation. The findings confirm the results in prior research on the critical role of home- and host-country linkages in making the operations easier for foreign firms (e.g. Li & Vaschilko, 2010). Additionally, positive, country-of-origin image (i.e. Turkey), ethical practices (above-average salaries for employees and focus on their skills development), fair relationships with local partner firms (and suppliers), and legitimacy were found to be relevant elements that can help to cope with risks and institutional voids. These aspects also positively influenced social value, which boosted the competitiveness of the case firm. Social value creation for BOP consumers especially in the construction sector is an under-researched area (e.g. Barraket & Loosemore, 2018), and our study has demonstrated specific aspects of value creation at employee, joint venture partner, and suppliers' levels. This sets the foundation for future studies to further theorise on these specific aspects while addressing firm operations in different BOP contexts.

Our chapter offers several managerial implications as well. First, even though Somalia is a volatile economy with the perpetual eruption of violence, foreign firms, especially of EM origins (China and Turkey), are operating there. This means that despite risks, the market potential is higher in certain sectors, and other firms can consider tapping into this potential if they develop an offering at a reasonable price. The second implication relates to the specificity of the construction sector. Our case study supported the notion presented in earlier studies that the construction industry has significant potential to contribute to the BOP segment in developing countries (e.g. McCutcheon, 1995; Del Castillo, 2008). The case firm served the BOP market both directly and indirectly. The BOP segment was served directly by the case firm through the development of affordable housing with modern amenities representing certain quality levels, an offering that was previously missing in the Somalian context. At the same time, the BOP segment is also served indirectly as the case firm offered above-average market salaries to the employees and gave significant attention to skills development of both local managers and contractual workers. These skilled employees can later also start their own businesses. This is a good example of social value creation, which can be benchmarked by managers of other firms aspiring to enter similar volatile BOP markets. Third, for any foreign firm wishing to operate in the BOP sector in similar countries, winning legitimacy from locals is essential, as mistrust of outsiders or foreigners is relatively high due to historical or colonial legacies. Hence, joint venture formation with local firm(s) as well as highlighting the value-creation aspect of their operations can be a good strategy for foreign firms to overcome this barrier and receive legitimacy.

Our chapter also has certain limitations. First, the empirical context is based on a single case study in a specific industrial sector and only comprises a limited number of interviewees. Therefore, the findings of the study cannot be easily generalised. Still, we believe that our study serves as a stepping-stone in the under-researched context of Somalia, and future studies can build on it to further explore dynamics of market entry, operations, and social value creations for BOP segments in other volatile contexts. In our case, the Somalian partner of the Turkish firm was a graduate student in Turkey who later returned to the home country to run the joint venture. Future studies can specifically focus on this aspect and analyse how such linkages (expatriates, students abroad) influence foreign firms' entry, operations, and service, especially in the BOP context. Finally, culture has been referred to as an essential determinant of firm strategies in many prior studies. Culture (cultural and religious similarity) also appeared to play a role in our case study. Hence, future studies can further probe culture and its dimensions, specifically in relation to firm operations in different BOP markets.

References

Acs, Z. J., Boardman, M. C., & McNeely, C. L. (2013). The social value of productive entrepreneurship. *Small Business Economics*, *40*(3), 785–796.

Arslan, A. (2011). Institutional distance – market conforming values in the host country and foreign direct investment choices of multinational enterprises (Doctoral Dissertation, University of Vaasa, Finland). (ISBN: 978–952–476–358–5)

Arslan, A., Larimo, J., & Dikova, D. (2019). Equity ownership strategy in greenfield investments: Influences of host country infrastructure and MNE resources in emerging markets. In A. Chidlow, P. N. Ghauri, T. Buckley, E. C. Gardner, A. Qamar, & E. Pickering (Eds.), *The changing strategies of international business: How MNEs manage in a changing commercial and political landscape* (pp. 95–116). Cham, Switzerland: Palgrave MacMillan.

Asiedu, E., & Lien, D. (2011). Democracy, foreign direct investment and natural resources. *Journal of International Economics*, *84*(1), 99–111.

Barraket, J., & Loosemore, M. (2018). Co-creating social value through cross-sector collaboration between social enterprises and the construction industry. *Construction Management and Economics*, *36*(7), 394–408.

Basuil, D. A., & Datta, D. K. (2015). Effects of industry- and region-specific acquisition experience on value creation in cross-border acquisitions: The moderating role of cultural similarity. *Journal of Management Studies, 52*(6), 766–795.

Bell, E., Bryman, A., & Harley, B. (2018). *Business research methods.* Oxford: Oxford University Press.

Biglaiser, G., & DeRouen Jr, K. (2006). Economic reforms and inflows of foreign direct investment in Latin America. *Latin American Research Review, 41*(1), 51–75.

Biglaiser, G., & DeRouen Jr, K. (2007). Following the flag: Troop deployment and US foreign direct investment. *International Studies Quarterly, 51*(4), 835–854.

Bouquet, C., & Birkinshaw, J. (2008). Managing power in the multinational corporation: How low-power actors gain influence. *Journal of Management, 34*(3), 477–508.

Calderón, C. (2009). *Infrastructure and growth in Africa.* World Bank. Retrieved from http://documents.worldbank.org/curated/en/365631467990387228/pdf/WPS4914.pdf

Casson, M., & da Silva Lopes, T. (2013). Foreign direct investment in high-risk environments: A historical perspective. *Business History, 55*(3), 375–404.

Cieslik, K. (2016). Moral economy meets social enterprise community-based green energy project in rural Burundi. *World Development, 83*(1), 12–26.

Collier, P. (2003). *Breaking the conflict trap: Civil war and development policy.* The World Bank. Retrieved from https://openknowledge.worldbank.org/handle/10986/13938

Dai, L., Eden, L., & Beamish, P. W. (2017). Caught in the crossfire: Dimensions of vulnerability and foreign multinationals' exit from war-afflicted countries. *Strategic Management Journal, 38*(7), 1478–1498.

Del Castillo, G. (2008). *Rebuilding war-torn states: The challenge of post-conflict economic reconstruction.* Oxford: Oxford University Press.

Dembek, K., Singh, P. & Bhakoo, V. (2016). Literature review of shared value: A theoretical concept or a management buzzword? *Journal of Business Ethics, 137,* 231–267.

Dunning, J.H. (2000). The eclectic paradigm as an envelope for economic and business theories of MNE activity. *International Business Review, 9*(2), 163–190.

Edwards, L., & Edwards, L. J. (1995). *Practical risk management in the construction industry.* London: Thomas Telford.

Eisenhardt, K.M., & Graebner, M.E. (2007). Theory building from cases: Opportunities and challenges. *Academy of Management Journal, 50*(1), 25–32.

Ferguson, B., Smets, P., & Mason, D. (2014). The new political economy of affordable housing finance and urban development. In J. Bredenoord, P. van Lindert, & P. Smets (Eds.), *Affordable housing in the urban global south* (pp. 66–80) Oxon: Routledge.

Finkel, G. (2015). *The economics of the construction industry.* Oxon: Routledge.

Frynas, J.G., & Mellahi, K. (2003). Political risks as firm-specific (dis) advantages: Evidence on transnational oil firms in Nigeria. *Thunderbird International Business Review, 45*(5), 541–565.

Ganson, B., & Wennmann, A. (2018). *Business and conflict in fragile states: The case for pragmatic solutions.* Oxon: Routledge.

Gligor, D.M., Esmark, C.L., & Golgeci, I. (2016). Building international business theory: A grounded theory approach. *Journal of International Business Studies, 47*(1), 93–111.

Grosso, M. G., Jankowska, A., & Gonzales, F. (2008). *Trade and regulation: The case of construction services*. OECD Publications, Retrieved from www.researchgate.net/publication/255656996_Trade_and_Regulation_The_Case_of_Construction_Services

Gu, J., Zhang, C.,Vaz, A., & Mukwereza, L. (2016). Chinese state capitalism? Rethinking the role of the state and business in Chinese development cooperation in Africa. *World Development, 81*, 24–34.

Guidolin, M., & La Ferrara, E. (2007). Diamonds are forever, wars are not: Is conflict bad for private firms? *American Economic Review, 97*(5), 1978–1993.

Haksöz, Ç. (2016). *Risk intelligent supply chains: How leading Turkish companies thrive in the age of fragility*. London: CRC Press.

Henisz, W. J., Mansfield, E. D., & von Glinow, M. A. (2010). Conflict, security, and political risk: International business in challenging times. *Journal of International Business Studies, 41*, 759–764.

Hillebrandt, P. M. (2000). *Economic theory and the construction industry*. London: Macmillan.

Hönke, J., & Thauer, C. R. (2014). Multinational corporations and service provision in sub-Saharan Africa: Legitimacy and institutionalization matter. *Governance, 27*(4), 697–716.

Jensen, N. M., & Young, D. J. (2008). A violent future? Political risk insurance markets and violence forecasts. *Journal of Conflict Resolution, 52*(4), 527–547.

Karakas, F., & Sarigollu, E. (2019). Spirals of spirituality: A qualitative study exploring dynamic patterns of spirituality in Turkish organizations. *Journal of Business Ethics, 156*(3), 799–821.

Kolk, A., Rivera-Santos, M., & Rufín, C. (2014). Reviewing a decade of research on the "Base/Bottom of the Pyramid" (BOP) concept. *Business & Society, 53*(3), 338–377.

Kuratko, D. F., McMullen, J. S., Hornsby, J. S., & Jackson, C. (2017). Is your organization conducive to the continuous creation of social value? Toward a social corporate entrepreneurship scale. *Business Horizons, 60*, 271–283.

Leposky, T., Arslan, A., & Dikova, D. (2019). Value co-creation in multinational enterprises' services marketing at the Bottom-of-the-Pyramid markets. In M. Marinov, S. Marinova, J. Larimo, & T. Leposky (Eds.), *International business and emerging economy firms, Volume I: Universal issues and the Chinese perspective* (pp. 89–116). Cham, Switzerland: Palgrave MacMillan.

Li, Q., & Vashchilko, T. (2010). Dyadic military conflict, security alliances, and bilateral FDI flows. *Journal of International Business Studies, 41*(5), 765–782.

Loosemore, M., & Higgon, D. (2015). *Social enterprise in the construction industry: Building better communities*. Oxon: Routledge.

Marvasti, A., & Silverman, D. (2008). Doing qualitative research: A comprehensive guide. Thousand Oaks, CA: Sage Publications.

Mata, R., Josef, A. K., & Hertwig, R. (2016). Propensity for risk taking across the life span and around the globe. *Psychological science, 27*(2), 231–243.

McCutcheon, R. T. (1995). Employment creation in public works: Labour-intensive construction in sub-Saharan Africa: The implications for South Africa. *Habitat International, 19*(3), 331–355.

Müllner, J. (2016). From uncertainty to risk—a risk management framework for market entry. *Journal of World Business, 51*(5), 800–814.

Newenham-Kahindi, A. M. (2011). A global mining corporation and local communities in the Lake Victoria zone: The case of Barrick Gold multinational in Tanzania. *Journal of Business Ethics, 99*(2), 253–282.

Njoku, R. C. (2013). *The history of Somalia.* Santa Barbara, CA: Greenwood Press.

Ofori, G. (2008). Leadership for future construction industry: Agenda for authentic leadership. *International Journal of Project Management, 26*(6), 620–630.

Ozkan, M. (2017). The Turkish way of doing development aid? An analysis from the Somali laboratory. In I. Bergamaschi, P. Moore, & A. Tickner (Eds.), *South-South Cooperation Beyond the Myths: Rising donors, new aid practices?* (pp. 59–78). London: Palgrave Macmillan.

Patton, M. Q. (2002). Two decades of developments in qualitative inquiry: A personal, experiential perspective. *Qualitative Social Work, 1*(3), 261–283.

Payaud, M. A. (2014). Marketing strategies at the bottom of the pyramid: Examples from Nestlé, Danone, and Procter & Gamble. *Global Business and Organizational Excellence, 33*(2), 51–63.

Prahalad, C. K. (2006). *The fortune at the Bottom of the Pyramid: Eradicating poverty through profits.* Upper Saddle River, NJ: Pearson Education.

Porter, M. E., & Kramer, M. R. (2011). The big idea: Creating shared value. *Harvard Business Review, 89*(1/2), 62–77.

Porter, M. E., & Kramer, M. R. (2014). A response to Andrew Crane et al.'s article by Michael E. Porter and Mark R. Kramer. *California Management Review, 56*(2), 149–151.

Raditloaneng, W. N., & Chawawa, M. (2015). *Lifelong learning for poverty eradication.* Heidelberg: Springer

Ramamurti, R. (2012). What is really different about emerging market multinationals? *Global Strategy Journal, 2*(1), 41–47.

Reilly, T. M. (1950). *Economic aspects of reconstruction after the Civil War* (Doctoral dissertation, Boston University). Retrieved from https://open.bu.edu/handle/2144/4961

Rohatynskyj, M. (2011). Development discourse and selling soap in Madhya Pradesh, India. *Human Organization, 70*(1), 63–73.

Schuster, T., & Holtbrügge, D. (2012). Market entry of multinational companies in markets at the bottom of the pyramid: A learning perspective. *International Business Review, 21*(5), 817–830.

Sinkovics, N., Sinkovics, R. R., & Yamin, M. (2014). The role of social value creation in business model formulation at the bottom of the pyramid–implications for MNEs? *International Business Review, 23*(4), 692–707.

Suchman, M. C. (1995). Managing legitimacy: Strategic and institutional approaches. *Academy of Management Review, 20*(3): 571–610.

Visser, W. (2011). *The age of responsibility: CSR 2.0 and the new DNA of business.* Hoboken, NJ: John Wiley & Sons.

Waibel, P. (2017). *Putting the poor first: How Base-of-the-Pyramid ventures can learn from development approaches.* Oxon: Routledge.

Xiaopeng, D., & Pheng, L. S. (2013). Understanding the critical variables affecting the level of political risks in international construction projects. *KSCE Journal of Civil Engineering, 17*(5), 895–907.

Yin, J., & Jamali, D. (2016). Strategic corporate social responsibility of multinational companies' subsidiaries in emerging markets: Evidence from China. *Long Range Planning, 49*(5), 541–558.

Yin, R.K. (2009). *Case study research. Design and methods.* Thousand Oaks, CA: SAGE.

5 BOP business models and partnerships in the context of state failure

Margaret Hanson

Introduction

In recent decades, multinational corporations (MNCs) have sought new markets at the Base of the Pyramid (BOP; Kolk, Rivera-Santos, & Rufín, 2014; Prahalad, 2004) and in some cases, ventures in Africa have stalled due to institutional failures (Parmigiani & Rivera-Santos, 2015). Institutional failures are often characterised as state failures, with the burden of responsibility put on governments to address critical social needs, infrastructure, security, and regulatory guidance, although market actors and social sector organizations may also play an important role in addressing institutional failure (Hutchison & Johnson, 2011; Jones, 2008). A proactive MNC strategy to address institutional challenges, including those surrounding BOP markets, has been to engage in cross-sector partnerships that specifically target institutional capacity building (Kramer & Pfitzer, 2016). These partnerships may include MNCs, social mission-driven global philanthropies, development agencies, transnational social entrepreneurs, as well as country-based actors, whether local government partners, social sector partners, or business partners.

The pursuit of profit in the BOP, and in Africa in particular, includes market segments at subsistence levels of consumption (Rangan, Chu, & Petkoski, 2011), alongside emerging concentrations of wealth (Freund & Oliver, 2016; Leke & Yeboah-Amankway, 2018). The view that improved market access to the BOP alone offers a pathway to development has long been criticised (Karnani, 2007). As such, MNCs' continued pursuit of profit in BOP markets has often been joined by careful efforts to extend practices of corporate social responsibility (CSR) and strategic philanthropy (Muthuri, 2013; Darty-Baah & Amponsah-Tawiah, 2011; Visser, McIntosh, & Middleton, 2017; van Cranenburgh & Arenas, 2014; Harrow, 2010). The impact of global influences on host country development continues to be an important area of continued debate and research (Kolk, Tulder, & Kostwinder, 2008; Kolk & Tulder, 2010; Selsky & Parker, 2005; Sullivan & Warner, 2004; Gold, Hahn, & Seuring, 2013; Schwab, 2008). This chapter frames the study of collaboration between MNCs, global philanthropies, and international development agencies with local partners in government, the social sector, and markets towards capacity building institutions. Further, it aims to contribute to a better understanding of the influence of global actors on the evolution of domestic institutions around BOP markets. Whether institutions are characterised as governance systems within larger market-based ecosystems (Kramer & Pfitzer, 2016) or mechanisms of social redistribution (Ruggie, 2004), scholars of business and development agree on the importance of institutions to sustainable market-based economic growth (Rodrik, 2008; Evans, 2012).

This chapter is organized into three parts. First, a review of the extensive business management literature on the challenges of access to BOP markets suggests that MNCs' market-centric bias has led them, on the one hand, to innovate around infrastructure challenges, and on the other hand, to engage directly with local entrepreneurs as partners. The question of local agency is central to this discussion, and the importance of local partners as agents of change is explored in the selected case studies of cross-sector knowledge-based partnerships in Kenya and Mozambique. The conceptual framework presented below highlights the link between local BOP partners and global partners, including MNCs, philanthropy, and development agencies, and each case represents a different sector-specific target for institutional capacity building.

In the first case, the Ministry of Health of the Government of Mozambique champions the adoption of Coca-Cola's expert advice to improve the national healthcare delivery system. In the second case, smallholder farmers use the Hello Tractor platform created by a social entrepreneur to address the affordability of tractors. In the third case, also in Kenya, small- and medium-sized enterprises (SMEs) in the emerging food processing industry use the mentorship and education platform, managed by Partners in Food Solutions (PFS), to consult global industry experts regarding their challenges within the emerging food processing industry. Together, the cases (1) illustrate local actors leveraging global partners' knowledge towards improving institutional capacity around BOP markets and communities, and (2) support the overarching argument that such institutional transformation may have sources in government, society, or markets.

Literature review: MNCs working in the shadow of institutional failure

MNCs have long formed partnerships with host governments, state-owned enterprises, and local corporations through formal public–private partnerships or joint ventures. The pursuit of the BOP market, however, is set apart from MNC historical ties by the aim to serve very low-income customers that had been marginalised. This aim – to address potential BOP demand – has had the effect of drawing MNCs into greater engagement with a host of local partners across governments, society, and markets. The BOP opportunity, imagined at first as a function of consumer behaviour and purchasing power (Hammond, Kramer, Katz, Tran, & Walker, 2008), has proven more dynamic, as barriers to access are overcome and BOP partners emerge as potential supply chain partners (Holt & Littlewood, 2014; Rosca, Moellering, Rijal, & Bendul, 2019). This journey for MNCs has been both a process of discovery and innovation.

BOP 1.0 to 2.0

Framed as a challenge of using markets to meet the needs and requirements of BOP customers, the MNC response has been characterised, first, by efforts to build better products, and second, by attempts to build a better business model to overcome the challenges of market access. Early cases of BOP success, such as Unilever's introduction of laundry soap, were characterised by the drive to adapt an existing product to the needs and requirements of the target consumer (Beers, Knorringa, & Leliveld, 2012). Product design and marketing experts sought local partners to provide insights into regional preferences, consumer requirements, and social dynamics so product and marketing managers could reformulate their products to meet consumer needs and requirements. Soap was repackaged at lower price points, for easy transport, and for a longer shelf life (Chikweche & Fletcher, 2012). Local business partners played an important role in product promotion and distribution channels through grassroots word of mouth marketing strategies or local sales (Simanis, Hart, & Duke, 2008). MNC distribution strategies that worked in one emerging market were replicated in another. For example Hindustan Unilever empowered women's groups to sell household goods through their Shakti programme in India. Likewise, Avon empowered women as micro-entrepreneurs to sell beauty products and household goods in South Africa (Dolan & Scott, 2009).

BOP 1.0 was revised to BOP 2.0 as MNCs' perception of the market broadened from consumers to co-producers (Dembek, Sivasubramaniam, & Chmielewski, 2019). MNCs used different strategies for engaging local partners in the innovation process (Muhia, Simanis, & Hart, 2008); for example S.C. Johnson led collaborative initiatives that engaged local partners in "deep dialogue" to better understand the needs and requirements of BOP customers (Simanis et al., 2008). Forming joint ventures with locally based enterprises, managers sought to develop products for BOP markets and, using "reverse innovation", found that such products also spurred demand in their more affluent markets (Govindarajan & Trimble, 2012). Local movements, such as "frugal innovation" and "jugaad innovation" in India, stood as models of how a context defined by its resource scarcity could be a productive starting point for the innovation process (Radjou, Prabhu, & Ahuja, 2012).

At the same time, some MNC product innovations were crippled by their reliance on assumed consumer access to basic services, resources, and infrastructure (Garrette & Karnani, 2010). For example Essilor International innovated a new, low-cost material for making strong and light lenses for prescription spectacles, crossing the low-cost threshold requirement that enabled it to compete in BOP segments (Seitanidi & Crane, 2013). Fitting spectacles to myopic customers, however, still required that customers overcome the challenge of access to healthcare services for diagnoses and prescriptions. Only after bundling market-based activities (lens manufacturing, grinding lenses, and fitting frames) with philanthropic-supported activities (eye testing, diagnosing cataracts, and delivering finished products) into a mobile unit that could travel from village to village could Essilor see a pathway to the BOP market.

Infrastructure failure itself was framed as a market opportunity, which MNCs often pursued through a product mindset. A host of consumer products came on the market that substituted infrastructure requirements with product features; rechargeable solar powered lamps, point-of-use water purification sachets, and battery-powered electrocardiograms sized into a backpack meant that supply chains could work within the constraints of the infrastructure voids (Parmigiani & Rivera-Santos, 2015). This innovation tack sometimes took on the same characteristics of innovating products for serving customers living off the grid, and in some cases, innovative products trickled up the pyramid to the recreational hiking and camping departments of big-box retail stores.

Sidestepping infrastructure challenges, however, has not always been feasible, as with the introduction of cell phones or with sanitation. With cell phones, the distribution of handsets could be scaled from urban populations to rural segments, relying on the extension of urban-based dealers, sub-dealers, umbrella men, and extending to villages. The extension of cell phone coverage, however, required distribution of cell towers throughout a region. In urban city centres, telecommunications companies might partner with the central government to secure and electrify the cell towers. In rural areas, however, depending on local governance and infrastructure, the installation, maintenance, and electrification of cell towers presented a different kind of hurdle. In the case of expansion into the rural BOP segments of Nigeria, Celtel introduced a micro-base station franchise business model to engage local entrepreneurs as business partners who could also take on the infrastructure challenges of tower maintenance, security, and energy access (Ebrahim & Rangan, 2014; Cooper & Boye, 2005). Likewise, with sanitation, the distribution of portable toilets presented one kind of product-based challenge, while the collection of portable toilets and sustainable waste management presented another kind of challenge that required a more comprehensive solution (Smith & Crawford, 2008).

In other emerging industries targeting the BOP, such as financial technical services, micro-finance institutions (MFIs) faced a chasm of regulatory failure around financial services that targeted the unbanked. In the case of M-Pesa's technology-based financial platform, entrepreneurs anticipated that they would need a reliable and capable regulatory partner operating at a national level if they were to successfully go to scale. The emergence of governmental regulation, however, lagged. That regulatory piece would eventually have to be added to the ecosystem, so M-Pesa approached going to scale strategically and in stages (Adner, 2013). In sum, when MNCs encountered infrastructure, security, and regulatory challenges, they often sought to work around them. In some cases, they re-bundled market-based and philanthropic activities; in other cases, they re-thought how to engage local partners in the social sector and in local government in their pursuit of market access. The early days of focusing on building better products to overcome the challenges of BOP access gave way to a fuller picture of the institutional context challenges.

Strategic philanthropy and cross-sector collaboration

Over the past two decades, macroeconomic trends have pointed to the changing character of opportunities in the BOP market. More low-income countries have graduated into lower-middle-income countries, while more lower-middle-income countries have also graduated into middle-income status. At the same time, the rise of the newly rich within emerging market countries offered proof of the dynamic potential of emerging markets (Freund & Oliver, 2016). Some pockets of poverty, however, have persisted, and this persistence has continued to check MNCs' optimism regarding the BOP. The emergence of social mission-driven investment, exemplified by the rise of "patient capital" (Novogratz, 2009) and efforts to address "the missing middle" (Dougherty & Dogandjieva, 2015), was driven by a rising awareness of institutional failures that undermined the effectiveness of narrowly focused market-based business models for the BOP (Boadi, 2016; Doran, McFayden, & Vogel, 2009; Milligan & Schöning, 2011; Schuster and Holtbrügge, 2012).

For MNCs, the promise of BOP markets has been joined by the push of corporate social responsibility, with all its variations among corporations based in North America, Europe, and Asia (Miska, Witt, & Stahl, 2016; Hah & Freeman, 2014; Matten & Moon, 2008). CSR programmes ranged from minimal environmental risk mitigation to community-based service projects, such as building schools or water treatment projects, as (Kolk & Tulder, 2010) observed through careful review in the case of Dutch MNCs. CSR-driven collaboration was more likely to be project-based with a single or small number of local partners and well-defined benchmarks of success (Gupta & Khilji, 2013).

Theory and conceptual framing

The study of cross-sector collaboration is far-reaching, joining the study of public administration, social entrepreneurship, and business management (Sullivan & Warner, 2004). Collaboration is often introduced as a challenge, with a discussion contrasting for-profit and non-profit motives among governmental agencies, social-sector organizations, and market actors (local or MNC) operating under very different constraints of governmental sector, social sector, and competitive markets (Austin, 2010). This conundrum of collaboration across sectors is typically solved by framing engagement as voluntary, and potentially complementary, albeit driven by actors holding different institutional positions and different motives (government, society, and markets). Further, cross-sector collaboration over capacity building institutions is often characterised by sharing knowledge framed as global industry standards, industry specific expertise, and management skills (Börzel, Hönke, & Thauer, 2012). Collaboration may also be characterised by learning across organizations, between individuals, or even across individuals and organizations (Kolk, van Dolen, & Vock, 2010). Further, this type of collaboration brings global philanthropies and MNCs together with a locally situated partner, and thus presents a potential site of impact on how institutions evolve around BOP markets, as well as an important area of research.

Viewing MNCs from a stakeholder perspective, the motives behind CSR programmes are framed as outreach strategies, through which MNCs seek approval from the local community as well as global stakeholders. In the cases discussed below, the USA-based MNCs demonstrate a willingness to engage broadly through cross-sector partnerships to address institutional context challenges of BOP markets with local partners as well as with global philanthropies, such as the Bill and Melinda Gates Foundation and TechnoServe. Given that MNCs often operate with a regional perspective towards their market opportunities, they may replicate a CSR project across a region, launching similar projects in neighbour countries.

The reasons why MNCs engage in knowledge philanthropy may be widely motivated. Through a strategic philanthropy paradigm, the CSR practice of giving back to the community is viewed as a proactive feature of corporate strategy where corporations act on the context conditions of competitive markets (Aguilera-Caracuel, Guerrero-Villegas, & García-Sánchez, 2017; Porter & Kramer, 2019; Kolk & Lenfant, 2010). Ongoing concerns with the reliability and quality of the global supply chain reinforce MNCs' attention to the institutional context of BOP markets (Amoako, 2016; Susha, Grönlund, & Tulder, 2019). That said, the focus of the conceptual framework offered in this chapter is less about why MNCs engage in knowledge sharing through cross-sector collaborations, and more about why and how local partners might be interested in engaging and adopting the ideas into institutional practice.

Alliance theory and cross-sector partnerships: leveraging resources towards local institutional capacity building

Framing a cross-sector partnership as an alliance subtly shifts the analysis away from the sometimes murky question of for-profit versus non-profit motives and towards an analysis of the distribution of resources among partners (Harris, Derdak, Lash, Uygur, Welch, & Zayer, 2013). For example in their study of a coffee cooperative in the emerging market context of Tanzania, Harris et al. (2013) used an alliance framework to analyse a "social enterprise alliance" formed around a coffee cooperative. Framing cross-sector collaboration in this way shifts the focus of analysis to explore the diversity of resources among partners – as diverse as a university, a non-profit, a small business, and a corporation. Further, the inquiry shifts to how partners value each other's resources opportunistically. Coffee farmers, for example were interested in supporting their market-based enterprise and leveraged their university and MNC partner resources – including "social capital", "expertise", "market access", and "human resources" (referencing the specific resources highlighted in their social enterprise alliance framework; Harris et. al, 2013, p. 121). The analysis then revolves around how these various resources are linked through organizational design. The discussion then turns to how partners' resources together are leveraged towards overall project aims. Given that resources may be embedded, attention is given to how a resource may be used without degrading it, for example through corrupt practices. Finally, this alliance framework returns to the question of motives, tying motives specifically to how resources are leveraged and by whom.

The linchpin to bringing about institutional change, highlighted in this framework, is the local partner who views the adoption of knowledge-based resources as serving their aims. Thus, the analysis shifts from the motive to give, to the motive to take advice, hypothesizing that the uptake of ideas and their adoption by local agents may point to how and why institutions are impacted by knowledge sharing practices. Framing the study of cross-sector partnerships between MNCs and local partners in the BOP, an alliance framework shifts the analysis of the distribution of valued resources among partners and how local partners are interested in leveraging those knowledge-based resources in practice. From the view of local producers, for example MNC quality standards may be a gateway to future supply chain partnerships. MNC expert advice may lead to higher rates of productivity, increased safety, or risk reduction, as well as local support for BOP-based communities. Further, ratcheting up quality standards may be specifically tied to increased access to targeted support through philanthropic grants or development aid.

Sector-based resources: state, social sector, and markets

The alliance framework proposed below (see Figure 5.1) identifies generic resources held by MNCs, namely, knowledge resources tied to the market, such as industry standards, expert advice, and management skills. While focused on market-based value creation, such knowledge-based resources can be shared, learned, and adopted by government actors, social mission-driven organizations, as well as local market actors such as SMEs. Local partners also have knowledge-based resources, but the MNC knowledge-based resources are highlighted for this study with the specific aim to further explore the impact of MNCs on capacity building in government, social sector, and markets across the African market. By contrast, the resources of social sector-based and government-based partners that are highlighted in this framework tend to be institutionally embedded resources and, therefore, not easily shared, transferred, or replicated. Focusing on the embedded resources of social sector and government actors, however, contributes to a theory of institutional change where local champions in government, social entrepreneurs, or local business partners adopt ideas into their organizational practice.

Governments, markets, and societies represent contrasting sectors-based actors, each enabled and constrained by their constituency, defined generally here as citizens, firms, and individuals (households, networks, and other social sector-based organizations). Government structures are

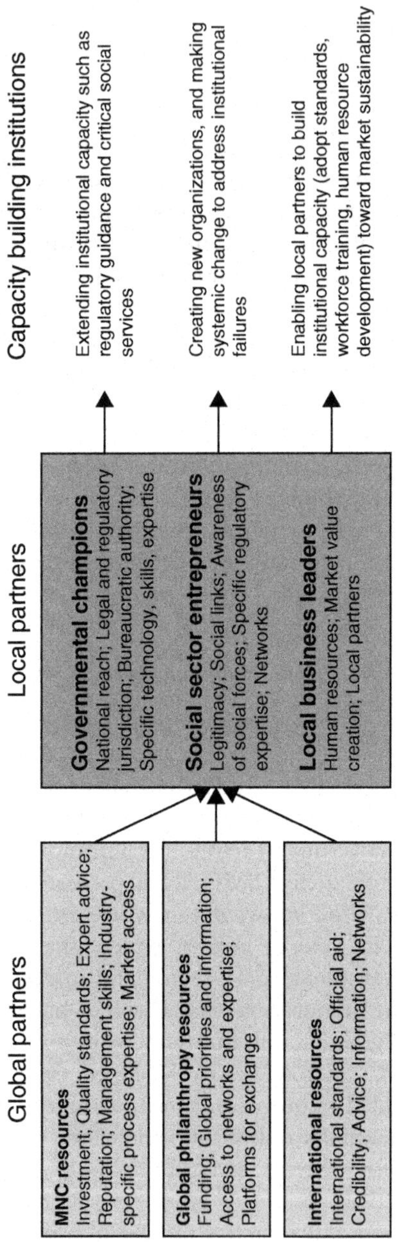

Figure 5.1 Local partners leverage global partners' resources for capacity building.

typically defined by their legal status and bureaucratic organization, with the role of securing, regulating, and guiding markets towards development, as well as underwriting a host of social services to secure their population. "Fragile", "failed", "corrupt", and "weak" are adjectives that have been used to describe governments in emerging market countries, and in Africa in particular, identifying an infrastructure or regulatory void (Gold et al., 2013). Such attributions, however, also imply that governments are the key drivers of change and hold the responsibility to address those failures. Social sectors and market sectors, however, also prove to be sources of institutional innovation, targeting social goods and public goods, usually associated with governments. While governments may play an important role in emerging market governance, other sources of institutional innovation, however, may emerge from non-state sources. Examples of non-governmental institutions that contribute to regulating markets include transnational business group networks, social sector or market-led non-governmental regulation, as well as the shared practices of MNCs.

Given the bureaucratic authority and bureaucratic capacity typically associated with governments, the institutional capacity building partnership with local government partners is often characterised by the extension of an existing national programme to underserved BOP communities. Building government institutional capacity to regulate and guide markets is informed by a multitude of international organizations, which together form a storehouse of knowledge regarding how governments may approach regulating and guiding markets. For example the OECD, the World Bank Group, the Food and Agriculture Organization (FAO) of the United Nations, the International Labour Organization (ILO), and the United Nations Conference on Trade and Development (UNCTAD) represent an impressive resource of governmental agency models and institutional practices, articulating standards of practice for states in general, and with specific reference to markets. For example with regard to a specific industry, such as the food processing industry, the FAO, the World Health Organization (WHO), and the World Trade Organization (WTO) all address issues related to safe food handling and safe food processing (Meagher, 2012; Meagher, De Herdt, & Titeca, 2014; Meagher, Mann, & Bolt, 2018; Kernen & Lam, 2014; Marjanovic, Hanlin, Diepeveen, & Chataway, 2013; Idemudia, 2011).

By contrast to governments, market-based organizations, such as MNCs, are constrained by the demands of market competition. That said, MNCs demonstrate how to replicate, through imitation and adoption, innovations or best practices across an industry, which represents a kind of knowledge-based practice. How firms organize internally as well as how firms reach out to their stakeholders, including supply chain partners, reflect different facets of knowledge and practice. From industry-led norms and standards to environmentally sustainable business practices, institutional capacity within the market sector may include forms of governance. These ideas illustrate how market-based actors are an active source of institutional innovation.

By contrast to both government and markets, the social sector is characterised by its voluntary and associational features and is often referred to as the citizen sector. Social sector organizations rely heavily on soft power, defined broadly by social links and characterised as "legitimacy, awareness of social forces, links to society, distinct networks, and specialised technical expertise" (Yaziji, 2004, p. 6). Social sector capacity therefore refers to organizational dimensions, such as the strength of social links and the ability to form and maintain links. The institutional capacity of social organization may include the ability to form networks around common interests, engage in intra-stakeholder communication, and voluntarily coordinate and advocate (e.g. for vulnerable groups). The exchange of information plays an important role in empowering individuals and social sector-based organizations. As such, social sector capacity often overlaps with capacities associated with democratic institutions.

In Africa, the social sector has emerged as an important demonstration of the power of society in its many organizational forms. Social sector-based organizations differentiate from each other not only by their missions, but also and increasingly by their roles and functions as explored in a recent study (Mair, Battilana, & Cardenas, 2012). Charities, philanthropy aggregators, activists, and social entrepreneurs are differentiated from each other in terms of roles. Charities are defined by their capacity to deliver a defined good or service within a pre-existing category of humanitarian relief, such as emergency relief goods or vaccines; meanwhile, a philanthropy acts strategically to fuel single mission-focused charities towards more comprehensive social missions. Activists, by contrast, play a crucial role in articulating and prioritising societal concerns; social entrepreneurs stand apart as innovators within the social sector, forging new social connections and new organizational forms. (Selsky & Parker, 2010; Mair et al., 2012; Mehta, Polsa, Mazur, Xiucheng, & Dubinsky, 2006; Santos, 2012; Yaziji, 2004). Social entrepreneurs tackle problems that existing institutions fail to address (Mair et al., 2012; Mair & Marti, 2009). They may, for example create and refine a service delivery organization and then hand it off to a scaling partner, such as a government or global philanthropy. In market contexts such as Africa, social entrepreneurs have demonstrated the capacity to create new societal links that have been able to tap into value creation through markets and increase access to BOP markets. Networks and platforms are examples of these new forms of social sector-based institutions where technology-based network platforms, in particular, have emerged as powerful spaces for market-oriented entrepreneurs and social entrepreneurs to meet and build access to BOP markets (Selsky & Parker, 2010; Kramer & Pfitzer, 2016).

Framing a cross-sector partnership as an alliance brings into focus the distribution of resources across a partnership and how those resources are leveraged to impact institutional capacity building. Figure 5.1 lays out a distribution of generic resources typically offered by MNCs, global philanthropies, and international organizations on the one hand, and local partners and how they may leverage those global resources on the other hand.

Cross-sector collaboration with local partners has proven to be an important strategy for many MNCs to explore opportunities on the ground in the context of longer-term pursuit of routes to BOP markets (Calton, Werhane, Hartman, & Bevan, 2013; Chikweche & Fletcher, 2012). Placing the agents of change at the centre of the analysis, whether situated in the state sector, social sector, or competitive market, directs the inquiry into how partners' resources may be adopted. Through this framework, the local–global link is brought into focus.

Cases of cross-sector partnerships for building institutional capacity

Taking the point of view of the local partner in the following case discussions serves to highlight how knowledge-based resources combine with the position of social sector partners and government sector partners to build institutional capacity. The seeds of institutional transformation around BOP markets may start in governments, but this change may also have sources in social sector entrepreneurship or markets. The empirical cases selected for this discussion feature institutional capacity building projects in each of the different sectors – government, society, and markets. This study aims to evaluate the traction of the conceptual framework offered for examining the local–global link between local agents of change and MNCs.

In the first case, the Ministry of Health in Mozambique worked with Coca-Cola's global and local subsidiary partners to champion the adoption of an improved logistics management system into the national healthcare delivery system, extending the national reach to better serve rural clinics, which overlap with BOP communities. In the second case, SMEs that work in the emerging food processing industry in Kenya, leveraged the mentoring and advice platform created by PFS in order to access advice from global food expert volunteers working at North American-based MNCs, such as General Mills. In the third case, social entrepreneurs introduced a digital platform, Hello Tractor, which offers affordable access to mechanised farming inputs for smallholder farmers in collaboration with John Deere's global and local subsidiary partners, the Kenyan government, and global philanthropic support. These three cases illustrate the local–global link wherein local agents of change – from governments, the social sector, or local industry – leverage the knowledge-based resources of their partners to build institutional capacity.

Case 1. Capacity building governmental agencies – Project Last Mile

The partnership, Project Last Mile, brings together the Coca-Cola Bottling Company and the Ministry of Health in Mozambique and illustrates a case of cross-sector collaboration in which government agencies leveraged MNC skills, quality standards, and technology to transform the institutional capacity of its national healthcare delivery system. The Centro de Colaboração em Saúde worked with implementing partners, Village Reach and local bottling subsidiary, Coca-Cola Sabco, to adopt network systems and logistics expertise to address the challenging last mile delivery of healthcare supplies across a national network of clinics (Foote, 2018).[1] Individuals with industry expertise (e.g. an Africa-based general manager, a human resource specialist, and a market research advisor) joined forces with local partners on three workstreams: route optimization through improved mapping and planning activities; supplier qualification to enhance distribution and tracking; and management capability enhancement through the development of training materials and performance metrics. The assembly of the learning team and its focus activities illustrates an approach to collaboration that leverages MNC expertise on the one hand, and well-positioned host governments and local implementing partners on the other, toward capacity building of the national healthcare management system.

A crucial piece of the explanation of institutional capacity building in this case is the role of the government as project champion. Having a champion in a position of bureaucratic authority is instrumental to the adoption of logistic capacity into the government systems. Without this high-level ministerial support, it is not clear that the resources available would have been effectively leveraged towards capacity-building. Resources such as grants from global philanthropies and development agencies, including USAID, the Global Fund, and the Bill and Melinda Gates Foundation, further supported the local adoption of the programme with both funds and social capital. This targeted capacity building of national healthcare delivery is complementary to the interests of Coca-Cola and may be viewed through a strategic philanthropy lens. Building community resilience and assisting in building domestic healthcare capacity reinforces the positive relations of the local subsidiary with the government and host community. Supporting this humanitarian initiative also offers a potential boost to the MNC brand value, as reputation works back to global stakeholders of Coca-Cola as an MNC.

Case 2. Capacity building society: organizing to support smallholder farmers – Hello Tractor

Described as an ag-tech social enterprise, Hello Tractor applies a model of a sharing economy that enables smallholder farmers in Kenya, who work plots of farmland averaging less than 100 acres, to gain access to a tractor that would otherwise be too costly to access. At the model's core is the digital platform that stands between tractor fleet manager and smallholder farmer, providing a matching function that forges new connections between stakeholders – smallholder farmers and suppliers of agricultural machinery, such as John Deere. A sharing model is used to ease the affordability constraint. Barriers to access are further reduced as the digital tractor-sharing application is accessible by phone and payable via the widely used banking app M-Pesa (Foote, 2018; Peters, 2018). Customer service agents are employed to facilitate the transaction.

Hello Tractor aims to scale the operation nationally, with 10,000 tractors pledged through formal public–private partnership agreements between John Deere, working with its local partners, and the Kenyan government. Motivated by the potential access to markets as a strategy to bolster food security, the cross-sector partnership model with Hello Tractor has been replicated with the Nigerian government as the host government partner. Global philanthropy and aid organizations lend their support to this market-driven collaboration, given the potential impact on greater food security.

The Hello Tractor initiative is illustrative of how a social sector-based IT platform (see the discussion in Okunlola & Adenmosum, 2017) serves the needs and requirements of smallholder farmers who can now have better access to mechanised farming inputs. The platform is reinforced by the employment opportunities of local entrepreneurs managing the tractor hiring, as well as MNC partners, such as John Deere, aiming to build greater market access to its tractors in Africa. While there is much development left to be done in the Hello Tractor initiative, John Deere has also engaged in other customer-based initiatives to create access for smallholder farmers, using a contractor model where farmers organized into small groups of about 20 to 30 can lease a tractor.[2] This contractor initiative illustrates how the modest but important re-organization of customer stakeholders may also be a route to greater access to higher impact farming inputs for smallholder farmers.

Case 3. Capacity building emerging industry: skills, quality standards, and technology – Partners in Food Solutions (PFS)

In this third case, PFS offers a mentoring and education platform to support SMEs in the emerging food processing sector in Africa. SMEs can access MNC quality standards, expert advice, and management skills to increase their safe food processing capacity and move the emerging industry, step by step, towards improved global quality standards.[3] Food security in Africa has drawn attention from global philanthropies, development agencies, as well as social entrepreneurs working at the local level (see, e.g. Hemphill, 2013). PFS collaborates with other global social sector organizations, including TechnoServe and the Bill and Melinda Gates Foundation, to catalyse reform in this emerging sector, reinforcing the adoption of international industry standards and strengthening the capacity of emerging African food businesses through knowledge transfer, one SME at a time.

For example PFS partners with Soy Afric, a growing soy processing enterprise that sought advice and mentoring from MNC volunteer industry experts, in order to raise quality standards. A key goal of the collaboration is to help Soy Afric meet the strict criteria of an approved supplier of soy to the global humanitarian foundations such as the World Food Programme. This case illustrates the capacity building dynamic wherein local SMEs are highlighted as adopters of the knowledge sharing PFS platform and use it to engage global food experts regarding their enterprise-based challenges. Second, SMEs in the growing food processing industry are adopters of MNC quality standards, expert advice, and skills. The adoption of quality standards into an emerging industry is challenging and difficult to verify without inspection.

At the time that this case was written, governmental regulatory agency capacity lagged behind the standards setting leadership of MNC-based global industry experts. Governments, nonetheless, hold the structural position as industry regulators. An important element in the evolving institutional context of the food processing industry in Africa will be the emerging role of domestic governmental regulatory agencies as they develop the capacity to regulate.

Case discussion

Together the three cases illustrate the local adoption of MNC knowledge-based practices and impact on institutional changes in different sectors that, overall, support BOP markets and communities. The Mozambique Ministry of Health's adoption of the logistics advice shared by Coca-Cola illustrates how government partners may build institutional capacity by extending an existing national programme to hard-to-reach communities. Smallholder farmers and local entrepreneurs in Kenya adopted the Hello Tractor platform that forged new links between stakeholders, by which it offered more affordable access to tractors for smallholder farmers. SMEs in the emerging food sector, also in Kenya, adopted the PFS mentoring and education platform through which they can consult experts from MNCs about improving their own quality standards and productivity as growing enterprises in the emerging food processing industry in Africa.

In the first case, the Mozambique Ministry of Health works with Coca-Cola, illustrating the importance of the embedded resources of local partners in government for leveraging MNC expertise towards improved healthcare delivery. Building capacity to extend healthcare service delivery is reinforced by the national government, serving target populations with better access to healthcare. Helping to improve healthcare delivery, supports the local Coca-Cola subsidiary's reputation vis-à-vis both government and the BOP community. For the MNC, this humanitarian initiative in Mozambique sits in line with their strategic philanthropy portfolio to support community resilience, which may work its way back to bolster the Coca-Cola brand value with MNC stakeholders globally (Yadav, Stapleton, & van Wassenhove, 2013). A similar cross-sector partnership model has been launched in other host countries in Africa, including Tanzania, reflecting the regional scope of this CSR initiative.

The Hello Tractor case, by contrast, demonstrates the impact of targeted capacity building in the social sector. Hello Tractor's digital platform creates opportunities for smallholder farmers to gain affordable market access to high-yield mechanised inputs offered by John Deere. Meanwhile, John Deere continues to experiment with new ways to reach its BOP customers, such as offering a contractor model to lease to a small group of farmers. This case illustrates the importance of the social sector dimension of how stakeholders are organized, and how MNCs might contribute to the intra-stakeholder relations of their potential customers. Finally, in the last case, PFS offers an educational platform where local SMEs in the emerging food processing industry in Africa can access advice from global food experts. MNC advisors build skills and capacity in the emerging food processing industry one SME at a time. Framing the cross-sector partnerships as an alliance brings into focus how essential it is that local actors (SMEs) leverage that expertise if there is to be any lasting impact.

While each case highlights a different sector-based institutional challenge, together, they illustrate how cross-sector collaborations bring together local and global partners to build institutional capacity around BOP markets and communities. Both the Hello Tractor and the PFS cases offer platforms that impact how cross-sector collaboration is organized towards greater impact on BOP market access. In both the agricultural and food sector industry cases, platforms for intra-stakeholder collaboration play an important role, facilitating collaboration. They also point to the importance of social entrepreneurs' role in forming new organizational forms for collaboration. The cases together suggest that knowledge-based philanthropy by MNCs and other global actors may have an important impact on institutions evolving around BOP markets and communities, and how that impact is tied to the agency of local government champions, social sector actors, or market-based enterprises.

Conclusions

Institutional failure around BOP markets has been an important area of concern and a driver of cross-sector collaboration including MNCs, global philanthropy, and development agencies that have targeted capacity building reforms in local government, society, and markets. The alliance framework offered in this chapter, and the case discussions, join ongoing research that shares concerns regarding the impact of local–global links on how institutional capacity develops and evolves in BOP markets and communities.

This chapter advances an alliance framework to shift emphasis from the different missions and motives brought together in a cross-sector collaboration in order to examine more closely how global resources are employed by local actors. An alliance framework highlights asymmetries of resources among partners, but the focus of the analysis is on how those resources are leveraged by interested partners who are instrumental in the local adoption of ideas and the capacity building of institutions. Local actors, such as government agencies, could offer a foothold for the extension of national programmes to serve unmet needs in the BOP across a country, as in the case with the extension of healthcare delivery in Mozambique. Building capacity in the social sector highlights a source of innovation based on technology-based platforms for intra-stakeholder coordination, such as the case of creating market access for smallholder farmers. Social sector-based resources may also be a wellspring for BOP communities to organize and engage in self-advocacy (Cairns, Harris, & Young, 2005). The

PFS platform allows local enterprises to consult global food processing experts to help build capacity in the emerging food processing industry.

Cross-sector partnering that supports institutional capacity building has become an interesting and potentially important part of MNCs' pursuit of profit in the BOP. Given different sector locations, however, local partners will vary fundamentally in how they build institutions, reflecting their sector constraints. The impact of MNCs, global philanthropies, and development agencies on institutional capacity that serves BOP markets is an area that demands continued research, particularly with attention to issues of accountability and responsibility. Reflecting broadly, the case discussion on capacity building partnerships that target different sectors suggests that there may be different pathways to national and regional institutional capacity to support BOP markets. That said, as institutions evolve, risks stem from the uncertainty surrounding the alignment of an emerging industry, such as food processing and the emerging capacity of governments.

Notes

1 See, for example case studies by parties in collaboration regarding Project Last Mile including the Global Fund, Coca-Cola, USAID, and local Coca-Cola subsidiaries (Project Last Mile, n.d.; The Global Fund, 2019; Coca-Cola n.d.; The Global Fund 2017).
2 See, for example discussions of this case in the business community (FarmBiz Africa, 2019; Hello Tractor, n.d.; Digest Africa, 2017).
3 See, for example PFS discussion of its collaboration with TechnoServe regarding food security in Africa (TechnoServe, 2012; Koigi, 2018; Melendez, 2018).

References

Adner, R. (2013). *The wide lens: What successful innovators see that others miss.* New York, NY: Penguin.

Aguilera-Caracuel, J., Guerrero-Villegas, J., & García-Sánchez, E. (2017). Reputation of multinational companies: Corporate social responsibility and internationalization. *European Journal of Management and Business Economics, 26*(3), 329–346. doi:10.1108/EJMBE-10-2017-019

Amoako, G. K. (2016). CSR practices of multinational companies (MNCs) and community needs in Africa: Evidence of selected MNCs from Ghana. In S. Vertigans, S. Idowu, & R. Schmidpeter (Eds.), *Corporate Social Responsibility in Sub-Saharan Africa* (217–240). Cham, Switzerland: Springer.

Austin, J. (2010). *The collaboration challenge: How nonprofits and businesses succeed through strategic alliances.* Hoboken, NJ: John Wiley & Sons.

Beers, C. V., Knorringa, P., & Leliveld, A. (2012). Frugal innovation in Africa: Tracking Unilever's washing-powder sachets. *Transforming Innovations in Africa, 11*, 55–78. doi: 10.1163/9789004245440_005

Boadi, I. (2016). Determinants of Ghanaian banks' credit to the "missing middle": A supply-side approach. *International Journal of Bank Marketing, 34*(6), 924–939.

Börzel, T., Hönke, J., & Thauer, C. (2012). Does it really take the state? *Business and Politics, 14*(3), 1–34. doi:10.1515/bap-2012–0023

Cairns, B., Harris, M., & Young, P. (2005). Building the capacity of the voluntary nonprofit sector: Challenges of theory and practice. *International Journal of Public Administration, 28*(9–10), 869–885. doi:10.1081/PAD-200067377

Calton, J. M., Werhane, P. H., Hartman, L. P., & Bevan, D. (2013). Building partnerships to create social and economic value at the base of the global development pyramid. *Journal of Business Ethics, 117*(4), 721–733.

Chikweche, T., & Fletcher, R. (2012). Franchising at the Bottom of the Pyramid (BOP): An alternative distribution approach. *The International Review of Retail, Distribution and Consumer Research, 21*(4), 343–360.

Coca-Cola. (n.d.). Coca-Cola Sabco (Mozambique) SARL. Retrieved from www.ccbagroup.com/outlets/coca-cola-sabco-mozambique/

Cooper, R., & Boye, A. (2005). The scramble for BOP penetration in telecommunications. *Greener Management International, 51*, 88–98.

Dembek, K., Sivasubramaniam, N., & Chmielewski, D. A. (2019). A systematic review of the Bottom/Base of the Pyramid literature: Cumulative evidence and future directions. *Journal of Business Ethics*, 1–18.

Dentoni, D., Bitzer, V. & Pascucci, S. (2016). Cross-sector partnerships and the co-creation of dynamic capabilities for stakeholder orientation. *Journal of Business Ethics*, (135), 35 –53.

Digest Africa. (2018). Hello Tractor, John Deere partner to deploy 10,000 tractors across Nigeria. Retrieved from https://digestafrica.com/hello-tractor-john-deere-tractors-nigeria/

Dolan, C., & Scott, L. (2009). Lipstick evangelism: Avon trading circles and gender empowerment in South Africa. *Gender & Development, 17*(2), 203–218.

Doran, A., McFayden, N., & Vogel, R. C. (2009). The missing middle in agricultural finance: Relieving the capital constraint on smallholder groups and other agricultural SMEs. *Oxfam Policy and Practice: Agriculture, Food and Land, 9*(7), 65–118.

Dougherty, J., & Dogandjieva, R. (2015). The elephant in the room: Financial inclusion for the missing middle. *Innovations: Technology, Governance, Globalization, 10*(1–2), 147–162.

Ebrahim, A., & Rangan, V. K. (2014). What impact? A framework for measuring the scale and scope of social performance. *California Management Review, 56*(3), 118–141. doi:10.1525/cmr.2014.56.3.118

Evans, P. B. (2012). *Embedded autonomy: States and industrial transformation.* Princeton, NJ: Princeton University Press.

FarmBiz Africa. (2019). John Deere employs contractor model to help Kenya's smallholder farmers mechanise. *FarmBiz Africa.* Retrieved from http://farmbizafrica.com/profit-boosters/2541-john-deere-employs-contractor-model-to-help-kenya-s-smallholder-farmers-mechanise

Foote, W. (2018). Meet the social entrepreneur behind Africa's Uber for the farm. *Forbes.* Retrieved from www.forbes.com/sites/willyfoote/2018/08/14/meet-the-social-entrepreneur-behind-africas-uber-for-the-farm/#728eab62bc56.

Freund, C., & Oliver, S. (2016). *Rich people poor countries: The rise of emerging market tycoons and their mega firms.* Washington, DC: Peterson Institute for International Economics.

Garrette, B., & Karnani, A. (2010). Challenges in marketing socially useful goods to the poor. *California Management Review, 52*(4), 29–47.

Gold, S., Hahn, R., & Seuring, S. (2013). Sustainable supply chain management in "Base of the Pyramid" food projects—A path to triple bottom line approaches for multinationals. *International Business Review, 22*(5), 784–799.

Govindarajan, V., & Trimble, C. (2012). Reverse innovation: A global growth strategy that could pre-empt disruption at home. *Strategy & Leadership, 40*(5), 5–11.

Gupta, V., & Khilji, S. E. (2013). Revisiting fortune at Base of the Pyramid (BOP). *South Asian Journal of Global Business Research, 2*(1), 8–26.

Hah, K. & Freeman, S. (2014). Multinational enterprise subsidiaries and their CSR: A conceptual framework of the management of CSR in smaller emerging economies. *Journal of Business Ethics, 122*(1), 125–136. doi:10.1007/s10551-013-1753-8

Hammond, A. L., Kramer, W. J., Katz, R. S., Tran, J. T., & Walker, C. (2008). The next 4 billion: Characterizing BOP markets. *Development Outreach, 10*(2), 7–26.

Harris, D., Derdak, T., Lash, N., Uygur, U., Welch, M., & Zayer, L. T. (2013). Alliance for social enterprise: A framework to develop social entrepreneurship in emerging economies. *International Review of Entrepreneurship, 11*(4).

Harrow J. (2010) Philanthropy. In R. Taylor (Ed.), *Third Sector Research*, 121–138. New York: Springer.

Hello Tractor. (n.d.). Collaboration announcement. Retrieved from www.hellotractor. com/john-deere-hello-tractor/

Hemphill, T. A. (2013). The global food industry and "creative capitalism": The partners in food solutions sustainable business model. *Business and Society Review, 118*(4), 489–511.

Holt, D. and Littlewood, D. (2014). The informal economy as a route to market in sub-Saharan Africa – observations amongst Kenyan informal economy entrepreneurs. In S. Nwanko & K. Ibeh (Eds.), *The Routledge Companion to Business in Africa* (198–217). London: Routledge.

Hutchison, M. L., & Johnson, K. (2011). Capacity to trust? Institutional capacity, conflict, and political trust in Africa, 2000–2005. *Journal of Peace Research, 48*(6), 737–752.

Idemudia, U. (2011). Corporate social responsibility and developing countries: moving the critical CSR research agenda in Africa forward. *Progress in Development Studies, 11*(1), 1–18.

Jones, B. G. (2008). The global political economy of social crisis: Towards a critique of the 'failed state' ideology. *Review of International Political Economy, 15*(2), 180–205.

Karnani, A. (2007). The mirage of marketing to the bottom of the pyramid: How the private sector can help alleviate poverty. *California Management Review, 49*(4), 90–111. doi:10.2307/41166407

Kernen, A., & Lam, K. N. (2014). Workforce localization among Chinese state-owned enterprises (SOEs) in Ghana. *Journal of Contemporary China, 23*(90), 1053–1072.

Koigi, B., (2018). USAID, Technoserve and Partners in Food Solutions in new alliance to point African farmers to profitable markets. *Africa Business Communities.* Retrieved from https://africabusinesscommunities.com/news/usaid-technoserve-and-partners-in-food-solutions-in-new-alliance-to-point-african-farmers-to-profitable-markets/

Kolk, A., & Lenfant, F. (2010). MNC reporting on CSR and conflict in Central Africa. *Journal of Business Ethics, 93*(2), 241–255.

Kolk, A., Rivera-Santos, M., & Rufin, C. (2014). Reviewing a decade of research on the "Base/Bottom of the pyramid" (BOP) concept. *Business & Society, 53*(3), 338–377.

Kolk, A., & Tulder, R. V. (2010). International business, corporate social responsibility and sustainable development. *International Business Review, 19*(2), 119–125.

Kolk, A., Tulder, R. V., & Kostwinder, E. (2008). Business and partnerships for development. *European Management Journal, 26*(4), 262–273. doi:10.1016/j.emj.2008.01.007

Kolk, A., van Dolen, W., & Vock, M. (2010). Trickle effects of cross-sector social partnerships. *Journal of Business Ethics, 94*(1), 123–137.

Kramer, M. R., & Pfitzer, M. W. (2016). The ecosystem of shared value. *Harvard Business Review, 94*(10).

Leke, A., Chironga, M., & Desvaux, G. (2018). *Africa's business revolution: How to succeed in the world's next big growth market.* Cambridge, MA: Harvard Business Press.

Mair, J., Battilana, J., & Cardenas, J. (2012). Organizing for society: A typology of social entrepreneuring models. *Journal of Business Ethics, 111*(3), 353–373.

Mair, J., & Marti, I. (2009). Entrepreneurship in and around institutional voids: A case study from Bangladesh. *Journal of Business Venturing, 24*, 419–435.

Matten, D., & Moon, J. (2008). "Implicit" and "explicit" CSR: A conceptual framework for a comparative understanding of corporate social responsibility. *Academy of Management Review, 33*(2), 404–424.

Meagher, K. (2012). The strength of weak states? Non-state security forces and hybrid governance in Africa. *Development and Change, 43*(5), 1073–1101.

Meagher, K., De Herdt, T., & Titeca, K. (2014). Unravelling public authority: Paths of hybrid governance in Africa. *IS Academy on Human Security in Fragile States.* Retrieved from https://blogs.lse.ac.uk/jsrp/2014/04/07/unravelling-public-authority-paths-of-hybrid-governance-in-africa/

Meagher, K., Mann, L., & Bolt, M. (2018). *Globalisation, economic inclusion and African workers: Making the right connections.* London: Routledge.

Mehta, R., Polsa, P., Mazur, J., Xiucheng, F., & Dubinsky, A. J. (2006). Strategic alliances in international distribution channels. *Journal of Business Research, 59*, 1094–1104.

Melendez, M. J. (2018). Lessons learned from my trip to Africa. Retrieved from https://blog.generalmills.com/2018/03/lessons-learned-from-my-trip-to-africa/

Milligan, K., & Schöning, M. (2011). Taking a realistic approach to impact investing: Observations from the world economic forum's global agenda council on social innovation. *Innovations: Technology, Governance, Globalization, 6*(3), 155–166.

Miska, C., Witt, M. A., & Stahl, G. K. (2016). Drivers of global CSR integration and local CSR responsiveness: Evidence from Chinese MNEs. *Business Ethics Quarterly, 26*(3), 317–345.

Marjanovic, S., Hanlin, R., Diepeveen, S., & Chataway, J. (2013). Research capacity-building in Africa: Networks, institutions and local ownership. *Journal of International Development, 25*(7), 936–946.

Muhia, N., Simanis, E., & Hart, S. (2008). *The Base of the Pyramid protocol: Toward next generation BOP strategy.* Ithaca, NY: Cornell University. doi:10.13140/2.1.5097.0402

Muthuri, J. N. (2013). Corporate Social Responsibility in Africa: Definition, issues and processes. In T. Lituchy, B. J. Punnett, & B. B. Puplampu (Eds.), *Management in Africa*, 110–131. London: Routledge.

Novogratz, J. (2009). Patient capital: A third way to think about aid. *International Trade Forum*, 4. Retrieved from www.tradeforum.org/Patient-Capital-A-Third-Way-to-Think-About-Aid/

Okunlola, F. O., & Adenmosun, A. (2017). Young ICT entrepreneurs provide solutions for agriculture. *Appropriate Technology, 44*(2), 22–23

Parmigiani, A., & Rivera-Santos, M. (2015). Sourcing for the base of the pyramid: Constructing supply chains to address voids in subsistence markets. *Journal of Operations Management, 33*, 60–70.

Peters, A. (2018). This startup lets African farmers hire an on-demand tractor to boost their harvests. *Fast Company*. Retrieved from www.fastcompany.com/90227534/hello-tractor-and-john-deere-bring-10000-tractors-to-africaPorter & Kramer (2006).

Porter, M. E., & Kramer, M. R. (2006). Strategy and society: The link between competitive advantage and corporate social responsibility. *Harvard Business Review, 84*(12), 78–92.

Porter, M. E., & Kramer, M. R. (2019). Creating shared value. In G. G. Lenssen & N. C. Smith (Eds.), *Managing sustainable business* (323–346). Dordrecht, Netherlands: Springer.

Prahalad, C. K. (2004). *The fortune at the bottom of the pyramid: Eradicating poverty through profits*. Upper Saddle River, NJ: Wharton School Publishing.

Project Last Mile. (n.d.). *If you can get a Coca-Cola product almost anywhere in Africa, why not life-saving medicines?* Retrieved from www.usaid.gov/sites/default/files/documents/1864/cii-pjt-last-mile-mozambique_508.pdf

Radjou, N., Prabhu, J., & Ahuja, S. (2012). *Jugaad innovation: Think frugal, be flexible, and generate breakthrough growth*. San Francisco, CA: Jossey-Bass.

Rangan, V. K., Chu, M., & Petkoski, D. (2011). Segmenting the base of the pyramid. *Harvard Business Review, 89*(6).

Rodrik, D. (2008). Second-best institutions. *American Economic Review, 98*(2), 100–104.

Rosca, E., Moellering, G., Rijal, A., & Bendul, J. C. (2019). Supply chain inclusion in base of the pyramid markets. *Management, 49*(5), 575–598.

Ruggie, J. G. (2004). How to marry civic politics and private governance. *The Impact of Global Corporations on Global Governance*. New York: Carnegie Council on Ethics and International Affairs.

Santos, F. M. (2012). A positive theory of social entrepreneurship. *Journal of Business Ethics, 111*(3), 335–351.

Schuster, T., & Holtbrügge, D. (2012). Market entry of multinational companies in markets at the bottom of the pyramid: A learning perspective. *International Business Review, 21*(5), 817–830.

Schwab, K. (2008). Global corporate citizenship: Working with governments and civil society. *Foreign Affairs, 87*(1), 107–118.

Seitanidi, M. M., & Crane, A. (Eds.). (2013). *Social partnerships and responsible business: A research handbook*. London: Routledge.

Selsky, J. W., & Parker, B. (2005). Cross-sector partnerships to address social issues: Challenges to theory and practice. *Journal of Management, 31*(6), 849–873. doi:10.1177/0149206305279601

Selsky, J. W., & Parker, B. (2010). Platforms for cross-sector social partnerships: Prospective sensemaking devices for social benefit. *Journal of Business Ethics, 94*(1), 21.

Simanis, E., Hart, S., & Duke, D. (2008). The base of the pyramid protocol: Beyond "basic needs" business strategies. *Innovations: Technology, Governance, Globalization, 3*(1), 57–84.

Smith, N. C., & Crawford, R. J. (2008). Unilever and Oxfam: Understanding the impacts of business on poverty. *Journal of Business Ethics Education, 5*, 63–112.

Sullivan, R., & Warner, M. (2004). *Putting partnerships to work: Strategic alliances for development between government, the private sector and civil society.* Sheffield, UK: Greenleaf Publishing.

Susha, I., Grönlund, Å. & Tulder, R. V. (2019). Data driven social partnerships: Exploring an emergent trend in search of research challenges and questions. *Government Information Quarterly, 36*(1), 112–128. doi:10.1016/j.giq.2018.11.002

TechnoServe. (2012). Partners in Food Solutions, USAID and TechnoServe expand partnership to improve food security in Africa. Retrieved from www.technoserve.org/news/partners-in-food-solutions-usaid-and-technoserve-expand-partnership-to-impr/

The Global Fund. (2017). *Coca-Cola's "Project Last Mile" expands to Liberia and Swaziland strengthening health systems across Africa.* Retrieved from www.theglobalfund.org/media/8706/publication_privatesectorcocacola_focuson_en.pdf?u=637066556880000000

The Global Fund. (2019). *Project Last Mile: The Coca-Cola Company.* Retrieved from www.theglobalfund.org/media/8706/publication_privatesectorcocacola_focuson_en.pdf?u=637066556880000000

Visser, W., McIntosh, M., & Middleton, C. (Eds.). (2017). *Corporate citizenship in Africa: Lessons from the past; paths to the future.* London: Routledge.

Van Cranenburgh, K.C. & Arenas, D., (2014). Strategic and moral dilemmas of corporate philanthropy in developing countries: Heineken in sub-Saharan Africa, *Journal of Business Ethics, 122*, 523. doi:10.1007/s10551-013-1776-1

Yadav, P., Stapleton, O., & van Wassenhove, L. (2013). Learning from Coca-Cola. *Stanf Soc Innov Rev, 11*(1), 51–55.

Yaziji, M. (2004). Turning gadflies into allies. *Harvard Business Review.* Retrieved from https://hbr.org/2004/02/turning-gadflies-into-allies

Part III

Roles, cooperation, and structure in BOP markets

6 Addressing social sustainability on Base of the Pyramid markets through business model innovations

A comparative study within Africa's fashion industry

Katja Beyer

Introduction

As a key provider of employment opportunities across the globe, the fashion industry holds enormous responsibilities for fostering social sustainability on the Base of the Pyramid (BOP) markets in both affluent as well as less affluent countries. BOP markets refer to impoverished regions of the world on different continents including Africa (Chikweche & Fletcher, 2013; Hill, 2016; Kistruck, Webb, Sutter, & Bailey, 2015). While definitions regarding size and market opportunities vary in the respective literature (Arnold & Valentin, 2013), there exists a certain agreement related to the core elements of such markets. They are typically characterized by (a) social problems, such as high rates of poverty, illiteracy and unemployment causing social exclusion; (b) institutional voids, including interwoven formal and informal institutions, weak legal and regulatory frameworks, as well as high bureaucracy; and (c) deficits regarding infrastructure and resource constraints (e.g. Agarwal, Chakrabarti, Brem, & Bocken, 2018; Arnold, 2017; Hahn & Gold, 2014; Howell, van Beers, & Doorn, 2018). At the same time, however, BOP markets offer enormous potential for creating employment and alleviating poverty by exploiting hidden entrepreneurial opportunities and developing local businesses (Agarwal et al., 2018; Davies & Torrents, 2017; London, Anupindi, & Sheth, 2010; Onsongo, 2017).

These characteristics of BOP markets are also reflected with particular regard to the African fashion industry. As will be shown later on in the study, the sector has been faced with huge challenges (e.g. Baden & Barber, 2005; Brooks & Simon, 2012; Frazer, 2008). This has resulted in severe negative socio-economic development including increasing rates of unemployment, thereby leaving even more impoverished and disenfranchised people on the continent. Yet, recent estimates have been predicting the potentially tremendous economic value of the continent's fashion industry, its significance for employment creation in local micro-, small-, and medium-sized companies, as well as inclusive growth (African Development Bank Group, 2016). An increasing Afrocentrism and changing perceptions of the uniqueness of African cultures, values, and traditions have contributed to this development (Douglas, 2016;

George, Corbishley, Khayesi, Haas, & Tihanyi, 2016; Langevang, 2016). So, the question arises: how can these potential benefits be harnessed and commuted into a sustained economic development of the African fashion industry while at the same time responding to the continent's challenges concerning social sustainability on BOP markets?

Previous research on business development in BOP contexts has repeatedly prompted consideration of radically new business models as well as alternative and inclusive corporate strategies and approaches in order to resolve urgent development problems and to enhance sustainability (Bittencourt Marconatto, Barin-Cruz, Pozzebon, & Poitras, 2016; Howell et al., 2018; Rosca, Arnold, & Bendul, 2017). By realigning development with inclusiveness (Dhahri & Omri, 2018), sustainable development enables "the creation of resilient ecological, social and economic systems by respecting the natural and given limits of ecological viability and capacity" (Arnold, 2018, p. 582). The need for inclusive, equitable, and people-centred development has been emphasized particularly in Africa's transition towards sustainability. This includes economic, structural, and social transformations with a focus on aspects such as adding value to local products, sustainability-oriented innovations, and addressing excluded groups (Economic Commission for Africa, 2015; Lawan, 2015; Maji, 2019; Swilling, 2013).

Taking a closer look, alternative business approaches are seen to predominantly engage in social innovation, thereby addressing the social dimension of sustainability (Gold, Hahn, & Seuring, 2013; Onsongo, 2017). Social sustainability refers to:

> development that is compatible with harmonious evolution of civil society, fostering an environment conducive to the compatible cohabitation of culturally and socially diverse groups while at the same time encouraging social integration, with improvements in the quality of life for all segments of the population.
>
> (Sierra, Yepes, & Pellicer, 2018, p. 496)

Social entrepreneurship represents such an innovative and alternative approach of social and inclusive value creation to alleviate social inequalities and to foster social welfare (Howell et al., 2018; Urban, 2008).

However, research on the relevance of social enterprises in Africa remains rather limited (Littlewood & Holt, 2017). Furthermore, despite studies focusing on social and inclusive business models in general (e.g. Goyal, Sergi, & Jaiswal, 2015; Hlady-Rispal & Servantie, 2016; Michelini & Fiorentino, 2012), there is a paucity of research exploring business model components of social enterprises and other innovative corporate strategies from an integrated sustainability perspective. Usually, only specific elements are considered for potential optimization, and thus, a systemic view is often neglected (Bocken, Boons, & Baldassarre, 2019). This, however, is an important concern for business model innovations for sustainability on BOP markets since they need to develop business ecosystems and to be adaptive to contextual challenges (Ausrød, Sinha, & Widding, 2017; Howell et al., 2018). In light of this, further research on what social sustainability-related effects can be derived from business model innovations on BOP markets in Africa becomes necessary.

Against this background, this study's purpose is to explore business model innovations for sustainability in the African fashion sector by investigating business model components from a holistic and inclusive sustainability viewpoint. Therefore, a conceptual framework for business model innovation for sustainability is developed and applied on a total sample of 12 African fashion companies. Split into several subsamples, the study considers both companies that appear to have social and sustainability-oriented missions with clear linkages to BOP segments as well as traditional business ventures for comparison. The following three research questions guide the conceptual as well as empirical analysis:

(1) *Which sustainability-related aspects are considered in main components of business model innovation for sustainability?*
(2) *Which trends and drivers of the global fashion industry are communicated in main components of business model innovation for sustainability on the company's web presence?*
(3) *What are the implications for addressing social sustainability on BOP markets in Africa?*

The chapter begins with a review of extant literature on business model innovation and social enterprises in Africa as well as their relevance for BOP contexts. This is followed by the development of a conceptual framework emphasizing a holistic and integrative perspective on business model innovations for sustainability. The methodology section describes the research context of Africa's fashion industry and the comparative case study design. Subsequently, findings relating to impacts as well as characteristics of components in business model innovations for sustainability are presented and comparatively discussed, thereby highlighting the social dimension of sustainability. The conclusion section illustrates theoretical and practical implications while reinforcing the significant role of social enterprises in addressing social sustainability-related challenges on Africa's BOP markets.

Literature review

The following section illustrates relevant literature on the connection between business model innovations for sustainability and BOP markets. Furthermore, in representing such alternative corporate approaches, social enterprises in Africa are highlighted with their characteristic features.

The BOP proposition claims that economic and business activity can help to alleviate poverty, thereby emphasizing the social responsibility and social embeddedness of companies (Ansari, Munir, & Gregg, 2012; London et al.,

2010; van den Waeyenberg & Hens, 2012). BOP markets are seen to comprise cognitively and socially vulnerable people with high levels of illiteracy and poverty and low levels of education, amongst other challenges (Arnold & Valentin, 2013). On the one hand, this results in the social exclusion of these people, leading to their exploitation by other members of the society. On the other hand, these vulnerabilities cause them to make use of and enhance more informal networks. While early conceptions have predominantly focused on profit opportunities of Western-based multinational corporations (MNCs) on BOP markets by simply adapting their products to local conditions, recent approaches show a different perspective and emphasize inclusivity and co-creation. In this vein, the concept of the BOP 2.0 has included the active engagement of the poor, local empowerment, and entrepreneurship in business activities. Yet, given limited success, a recent shift in the conception of the BOP market has been calling to strive for more inclusion and collaboration in such market-based approaches in order to facilitate solutions for quite complex societal challenges, systemic change, and true poverty eradication (Arnold, 2017; Bendul, Rosca, & Pivovarova, 2017; Chmielewski, Dembek, & Beckett, 2018). This notion of the BOP 3.0 highlights the importance of local businesses and enterprises. Given local entrepreneurs' highly valuable resources, such as social networks, local cultural knowledge, and reputation in the community, they are considered to essentially reduce poverty (Davies & Torrents, 2017). This is even more important since research on BOP markets has been criticized of mainly adopting Western and multinational companies' perspectives (Chmielewski et al., 2018).

To engage in BOP contexts, fundamentally new business models and innovations in existing business model components have repeatedly been called for (e.g. Bittencourt Marconatto et al., 2016; Gebauer, Haldimann, & Saul, 2017a; Gebauer, Saul & Haldimann, 2017b; Jose, 2008). Drawing on Geissdoerfer, Vladimirova, & Evans (2018), business models are "simplified representations of the value proposition, value creation and delivery, and value capture elements and the interactions between these elements within an organisational unit" (p. 402). In light of the contextual peculiarities on BOP markets, reinventing one or multiple of these business model components is suggested to overcome challenges and barriers (Gebauer et al., 2017a), yet it is also considered rather demanding (Howell et al., 2018).

Innovations in business models challenge the dominant regime logic as they change value creation and capture (Bidmon & Knab, 2018; Rauter, Jonker, & Baumgartner, 2017). Previous research on business model innovations in the context of BOP markets has emphasized important dimensions and elements to be included in order to transform corporate strategies (Bittencourt Marconatto et al., 2016; Gebauer et al., 2017a, b; Howell et al., 2018; Jose, 2008) and to circumvent the various constraints on BOP markets (Bendul et al., 2017). Gebauer et al. (2017a) characterize business model components on BOP markets as inclusive, complex, collaborative, and scalable. In this vein, they should promote close interaction with local people and communities as well as integrate local and indigenous knowledge and culture. This enables firms to develop native capabilities and build upon the local environment (Ausrød et al., 2017).

In order to address challenges regarding sustainability and development in BOP contexts, business model innovations for sustainability have recently been advocated. In an attempt to link business with sustainability concerns, such innovations in business models and their components aim at shared value creation for the company, the community, and society (Bittencourt Marconatto et al., 2016; Howell et al., 2018). Despite conceptual variations in the literature (Morris, Schindehutte, & Allen, 2005), it is acknowledged that such business models alter and extend the traditional business model concept by integrating sustainability considerations. They embed economic, ecological, and social elements in value offering and value creation processes. Further, they foster equitable, pro-active stakeholder relationships, promote fair and balanced revenues including their distribution, and involve a long-term orientation (Bocken, Short, Rana, & Evans, 2014; Dentchev et al., 2018; Geissdoerfer et al., 2018; Matos & Silvestre, 2013; Ritala, Huotari, Bocken, Albareda, & Puumalainen, 2018; Schaltegger, Lüdeke-Freund, & Hansen, 2012; Tolkamp, Huijben, Mourik, Verbong, & Bouwknegt, 2018; Yang, Evans, Vladimirova, & Rana, 2017). In deviation from profit maximization goals in traditional business models, business model innovations for sustainability are seen as a mechanism to create significant positive societal impacts. Thus, they have the potential to enable systemic change (Koistinen, Laukkanen, Mikkilä, Huiskonen, & Linnanen, 2018; Nußholz, 2017). For companies to successfully adopt and implement business model innovations for sustainability, internal capabilities and stakeholder collaborations play key roles (Matos & Silvestre, 2013). This is even more so because they often require the solution of trade-offs and conflicts concerning sustainability objectives and dimensions as well as stakeholder interests and their roles (Bocken, Miller, Weissbrod, Holgado, & Evans, 2017; Lüdeke-Freund, Gold, & Bocken, 2018).

Research concentrating on sustainable business models for BOP contexts has emphasized the need for including low-income segments in the value proposition in order to eventually address the problem of poverty and, thus, the social pillar of sustainability (Bittencourt Marconatto et al., 2016). This is an innovative approach, particularly considering social sustainability in business models represents social entrepreneurship (Howell et al., 2018). Social enterprises focus on developing innovative solutions to realize social missions and to improve human well-being. They further promote the mutual consideration of economic and social or environmental aspects in value creation processes (Cherrier, Goswami, & Ray, 2018; Goyal et al., 2015; Luke & Chu, 2013; Rivera-Santos, Holt, Littlewood, & Kolk, 2015; United Nations Development Program, 2014). Social entrepreneurship aims at stimulating social change and social wealth creation by offering employment opportunities, developing industries, or addressing gender inequity and social exclusion, amongst others (Rahdari, Sepasi, & Moradi, 2016; United Nations Development Program, 2014). Against this background, previous academic studies have focused on explicit social impact approaches and inclusivity (Howell et al., 2018).

In BOP contexts, social enterprises usually involve poor people primarily living in rural and remote areas. In doing so, they are faced with multiple obstacles stipulated by the BOP environment as aforementioned. These involve environmental dynamics, balancing the duality of social and commercial object-ives as well as the management of an underdeveloped market-based ecosystem (Goyal et al., 2015).

Considering the prevailing socio-economic environment in Africa, signifi-cant challenges and opportunities for social enterprises and other ventures have been enunciated in prior research. Table 6.1 provides a summary of these con-textual elements and maps them with opportunities for sustainable develop-ment from a corporate perspective. Thus, it shows framing conditions in terms of business models and market strategies as well as sustainable and inclusive innovations. By exploring them, previous studies on social enterprises in Africa have examined a variety of topics. They include, for instance, self-perceptions as well as impacts on founders (Littlewood & Holt, 2018; Rivera-Santos et al., 2015), the connection between strategy and resilience (Littlewood & Holt, 2017), the emergence of hybrid approaches (Calvo & Morales, 2016), or the nexus between interest in pursuing social entrepreneurship and concomitant skills (Urban, 2008).

Furthermore, given the variations across the continent, social enterprises are also likely to be different within Africa. This becomes emphasized by a potentially broad range of social venture forms, long histories of the phe-nomenon in single countries, as well as multiple context-specific factors to influence their evolution, as shown in Table 6.1 (Karanda & Toledano, 2012; Littlewood & Holt, 2018; Rivera-Santos et al., 2015). For instance, a likely different understanding and reinterpretation of the "social" in social enterprises in Africa can be affirmed (Karanda & Toledano, 2012). According to Mirvis and Googins (2018) social entrepreneurship on the continent is closely related to cultural beliefs and values such as interdependence, reciprocity, and collectivist orientations. Especially relations within communities as well as their ideological and cultural links can be considered to highly affect the activities of social enterprises (Cieslik, 2016; Rivera-Santos et al., 2015). In this vein, Karanda and Toledano (2012) point to different narratives on social enterprises and the role of the social entrepreneur in the South African context. Thus, the significance of cooperative relationships and reciprocal relations between satisfying the social needs of the entrepreneur and the community is highlighted, involving high levels of commitment, embeddedness, and responsibility. This also includes aspects such as passion on the part of the social entrepreneur, reflected in acting as a change-agent or by fostering an internal change of people's and com-munities' mindsets as precursors for successful social enterprises (Karanda & Toledano, 2012; Thorgren & Omorede, 2015).

Social enterprises in Africa are also seen to create social values and benefits on a local and small-scale level (Karanda & Toledano, 2012). Focusing on

Table 6.1 Stressed contextual elements of the African continent and sustainability-related implications for domestic and international business and management

Aspect	Key features of the African continent (by the author*)	Opportunities and challenges for sustainable development (by the author*)
Size	• World's second largest continent • 5 regions with 54 countries	• National, regional, and local differences
Natural conditions	• 30% of the world's minerals • Largest reserves of precious metals • 90% of soils unsuitable for agriculture • 0.25% of soils with potential for sustainable farming • Water scarcity	• Natural resource management • Local ecosystems and social embeddedness of communities • Stakeholder management in key industries • Organizational responses to institutional changes • Capacity building • Aggregation of natural conditions (e.g. water) due to global warming and climate change
Demography	• Population growth • Acceleration in urbanization • High number of people under the age of 25	• Growing consumer markets for goods and services • Employment opportunity creation • Human resources (e.g. employee training) • Health care • Inclusive education
Institutional, infrastructure, governance, mechanisms, and ethical business practices	• Institutional plurality and complexity • Institutional voids • Lack of enforcement of property rights • Differences in transaction costs and firm competitiveness • Fraud and corruption • Peaceful transfer of power through democratic electoral processes in single countries • Resource constraints (e.g. basic infrastructure, credits, technology)	• Resilient social and economic institutions • Competitive value chain activities based on (local) market liberalization and business entities' networks • Institutional reforms • Positive political engagement and stakeholder relations • Ethical stewardship • Embeddedness of CSR practices • Orientation to long-term market success • Governance models that meet or exceed local needs
Ethnicity and linguistics	• Tribal and ethnic variety • (Local) variety of subcultures, rites, norms, values, and traditions	• Understanding of culture- and society-based constructs (e.g. trust)

(continued)

Table 6.1 Cont.

Aspect	Key features of the African continent (by the author*)	Opportunities and challenges for sustainable development (by the author*)
	• Importance of local identities and leaders • Unrest	• Cultural affinity • Professional social identities • Legitimacy-establishing adoption to local languages and regional "lingua francas" • Local stakeholder relationship management • Modification of corporate organizational structures
Poverty	• 26 out of 54 countries with middle-income status • 22 countries ranked among the world's 25 poorest countries in GDP • Decline of people living in extreme poverty (from 51% in 2005 to 42% in 2014)	• Social welfare • Delivery of goods and services • Human development • No discrimination
Social norms and relations	• Reliance on entrepreneurial resources within family or community context • Social obligations and demands	• Social capital and managerial networking relationships with external entities
Inclusive growth	• Inequalities of market access • Limited market access to (financial) services • Gender discrimination	• Policy initiatives • Workplace equality • Market transformations impact rural and semi-urban areas
Security	• Conflicts and wars • 20 of the world's 36 fragile states • Post-conflict tensions	• Supply chain and distribution channel management in unsafe and turbulent regions • Decision-making in conflict-driven regions • Investment risks • Embeddedness in local networks
Market and investment behavior	• Average growth rate of 5% over 15 years • Largely agrarian economies • Dominance of the informal sector • Foreign (direct) investment (e.g. China)	• Different forms of social capital • New organizational forms or alternative governance arrangements in low-cost settings • Specific consumption behaviors and cultural preferences • Rural entrepreneurial opportunity • Different market entry modes • Impacts regarding global strategic dependencies • Adaptation of corporate practices to local contexts

Table 6.1 Cont.

Aspect	Key features of the African continent (by the author*)	Opportunities and challenges for sustainable development (by the author*)
Private sector	• Generation of 90% of employment, two-thirds of investment, and 70% of economic output • Lack of access to financial resources and venture capital funding • Lack of business expertise in formal sectors • High failure rates of SMEs	• Local entrepreneurship • Alternative operating banking models • New business models • Embeddedness of business (models) in communities • Entrepreneurial opportunity identification within non-supportive ecosystems
Labor	• Limited access to human capital (e.g. shortages in high-quality, technically educated workforce) • Lack of employee training and development • Union relations • Migrant flows • Variety of workplace practices, regulations and processes	• Diffusion of management practices across cultures • Modification of Western-based human resource management • Employee relations in the informal sector • Organizational improvements based on communication, trust, and team building • In-house training of workers • Effects of varying labor relations and their conditions
Management and organization	• Lack of access to managerial capabilities • Denied or limited access to management structures for certain ethnic groups	• (Basic-level) managerial capacity development • Management effectiveness and achievement of organizational goals • Human capital development • Inclusive organizational culture • Diverse management team • (Global) implications of leadership practices in the African context

Source: * author's summary; inspired by and adopted from George et al. (2016); Kolk and Rivera-Santos (2018); Zoogah (2008); and Thomas and Bendixen (2000).

BOP contexts in Kenya, Panum, Hansen, and Davy (2018) stress that social enterprises equally and mutually pursue social and commercial objectives, thereby hinting to the fact that, in such environments, "social impact is seen as a function of the enterprise's commercial success" (p. 19). However, due to conflicts between internal and external social objectives, large-scale social impacts in these settings are constrained. Furthermore, the authors find that the perceived competitive advantage of social enterprises at the BOP establishes difficulties concerning their conceptual attributes and distinctions with other companies, thereby questioning their legitimacy. Based on these arguments, the authors contend that the concept of social enterprises "becomes illusive at the BOP" (p. 20) while calling for further examination. The present study builds on this and undertakes such an exploration in the context of social enterprises on BOP markets in the fashion industry. Furthermore, while there is scholarly research focusing on social enterprises in single African countries, there have been increased calls for conducting more cross-country studies as well as for further focusing on sub-Saharan Africa (Littlewood & Holt, 2017). Thus, the present study also attempts at responding to these calls.

Theoretical synthesis and conceptual framework development

In order to answer the research questions, and in particular the first one, this study draws on a conceptual framework for business model innovation for sustainability. This framework is grounded in six research studies that account for seminal and prominent work in the fields of business models, social and inclusive business models, business model innovations for sustainability, as well as business models for frugal innovations in developing countries and business model innovations in the fashion industry. These investigations and their relevance to this study's framework are as follows: (1) Richardson (2008) provides a generic and strategic view on business models, whereas (2) Yunus, Moingeon, and Lehmann-Ortega (2010) focus on a social perspective in terms of business models. This is continued by the third study conducted by (3) Michelini and Fiorentino (2012) who offer a social and inclusive perspective on business model innovation, distinguished according to four business model areas, namely offer, eco-system, market, and economic features.

The highly cited article by (4) Bocken et al. (2014) points to a sustainability view on business model innovation by presenting several technological, social, and organizational business model archetypes. Furthermore, the research by (5) Rosca et al. (2017) was included in the development of the present framework since the authors present a sustainability view on business models centring on innovations in developing countries. This was considered especially important given the present study's focus on Africa and the role of frugality and inclusivity in such developing contexts. Finally, in light of the limited research on the integration of sustainability in business models in the fashion industry (Thorisdottir & Johannsdottir, 2019), the framework is based on the study by (6) Todeschini, Cortimiglia, Callegaro-de-Menezes, and Ghezzi (2017). They – to the best of the author's knowledge – for the first time employ a complex fashion industry-related view on conceptualizations for sustainable and innovative business models. Other than the study by Morgan (2015), who focuses mainly on the consumption side for business model innovations in clothing retail, Todeschini et al. (2017) emphasize both production as well as consumption views in business model innovations for sustainability by categorizing several trends and drivers that influence alternative entrepreneurial approaches. These are depicted in Table 6.6 in the Appendix. Since the present study's purpose is to analyse sustainability-driven companies in the African fashion industry, the conceptualization developed by Todeschini et al. (2017) was considered to offer a blueprint for the subsequent empirical analysis, thereby gaining theoretical insights into the context-specificity of business model innovations.

While the efforts made by all six research studies are highly appreciated, there are several shortcomings in each of the approaches. By way of illustration, Yunus et al. (2010) introduce the term "social profit equation", which combines aspects of social and environmental sustainability. Yet, an exact distinction between each dimension is not made, thereby contributing to a certain vagueness as already criticized in previous studies on particularly social enterprises. Furthermore, the value proposition as described by Yunus et al. (2010) does not explicitly relate to or distinguish between different dimensions of sustainability. Next, the research by Todeschini et al. (2017) seminally introduces linkages between trends and drivers in the fashion industry as well as the concept of business model innovation, but leaves some margin for interpretation as to how those have been elaborated.

Given similar theoretical, conceptual, and methodological drawbacks in the other studies, the present study was induced by developing a more holistic and inclusive framework for business model innovations for sustainability. As shown in Figure 6.1, this was achieved in a first step by analysing the similarities among the six previous studies concerning single components of business model innovations. Based on this, the common features and understanding of main business model components as construed in the extant literature were summarized in a second step. The objective here was to synthesize existent business model components. Identified gaps laid the foundation for the final step of further nurturing them by explicitly integrating a systemic and embedded perspective on sustainability in business model components. In doing so, single components were refined and expanded (e.g. adding of social and environmental value proposition).

Figure 6.2 illustrates the final conceptual framework, its basic attributes, as well as components and elements developed and employed in this research. In light of the challenges in BOP contexts and with particular regard to the detrimental effects of poverty, integrating a holistic and integrative view on sustainability in each business model component was considered crucially important since "sustainability can only be attained when each subsystem, economic, social and environmental, is vital and resilient individually and jointly" (Kirchgeorg & Winn, 2006, p. 172). Furthermore, balancing the three dimensions of economic, environmental, and social sustainability is essential in sustainable business models and performance objectives due to their interrelations and interdependencies (Dhahri & Omri, 2018; Li, Zhao, Shi, & Li, 2014; Matos & Silvestre, 2013). In addition, organizational aspects were included in the differentiation of single components since previous literature has pointed to the relevance and necessity of building organizational and internal capabilities, particularly in sustainable business models

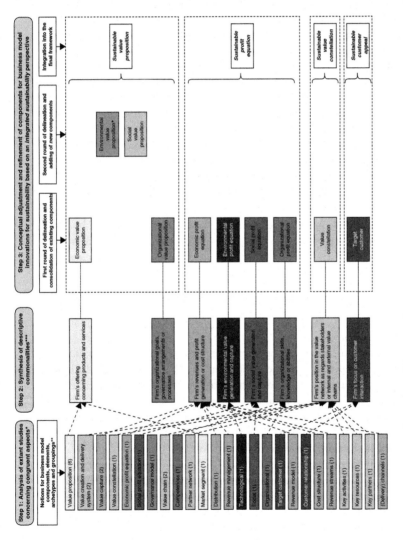

Figure 6.1 Derivation of conceptual framework.

Note: * as emphasized by the author and based on the following seminal and prominent work: Richardson (2008), Yunus et al. (2010), Michelini and Fiorentino (2012), Bocken et al. (2014), Rosca et al. (2017), and Todeschini et al. (2017). Similar shaded markings represent congruent components, elements, and aspects in business models among the studies cited and their adjustment for this study's framework; they are identical with the shaded markings in the conceptual framework in Figure 6.2 in order to highlight congruency. ** The italic numbers given in brackets indicate the number of times the respective business model component was considered in business model conceptualizations across the six studies mentioned in (*). **Based on seminal and prominent work as listed in (*). ◆ This component is also in line with the study by Abdelkafi and Täuscher (2016).

Source: author's own.

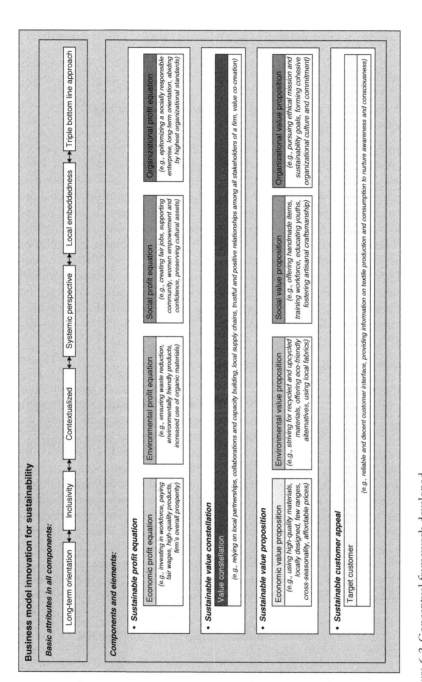

Figure 6.2 Conceptual framework developed.
Source: author's own derivation and illustration.

as well as social enterprises (Hlady-Rispal & Servantie, 2016; Rauter et al., 2017; Stubbs & Cocklin, 2008). In line with this, the present research also assumes that particular corporate preconditions are required in order to offer social value as well as to create a wider and true impact on society through social enterprises.

Methodology

Research context: the significance of sub-Saharan Africa's fashion industry for social enterprises

The textile and apparel sector in sub-Saharan Africa has been facing various challenges to sustainable and sustained development based on several levels and factors, thereby displaying different trajectories within single countries and regions. This involves aspects such as the role of increasingly globalized value chains, Asian investments, and second-hand clothing trade or structural problems relating to shortages in power supply and inadequate financing (e.g. Baden & Barber, 2005; Brooks & Simon, 2012; Essel, 2017; Frazer, 2008; Nørup, Pihl, Damgaard, & Scheutz, 2019; Traub-Merz, 2006; Wrede, 2018; Xiaoyang, 2014). However, specifically when taking the perspective of business model innovations for sustainability on BOP contexts in general and social enterprises in particular, focusing on the fashion industry in sub-Saharan Africa is particularly justified for the following three reasons.

(1) Tremendous economic scope and entrepreneurial opportunities

According to recent forecasts, the apparel and footwear industry in sub-Saharan Africa unfolds a potentially significant scope with an economic value of US $31 billion. The overwhelming majority of ventures in this sector are small- and medium-sized companies that are exposed to severe challenges, constraining operations and growth expectations (Douglas, 2016). Yet, by improving conditions as well as promoting indigenous entrepreneurial ventures that address sustainability challenges, local (end-) market development, brand building, regional investment, and linkages to other sectors are considered to play a key role in realizing the sector's potential for sustainable value chains as well as local and regional industrialization and integration at the global level (African Development Bank Group, 2016 Morris, Staritz, & Plank, 2014; Sneyd, 2015). Significant business opportunities therewith are also related to an environmentally sustainable textile value chain, including organic cotton production, or engaging in recycling activities (African Development Bank Group, 2016).

(2) Priority sector for employment generation, socio-economic, and structural transformations

The labour intensiveness of the fashion industry provides essential chances for job creation at the local and community level. Against the background of severe

Table 6.2 Sample inclusion and exclusion criteria (Author's own illustration and emphasis)

Inclusion criteria	Exclusion criteria

General criteria:
• Primary textile focus:
  ✓ Garments and shoes
  ✓ Plant and animal fibres (e.g. cotton, leather)
• Main product segments:
  ✓ Clothing companies (e.g. womens- and/or menswear)
  ✓ Footwear companies (e.g. sandals, shoes, boots)
  ✓ Companies offering accessories (e.g. bags, belts, scarfs)
• Location of production process and/ or headquarters in Africa
• Location of companies in different countries and regions of Africa (at least 2 countries per group)
• Direct-to-customer brands (companies with an updated, ovm corporate website and an online shop)
• Recognition and reputation of companies (e.g. awards, international and African fairs, trade shows and exhibitions, media and press coverage including interviews, Fair Trade certification)
 	
Specific criteria for each group of companies:
• **Social enterprise-specific criteria:**
  ✓ <u>Explicit</u> reference on corporate website to the fact that the company is a social enterprise or a socially responsible company
  ✓ List of main keywords on corporate websites primarily relates to social sustainability (e.g. social responsibility, inclusion, African culture and heritage, job creation, community dedication, wages, artisanal crafts and skills, handmade items, women and youth empowerment, disadvantaged, education and training, local production)
	• Exclusion of non-accessible corporate websites or parts thereof (e.g. beta versions of websites)
	• Exclusion of companies that are – according to their website – currently in a phase of strategic reorientation and period of charge (e.g. closing factories and/or shifting production location to another African country)
	• Exclusion of non-updated corporate websites and online shops (e.g. no contact options, outdated copyright clams)
	• Exclusion of non-African based production of brands and labels
	• Exclusion of platform-based, integrated networks of social enterprises or artisans in Africa
	• Exclusion of individual designers
	• Exclusion of specific segments and products:
	  ✓ Solely yarn and fibre manufacturing companies
	  ✓ Supplying technology companies (e.g. spinning technologies)
	  ✓ Fabrics (e.g. home textiles)
	  ✓ Jewellery
	  ✓ African premium, haute couture, and luxury labels
	• Exclusion of corporate websites displayed in a language other than English (e.g. French)

(continued)

Table 6.2 Cont.

Inclusion criteria	Exclusion criteria
• **Sustainability-focused company-specific criteria:** ✓ Explicit reference on corporate website to sustainability ✓ Precise, comprehensive and traceable view of corporate sustainability efforts and initiatives presented on website ✓ List of main keywords on corporate websites primarily relates to environmental sustainability (e.g. organic cotton, naturally grown fibres, recycling, environment, waste reduction, water, energy, sustainable and local production, audits) and social sustainability (e.g. CSR, employment opportunities, wages, ethical fashion production, transparency) • **Traditional company-specific criteria:** ✓ Non-specific and non-traceable information concerning sustainability offered on corporate website; if presented at all, then only marginally with low accuracy ✓ List of main keywords on corporate websites primarily relates to the brand, its products, conventional materials used, and customers' shopping experience (e.g. mass production and market, international label, fast fashion, ready-to-wear, wholesale, large scale, shopping, latest fashion trends and styles, synthetic fibres, polyester)	

Source: author's own.

poverty challenges, entrepreneurial ventures in the fashion industry can help address the problem of women's and youth's unemployment by integrating poorly educated, low- or unskilled workers, and marginalized groups who have little – if any – alternative opportunities (African Development Bank Group, 2016; Traub-Merz, 2006; Vlok, 2006). Eventually, given the important role of women in sub-Saharan Africa's fashion industry (Damoah, 2018), this sector can decisively contribute to female empowerment and the social security of entire households. Further opportunities are seen in providing ethical, safe, and rewarding working conditions. Creating dignified, formal employment opportunities, developing markets, and exports targeting other countries and regions within Africa could help alleviate poverty and improve human development across the continent (Kao, 2016).

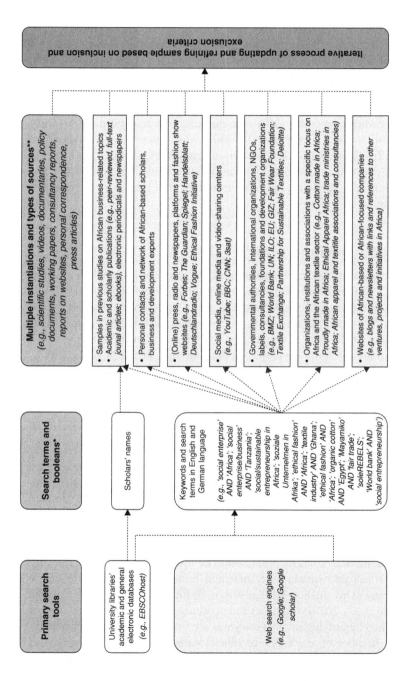

Figure 6.3 Case selection procedure.

Note: * here, the search terms and booleans are not an exhaustive list of keywords; instead, a variety of textile- and fashion-related synonyms and keywords (e.g. other countries with relevance for Africa's fashion industry and located in sub-Saharan Africa) was referred to during this research step of screening and identifying suitable companies. ** Following the systematization of literature as presented by Adams, Smart, and Huff (2017).

Source: author's own schematic visualization.

(3) Importance for social sustainability, local, and inclusive development impacts

The third argument for choosing the fashion sector as the empirical setting in the present study relates to its strong traditions (Essel, 2017) and cultural artefacts associated therewith, such as local fabrics and craftsmanship in African cultures. The specific roles and features of African culture, diversity, and creativity (as shown in Table 6.1) are considered a unique selling point for self-identification with the continent (African Development Bank Group, 2016). Practice shows the sector's potential for engaging in ethical fashion, thereby focusing on aspects such as artisanal cotton and hand-woven items (Cartier, 2017). Furthermore, previous studies have pointed to developing industry-specific skills and providing formal training to multiple stakeholders such as personnel, technicians, supervisors, managers, or farmers (Baffes, 2009; Kao, 2016; Morris, Staritz, & Plank, 2014). The need to promote cooperation among farmers has also been highlighted (Baffes, 2009), reflecting a further requirement when attempting to engage the BOP context in an inclusive way.

Research design: comparative case study

This research adopts an exploratory multiple and comparative case study approach. To gather data, typical and exemplifying cases were selected and analysed, enabling in-depth explanations as well as cross-contextual interpretation and pattern-matching (Bryman, 2015; Corbett, Webster, & Jenkin, 2018). The procedure of theoretical sampling was used, as the purpose of the study was to contribute to theory development (Zimmerling, Purtik, & Welpe, 2017). Several general and sustainability-related criteria for case selection were defined in advance in order to ensure rigor. Those criteria, as shown in Table 6.2, were partly based on common-sense intuitive reflection and partly derived from previous publications relevant to addressing the three research questions (e.g. Allianz Nachhaltige Universitäten in Österreich, 2014).

To answer the three research questions, sub-Saharan Africa was chosen as the empirical context. This was justified given the fact that this region is severely affected by extreme poverty and other challenges hampering sustainable development (L'Huillier, 2016; Maji, 2019; Qafa, 2017; Valente & Oliver, 2018). In fact, with an average poverty rate of about 41% and comprising 27 (out of 28) of the world's poorest countries, the area represents one of the largest BOP markets in the world (Davies & Torrents, 2017; Patel, 2018). This, in turn, provides manifold imperatives of social impacts by businesses. The preparatory work for exploring appropriate social and sustainability-oriented businesses proceeded iteratively through several steps. In line with previous qualitative research (e.g. Arnold, 2018; Rosca et al., 2017), multiple instantiations and supplementary sources were used since identifying suitable cases was accompanied by several challenges (e.g. limited number of and access to official statistics on social enterprises in Africa). This procedure for identifying relevant cases is illustrated in Figure 6.3.

In the initial phase of case sampling, nearly 70 ventures and companies were identified and documented in an Excel spreadsheet. Following several iterations of screening and refining in line with the case selection criteria as shown above, a final convenience sample was acquired consisting of 12 companies. This sample then was classified into three subgroups, comprising a first group of social enterprises, a second group of sustainability-oriented companies, and a third group of traditional companies. The latter functions as a control group in order to provide greater reliability and validity during the analysis. Furthermore, contrasting with traditional companies and, thus, eventually building on a comparison of positive and negative cases (Bryman, 2015) was considered to be useful in this explorative research approach for revealing "similarities and differences across cases towards theoretical generalizations" (Morioka & Carvalho, 2016, p. 127).

The companies selected are located in eight sub-Saharan African countries: Ghana, Burkina Faso, Nigeria, Ethiopia, Uganda, Tanzania, Malawi, and South Africa. Inspired by common case-based research criteria (Eisenhardt, 1989), at least two sub-Saharan African countries and four companies were included per subgroup of the sample in order to preserve methodological rigor and to allow for finding cross-contextual patterns. With regard to the BOP setting in the present study, the subsample of traditional companies comprised three cases located in two of Africa's largest BOP markets, Nigeria and South Africa (Hodgson, 2017). The case characteristics are presented in Table 6.3.

In line with previous research, content analysis of corporate websites was used (Kühn, Stiglbauer, & Fifka, 2018; Utgård, 2018). Data gathering took place during two time periods (June–August 2018; February–April 2019). For each of the 12 cases, the corporate statements were manually traced and stored in single files. Formal differences across corporate websites prompted to exclude additional material such as magazine interviews with founders of social enterprises, thereby seeking rigor and consistency.

Data analysis was based on a hybrid approach involving inductive and deductive techniques for qualitative content analysis, thereby following a detailed coding process (Lock & Seele, 2015; Mayring, 2015). The analysis was conducted in four steps: First, by using open coding, single statements and meaning units were inductively aligned with each business model component from the framework, as shown in Figure 6.2, thereby developing a code category system (Corbett et al., 2018; Fichter & Tiemann, 2018). Highlighting major themes and patterns in main business model components, a comparative theoretical synthesis across the sample was drawn for each component of business model innovation for sustainability in a second step. Thereafter, in the third step, the business model components for sustainability for each company were aligned to the trends and drivers of the fashion industry, as outlined by Todeschini et al. (2017). Thus, during this methodological step, literature-based deductive coding was applied and conceptual generalizations formed. Based on this, the fourth step comprised a summary of business model components affected for each subgroup of the sample. This again involved cross- and

Table 6.3 Overview of sample subgroups and company cases included in this research*

No.	Company	Corporate website	Country	Region	Year of inception	Employees	Primary textile fibres, fabrics, and materials**	Main product focus	Awards, accolades, and events illustrating local and international recognition
Social enterprises									
1	YEVU	https://yevu clothing. com	Ghana	Western Africa	2012	30	Cotton	Wearing apparel (Womens– and menswear)	2017 winner of InStyle and Audi Women of Style scholarship
2	Kitenge	https://kitenge store.com	Tanzania	Eastern Africa	2014	6		Wearing apparel (Womens– and menswear)	2019 showcasing at Bristol's Fabric Africa Fashion Show in the UK
3	KoliKo Wear	https://koliko wear.com/ index.html	Ghana	Western Africa	2017	No data available	Leather; rubber; cotton	Footwear	Supported by Managers without Borders, Ghana Climate Innovation Center, and iN4iN (Intelligence for Innovation)
4	Fairsole	https://fair sole.com/	Uganda	Eastern Africa	2017	No data available	Leather; rubber; banana fibres	Footwear	Appreciation by the Fair Fashion Blog as a sustainable crowdfunding project worth supporting

Sustainability-oriented companies

5	Xoomba	www.xoomba.com	Burkina Faso	Western Africa	2010	No data available	Organic cotton	Wearing apparel (Womens- and menswear)	2019 organizer of the ethical fashion project Future Fashion: For People Who Love Life On Earth; Repeated media coverage (e.g. OurGoodBrands, CNY Woman Magazine, The Afropolitan)
6	Mayamiko	www.mayamiko.com/	Malawi	Eastern Africa	2013	No data available	(Organic) Cotton	Wearing apparel (Womenswear)	2019 winner of the C010 Leadership Awards; Repeated media coverage (e.g. Cosmopolitan Conscious Issue, Vogue USA, Die Zeit)
7	soleRebels	www.solerebels.com/	Ethiopia	Eastern Africa	2004	3.000	Leather; (organic) cotton; koba; jute; rubber	Footwear	2016 winner of Business Women of the Year Award; Repeated media coverage (e.g. Forbes, CNN); Key Note at 2018 Swiss Economic Forum
8	Wazi Shoes	www.wazishoes.com/	Tanzania	Eastern Africa	2017	120	Leather	Footwear	Repeated media coverage (e.g. Outside Magazine, Santa Barbara Magazine)

(*continued*)

Table 6.3 Cont.

No.	Company	Corporate website	Country	Region	Year of inception	Employees	Primary textile fibres, fabrics, and materials**	Main product focus	Awards, accolades, and events illustrating local and international recognition
Traditional companies									
9	Loin Cloth & Ashes	https://loin cloth and ashes.my shopify.com	South Africa	Southern Africa	2008	No data available	Cotton; silk; synthetic fibres	Wearing apparel (Womens- and menswear)	2013 winner Emerging Designer of the Year by Africa Fashion International; Repeated media coverage (e.g. Entrepreneur Magazine, Daily Sun)
10	KIKI Clothing	https://kiki clothing.com/	Ghana	Western Africa	2002	No data available	No data available	Wearing apparel (Womenswear)	Repeated media coverage (e.g. CNN, Vogue US); part of the 2017 African Prints Fashion Now exhibition at the Fowler Museum in the US
11	Hesey Designs	www.hesey designs.com/	Nigeria	Western Africa	2012	No data available	No data available	Footwear	2013 winner of the Google Africa Connected Competition, Repeated media coverage (e.g. British Vogue, CNBC Africa)
12	Tsonga	www.tsonga.com/	South Africa	Southern Africa	1999	250	Leather; rubbers; polyurethane; microfibers; thermoplastic	Footwear	Repeated media coverage (e.g. BBC, Entrepreneur Magazine)

Note: ★ selection of data as emphasized by the author (as of April 30, 2019); this collection makes no claim to completeness. ★★ Based on selected product descriptions and product images at corporate websites.

within-case examination for and within each subgroup in the sample, thus enabling identifying similarities and differences as to the question of whether – if at all – single trends and drivers influence business model components as verbally communicated on corporate websites. The results of this approach are shown in the section on findings. Given the fact that – to the best of the author's knowledge – the focus of the present research is quite new to the African context, and previous studies on business model innovations for sustainability in the African fashion industry are largely absent, the overall methodological approach was considered appropriate.

In order to seek construct validity, the study is grounded in theoretical and conceptual constructs from the literature (e.g. BOP, business model innovations for sustainability). Internal or logical validity was ensured by defining three clear research questions as well as by using both inductive and deductive content analysis techniques. Moreover, data analysis for each company was carried out within the same time periods, thereby limiting potential biases in the coding of relevant meaning units. The approach of cross- and within-case analysis as well as including a subgroup of negative cases (traditional companies in the African fashion industry) further supported internal validity. Furthermore, presenting the research context of the African fashion industry as well as the selection criteria and characteristics of case companies (Tables 6.2 and 6.3) provided for external validity. Reliability was established by uncovering the methodological design, the data analysed (e.g. quotes of corporate websites), and the comprehensive coding material during the review and publication process.

Findings

This section comparatively highlights the results from the empirical analyses, thereby identifying similarities and differences across all three subgroups of the sample. The first part presents influencing factors on business model components that particularly drive sustainability efforts in the fashion industry as outlined in research by Todeschini et al. (2017). The second part of this section briefly highlights the generic characteristics of business model components as depicted in this study.

(1) Impacts on components of business model innovation for sustainability in the fashion industry.

With regard to the second research question, the results show that all components of business model innovation for sustainability can be aligned for the two subsamples of social enterprises and sustainability-oriented companies with trends and drivers shaping corporate strategies in the fashion industry. This can be seen in Table 6.4. In contrast to this, in the third subgroup of traditional companies, several business model components cannot be aligned. These

Table 6.4 Overview of business model components affected by drivers in the global fashion industry

Business model component*	Drivers for business model innovation in the fashion industry**														
	Recycling	Vegan	Upcycling	Sweatshop free	Fair trade	Locally sourced	Fashion library	Second hand	Collaboration	Sustainable raw materials	Zero waste	Wearables	Capsule wardrobe	Low-sumerism	Slow fashion
Target customer	1			2 2	4 2	2 1 1			2		1				4 2
Economic value proposition	2 3		1 2	1 2	1 2	2 2 4			2 1	2	2 2			1 / 2 3 / 3	3 4 / 4 4 / 4 3
Environmental value proposition	2 4		1 2		1	2			2 / 3 4	2 / 3 4				1	2
Social value proposition				1 3 1	1 3 / 3 4	1 1 3 / 4 1 1			3 / 4 / 3 3	2 / 2 / 1					3 4 / 4 4 / 4 1
Organizational value proposition	1			1 2	1 4 3	2 3 1			3 2	1 2	1			1	2 2 / 2 2
Value constellation			1		2 1	1 3 3			3	1 2					
Economic profit equation	2 2		2	2 2	3 1	3 2			3 2		2 2				2 2 / 2 2
Environmental profit equation					1				1	1	2 3 1			2	1 2
Social profit equation				4 4	4 4 / 4 2	4 2 4 / 3 2			4 / 3 1	1					4 4 / 4
Organizational profit equation				1 2	3 2	2			3 2	1					4 1

Note: * as illustrated in Figure 6.2 in this study. ** Numbers in italics indicate the frequency of occurrence among the companies; however, unless all companies are involved, it does not set up any correlation as regards to which company is affected. Light grey = Social enterprises; Middle grey = Sustainability-oriented companies; Dark grey = Traditional companies.

Source: drivers adopted from Todeschini et al. (2017)

include "environmental value proposition", "economic profit equation", and "organizational profit equation". Findings also reveal that the alignment for each company in the sample differs to a certain extent.

Within each subgroup of the sample, not all trends and drivers are included. For example the driver "vegan" does not play any role for the companies investigated; thus, it also does not affect any component for business model innovation. Similar results can be derived for the drivers "fashion library", "second hand", "wearables", and "capsule wardrobe". With particular regard to the subgroup of traditional companies, the following drivers further do not affect any business model component: "recycling", "upcycling", and "sustainable raw materials". As a result, in the subsample of traditional companies, less than half of the 15 drivers for business model innovation in the fashion industry are of any relevance.

Next, several drivers are only important for selected companies. As an example, the driver "upcycling" only has an impact on business model components in two of the four social enterprises. Similarly, the drivers "sustainable raw materials" and "zero waste" are only found to affect the business model components in three of the four social enterprises. Furthermore, findings show that no driver has an impact on all four companies within the subsample of traditional companies and their business model components. Conversely, if a driver influences the business model component of a traditional company, the same business model components of the companies in the two remaining subgroups are affected as well.

The two subgroups of social enterprises and sustainability-oriented companies are characterized by a great number of single drivers that affect various business model components. This finding includes the drivers "fair trade" and "slow fashion". Interestingly, the latter driver influences all ten business model components of one sustainability-oriented company in the sample, Xoomba. As opposed to this, the maximum amount of affected business model components in the subgroup of traditional companies equals five. This finding pertains to the driver "fair trade". In general, the overview, as shown in Table 6.4, clearly represents that drivers of business model innovation in the fashion industry are less likely to affect the subgroup of traditional companies.

Obviously, several drivers affect components of business model innovations for sustainability in relation to exclusively single sustainability dimensions. In the subsample social enterprises, this can be seen especially concerning the drivers "upcycling" and "zero waste": both the business model components value proposition as well as profit equation are only addressed from the perspective of environmental sustainability. At the same time, several drivers – if any – affect only marginally certain business model components of all companies analysed. For instance, the driver "slow fashion" affects business model components referring to environmental sustainability solely in one (of the four) social enterprises. This result again embraces the business model components environmental value proposition and environmental profit equation. Furthermore, the driver "sweatshop free" does not refer to the two business model components relating to environmental sustainability in any of the four social enterprises explored. This finding also applies to the two remaining subgroups.

Concerning the trends for business model innovations in the fashion industry, all drivers differently shape the three subgroups. As regards the subgroups of social enterprises and sustainability-oriented companies, for one out of five trends, namely "corporate social responsibility", all three drivers ("sweatshop free", "fair trade", and "locally sourced") are influencing all four companies in at least one out of ten business model components. In contrast, regarding the remaining subsample of traditional companies, in the same trend, "corporate social responsibility", the number of companies affected is always less than four.

With particular regard to the third research question and the social dimension of sustainability, the three sample subgroups show that, both the same five drivers ("sweatshop free"; "fair trade"; "locally sourced"; "collaboration"; and "slow fashion") and the same three trends ("corporate social responsibility", "sharing economy", and "consumer awareness") are affecting the two business model components, "social value proposition" and "social profit equation". However, again, this occurs to a different extent in all companies examined. With particular regard to the business model component "social profit equation", all four companies in the subgroup of social enterprises are affected by five different drivers ("sweatshop free"; "fair trade"; "locally sourced"; "collaboration"; and "slow fashion"). Whereas in the subgroup of sustainability-oriented companies, two of these drivers ("locally sourced" and "collaboration") are not at all affecting this particular business model component in one company, Xoomba. In sum, they also have less of an impact on the business model component "social profit equation" in the subsample of traditional companies. Moreover, concerning the latter, the driver "sweatshop free" does not at all affect the business model component "social profit equation" in traditional companies.

Furthermore, the business model component "target customer" is addressed among all companies in the subgroup social enterprises in regards to the two drivers, "fair trade" and "slow fashion". In line with this, the business model component "target customer" is also addressed to a greater extent among all companies in the subsample of social enterprises compared to the two remaining subgroups. Surprisingly or not, the component "environmental value proposition" is not addressed by all four companies in the subsample of social enterprises in any of the 15 drivers. In general, the different drivers also affect this particular business model component less than the subsample of sustainability-oriented companies. With regard to the reference group of traditional companies, the business model component "environmental value proposition" does not play any role at all. That is to say, none of the 15 drivers affects this particular component among the companies investigated.

(2) Characteristics of components of business model innovation for sustainability.

Based on the application of the conceptual framework (see Figure 6.2) and the general alignment of single corporate statements to business model components, Table 6.5 provides a comprehensive and detailed illustration of

Table 6.5 Synthesis of aspects relating to components of business model innovation for sustainability addressed by case companies in Africa's fashion industry

Business model component*	Social enterprises	Sustainability-oriented companies	Traditional companies
Sustainable customer appeal — Target customer	✓ Informing and guiding towards company products and their quality ✓ Fostering responsible consumption ✓ Supporting sustainable communities and projects, thereby developing emotional attachment and involvement ✓ Promoting positive feelings, mindfulness, and uniqueness ✓ Raising consumer knowledge on sustainability and textiles as well as contextual features in Africa	✓ Informing and guiding towards company products, their quality, and sustainable materials ✓ Fostering responsible consumption and changes in consumer habits ✓ Supporting sustainable development ✓ Promoting positive feelings, mindfulness, and uniqueness ✓ Raising consumer knowledge on (un)sustainability and textiles as well as contextual features in Africa	✓ Informing about company products and presenting their features ✓ Promoting positive feelings, attractiveness, and luxury ✓ Desire to satisfy customer needs
Sustainable value proposition — Economic value proposition	✓ Offering durable, high-quality products ✓ Offering a limited number of items and collections ✓ Focusing on local (African) content and design, materials, and community-based production	✓ Offering eco-friendly products and materials reinforcing uniqueness ✓ Providing high quality, cross-seasonal products of limited number and produced at request ✓ Pointing to local (African) content and materials	✓ Providing high quality, seasonal as well as cross-seasonal products ✓ Using conventional and synthetic fibres and materials ✓ Offering customization services ✓ Pointing to local (African) content
Sustainable value proposition — Environmental value proposition	✓ Using up- and recycled materials ✓ Using natural fibres and sustainable materials ✓ Commitment to reducing waste during production	✓ Using up- and recycled materials ✓ Using natural plant-based traditional textile production techniques ✓ Using natural fibres and sustainable materials, thereby acknowledging their value ✓ Environmental protection based on local sourcing and using renewable energy ✓ Fostering sustainable production facilities	✓ Pointing to natural properties of fibres and materials

(continued)

Table 6.5 Cont.

Business model component*	Social enterprises	Sustainability-oriented companies	Traditional companies
Social value proposition	✓ Offering handmade products, acknowledging the value of (artisanal) work and the people involved ✓ Acknowledging, engaging, and training skilled people ✓ Fostering empowerment of women, youth, and local communities ✓ Promoting ethical employment opportunities ✓ Supporting artisan training and craftsmanship ✓ Keeping traditions alive	✓ Offering handmade products, pointing at the value of the people involved ✓ Fostering empowerment of women, marginalized, and local communities ✓ Promoting ethical and healthy working conditions and sustainable employment opportunities ✓ Keeping cultural identity, traditions, and heritages alive	✓ Promoting Africa's cultural identity, traditions, and heritages in product designs (e.g. prints), thereby pointing to the value of handmade and artisanal crafts ✓ Pointing to societal empowerment
Organizational value proposition	✓ Grounded in a sustainable and ethical business philosophy ✓ Pursuing a purposeful mission ✓ Committing to societal transition and changes ✓ Promoting a sustainable fashion industry in Africa ✓ Providing a sustainable, inclusive work environment and organizational structure	✓ Grounded in a sustainable and ethical business philosophy and values ✓ Fostering and abiding by fair trade principles and legal compliance ✓ Committing to societal transition and changes ✓ Promoting a sustainable fashion industry, thereby focusing on Africa ✓ Pointing to long-term orientation ✓ Striving for ethical market growth ✓ Fostering ethical work environment	✓ Pointing to ethical and sustainable work environment ✓ Embedding African culture into creation of new and contemporary designs ✓ Striving for global business operations
Sustainable value constellation — **Value constellation**	✓ Offering close customer relationships ✓ Facilitating a sustainable fashion value chain ✓ Promoting close collaborations and partnerships with other stakeholders, thereby also including international partners	✓ Facilitating sustainable and steadily fashion production processes ✓ Promoting close collaborations and partnerships with other stakeholders ✓ Based on local sourcing and eco-friendly materials	✓ Promoting collaboration and partnerships with other stakeholders ✓ Promoting customer relationships ✓ Engaging local suppliers

Sustainable profit equation			
Economic profit equation	✓ Delivering quality and innovative products ✓ Using revenues and financial profits for investing in projects, workforce and external funding ✓ Supporting local economies' development in Africa ✓ Ensuring sustainable payments of workers	✓ Using revenues for re-investing in the company or community ✓ Transactions based on sustainability considerations ✓ Supporting local economies' development in Africa ✓ Ensuring cost reductions as well as adjusting to economic rationales ✓ Promotion of ethical buying decisions while adding value to products	✓ Producing fashionable items and varieties of collections
Environmental profit equation	✓ Producing environmentally friendly products ✓ Protecting the environment	✓ Avoidance of over-production ✓ Minimizing waste by fostering on-demand production processes ✓ Protecting the environment	–
Social profit equation	✓ Supporting young people, unemployed and disadvantaged ✓ Providing job opportunities, thereby reducing local unemployment rates ✓ Affecting livelihoods in a positive and sustainable manner ✓ Promoting sustainable working conditions and ethical payment practices ✓ Fostering skills development of workers ✓ Supporting workers' extended families and friends ✓ Investing into community development	✓ Supporting young people, unemployed and disadvantaged ✓ Promoting sustainable working conditions and ethical payment practices ✓ Pointing to skills development of workers ✓ Investing into community development, including social-oriented partnerships ✓ Striving for meeting local challenges in the particular country	✓ Securing job opportunities ✓ Commitment to contemporary African fashions, stylistic preferences and trends ✓ Pointing to an engagement in community development ✓ Pointing to eduction and vocational initiatives

(continued)

Table 6.5 Cont.

Business model component*	Social enterprises	Sustainability-oriented companies	Traditional companies
Organizational profit equation	✓ Epitomizing a company with a social mission ✓ Assuming social responsibility ✓ Fostering an organizational culture of mutually acknowledging team spirit, close relationships, individual skills and empowerment	✓ Adherence to sustainable and ethical production standards and working environments ✓ Being change agents and trendsetters in the transition processes towards a sustainable textile industry	✓ Raising brand awareness ✓ Ensuing options for market growth

Note: * Shaded markings refer to the conceptual framework of business model innovation for sustainability as illustrated in Figure 6.2 in this study.

Source: author's own.

how the components are characterized in each of the three subgroups of the sample. Though lacking a direct linkage to the trends and drivers in the textile industry as outlined in the research by Todeschini et al. (2017), this aggregation of mapping results presents interesting insights relating to business model innovation for sustainability. In this context, it becomes evident that in the subsample of traditional companies, business model components related to social and environmental dimensions of sustainability are considered less – if at all. Furthermore the remaining business model components are addressed less on the respective corporate websites. With particular regard to the group of social enterprises, the findings reveal that the two business model components "social value proposition" and "social profit equation" are comprehensively illustrated. Next, aspects aligned to the business model component "social value proposition" are directly linked with the business model component "social profit equation". Thus, there seems to be a real implementation of social offerings and social value creation among the social enterprises examined. This relationship can be retraced for the following examples: "supporting communities" shifts to "investing into community development"; "providing job opportunities" leads to "reducing local unemployment"; and "value of work and craftsmanship" stipulates "sustainable working conditions and ethical payment practices".

In contrast to the subgroup of traditional companies, results reveal a different design of the business model component "target customer". Similar to the group of sustainability-oriented companies, social enterprises attempt to enhance the knowledge and consciousness of their customers in regards to contextual features of the African continent as well as local conditions and environments. However, in contrast to sustainability-oriented companies, social enterprises appear to focus on a stronger emotional attachment to and involvement in their customer relationships. This can also be seen in the fact that they assume social responsibility not only for their workers' families and livelihoods (e.g. support for tailors' children and extended families), but also for their customers. For example the social enterprise YEVU illustrates the harsh living conditions of women in Ghana quite comprehensively on its corporate website:

> *Women are the backbone of a community, an economy, a country. They are entrepreneurs, mothers, sisters, teachers and community leaders. In Ghana, it's women that dominate the informal sector, owning and operating the vast majority of little business that scatter the roads, markets and remote communities. . . . Yet, working in this informal sector is a vulnerable place to be – it's characterised by underemployment, unsafe working conditions, precarious work relationships, low wages and no safety net. . . . In a nutshell, when it comes to jobs, income, opportunity and choice, women in Ghana are left behind. Which is kind of ironic, considering that women are the ones most likely to spend whatever income they do make on the health and education of their families and immediate communities.*
>
> Yevu Clothing (2019)

Discussion

Wrapping up the findings of this research, it becomes clear that the salient characteristics of the business model component "social profit equation" in social enterprises can enable and develop solutions for overcoming particularly social challenges and obstacles in the African context, as shown in Table 6.1. Recalling the third research question, the results suggest that social enterprises provide enormous potential and opportunities for acting locally, including among vulnerable and marginalized groups, involving communities as well as integrating educational and cultural rationales into their business models. Consequently, they promote social and inclusive approaches towards sustainable development on the African continent. The analysis has also revealed that social enterprises are eligible to leverage Africa's context-specific opportunities. In doing so, these alternative business models particularly acknowledge handmade products and promote traditions and craftsmanship as well as artisanal skills, amongst others. This, in turn, mirrors the potential of sub-Saharan Africa's fashion sector as officially proclaimed, whereby the cultural variety and uniqueness across the continent is considered a distinctive selling point and a source for promising exploitation of opportunities (African Development Bank Group, 2016). From a general perspective, this could also likely contribute to a different (self-)perception of the continent less simplistically characterized and disparaged as risk- and crisis-ridden, but appreciating and respecting its specificities as a valuable and valued resource for doing business (Adams, Nayak, & Koukpaki, 2018; Mezzana, 2005) and for indigenous knowledge creation (Jackson, 2013). Accordingly, highlighting the appreciation of workers and their skills – rather than the widespread and repeatedly summoned view of low-skilled labour across the continent in the economics and management literature (e.g. Traub-Merz, 2006; Vlok, 2006) – could not only emphasize other narratives concerning roles, objectives, salient features, and capabilities of social enterprises in Africa, but also support a change in mindsets, beliefs, and stereotypes of the continent, in general insisted by the relevance of local-driven development (Asante, 2013; Jamme, 2010; Poncian, 2015; Scott, 2009). Overall, this can be illustrated by the following quote from KoliKoWear:

> *We engage skilled young people who have talent but do not have the opportunity to start their own business.*
>
> KoliKoWear (2019)

Furthermore, given the significance of the youth in Africa as well as local BOP markets and informal sectors, the findings in the present study stress that social enterprises are crucial to foster the empowerment of young people and women, thereby contributing to reducing inequality, to improving livelihoods, and to promoting human development towards multi-dimensional well-being (DeJaeghere & Baxter, 2014). Africa's range of socio-cultural diversity enables them to uncover these more or less hidden, yet immensely important, entrepreneurial as well as social opportunities.

The findings display that aspects involving community dedication are more comprehensively addressed by social enterprises compared to the two other subgroups in the sample. They play a particularly important role in the business model component "social profit equation", thereby corroborating existing views in the literature concerned with the importance of communities and their relational as well as cultural systems in Africa (Cieslik, 2016; Juma, James, & Kwesiga, 2017). Even more important, results in the present study indicate that addressing social needs of communities is also prominently reflected in the two business model components "economic value proposition" and "economic profit equation". This implies that social enterprises in Africa's fashion industry obviously pursue social and commercial objectives in parallel (Agarwal et al., 2018; Goyal et al., 2015).

Community support can be retraced by statements concerning, amongst others, reinvestments of financial revenues in social impact projects and the social enterprises' workforce training and development as well as their commitment to local, community-based production. In light of the fashion sector and the contextual specifics of Africa, local community involvement and development thus can be considered as highly important drivers for fostering business model innovations towards social sustainability as well as for enhancing a shared-value paradigm that is pivotal in addressing challenges associated with social sustainability (Matinheikki, Rajala, & Peltokorpi, 2017). The importance of the community in the African context is also illustrated by the following quotation taken from the corporate website of another social enterprise in Africa's textile sector, Five and Six:

> *The community functions as a social, artistic, and economic hub where traditions are passed down from generation to generation. By working directly with the master weavers at Waraniéné, we can help preserve this craftsmanship so it can endure, continue to evolve, and become a reliable source of income to anyone who wants to make this their livelihood.*
>
> Five and Six Textiles (2019)

As opposed to traditional companies and social enterprises, the subgroup of sustainability-oriented companies highlights especially aspects on their corporate websites that can be aligned to the business model components "environmental value proposition" and "environmental profit equation". This includes issues concerning the use of natural fibres and sustainable materials like organic cotton, thereby acknowledging their value. Next, they are promoting the reduction of waste by producing at request of the customer and refusing over-production, thus promoting environmental protection. This finding can signify different meanings. From a theoretical–conceptual view, it emphasizes a lesser importance of objectives relating to environmental sustainability in social enterprises. This becomes comprehensible when recalling the social burden across Africa. At the same time, given significant natural resources on the African continent, the result could indicate increasing aspirations among sustainability-oriented companies to open up context-specific new pathways for sustainable value creation (Grenier, 2019). Thus, the companies realise calls concerning the important role of fashion businesses in responsibly addressing environmental challenges of the industry (Thorisdottir & Johannsdottir, 2019).

Finally, the subsample of social enterprises gives evidence that the business model components "organizational value proposition" and "organizational profit equation" are reflecting basic attributes of the conceptual framework in Figure 6.2. In particular, this finding pertains to the social enterprises' efforts in offering sustainable and inclusive work conditions as well as assuming social responsibility. In this vein, the findings support existing literature claiming that ventures in BOP contexts distinctively address social sustainability (Gold et al., 2013). Even more, the results from the empirical analyses reinforce extant views that social enterprises in Africa require high levels of commitment on the part of the entrepreneur and certain internal capabilities (e.g. mindsets) as essential prerequisites to make the social enterprise a successful one (Karanda & Toledano, 2012; Rauter et al., 2017). The following quote exemplifies this by providing the vision of Kitenge's founder:

> *The people who make our clothes should be paid fairly, treated with respect and dignity and work in a safe environment. . . . It was a light-bulb moment when I realised I could set up a local supply chain to create modern, authentic African fashion – in a responsible way.*
>
> Kitenge (2019)

There are a great number of aspects causing the above-mentioned findings. First, the composition of the sample investigated may shape the findings according to the main products of the companies. For instance, at the time of data collection, none of the social enterprises used animal-based fibres or other animal products. Consequently, there is no reason to replace these raw materials, thus the driver "vegan" does not play any role. Yet, changes in the sample's composition might reveal different results.

Second, as the sample only includes companies operating in Africa, the findings regarding the marginalized or neglected impact of trends and drivers on business model components for environmental sustainability might be explained by a different viewpoint on this dimension of sustainability in Africa. This could also imply a generally smaller relevance of this particular dimension in the African context. In line with this, this finding might reveal that the adaptation or development of new and innovative fibres, environmentally friendly materials, and technologies could be of less relevance on the African continent. Conversely, the analysis illustrates that aspects concerning social sustainability are of greatest significance among all four companies in the subsample social enterprises. In fact, the business model component "social profit equation" is affected by different trends and drivers across the entire subsample. Against the background of Africa's social challenges and critical issues, including, amongst others, high rates of poverty and unemployment, this result is quite plausible. Finally, the presentation on corporate websites varies in contents and amount as well as wording. This causes differences in the mapping to business model components, thereby shaping the overall results of this empirical analysis.

Notwithstanding these results, the study has several limitations. First, the research is primarily conceptual. Despite efforts in holistically and comprehensively synthesizing and capturing the main business model components, as shown in Figure 6.2, the effective consideration of an integrated sustainability view on single components might be limited. This especially proves true for the business model component "sustainable customer appeal". In this vein, the alignment and interpretation of verbal statements on corporate websites to single components of business models inevitably is induced by a certain degree of subjectivity since a single person performed the coding (Fichter & Tiemann, 2018). Potential drawbacks of the methodological approach concerning data analysis employed in this study were reduced by enhancing internal validity and reliability.

Second, by using web pages as the primary material, the research findings and interpretation thereof are limited to the verbally presented information. Consequently, this does not allow conclusions about the companies' integrity and actual implementation of business model innovations for sustainability. The latter argument is even further strengthened when considering potential language biases and the assumed inclusion of colloquial speech and marketing intentions in corporate statements. A further limitation of the study relates to the relatively small number of cases included as well as the exclusion of corporate websites in languages other than English, thereby restricting transferability and scope of interpretation. Finally, including also supplementary material (e.g. social media accounts, blogs, and interviews) in prospective research might bring forth more comparative findings.

Conclusion

This study's purpose was to identify components of business model innovation for sustainability in social enterprises as well as their linkages to the contextual features on the African continent. As a result, the study focused particularly on local BOP markets. In light of this, the study makes a number of important theoretical contributions. The conceptual and empirical research as conducted in this study contributes to existing research on business model innovations for sustainability by characterizing and fine-tuning business model components particularly relevant to social enterprises from a holistic and integrated sustainability perspective.

Existing business model components were conceptually synthesized and expanded based on economic, ecological, social and organizational sustainability considerations. The study shows clearly that, in particular, the two business model components "social value proposition" and "social profit equation" are comprehensively addressed by social enterprises in sub-Saharan Africa's fashion industry. Thereby, social enterprises effectively realize elements of both the BOP 2.0 and the BOP 3.0 concept as discussed in previous literature (e.g. Arnold, 2017; Bendul et al., 2017; Chmielewski et al., 2018; Dembek, Sivasubramaniam, & Chmielewski, 2019).

Next to involving local people as economic actors, all four social enterprises use their economic and social profit equations to reinvest into community development (e.g. sustainable livelihoods, education and training) as well as to support community members (Sinkovics, Sinkovics, & Yamin, 2014). Thus, there is an actual implementation of social value creation processes, which adds to the current understanding of these ventures' fundamental characteristics as construed in the extant literature. The present study further contributes to existing research on the role of social entrepreneurship and social enterprises in sub-Saharan Africa by delineating their potential for sustainable development and social value creation in the continent's BOP contexts. Findings reveal that social enterprises in Africa's fashion industry play a key role in leveraging the pressing social challenges for sustainable development on the continent while creating options for social inclusion and systemic change.

The theoretical outcomes concerning components of business model innovations for sustainability are further deepened by exploring and examining fashion industry-related trends and drivers that impact them. These results add, in turn, valuable insights to existing research on the connection between business and sustainability in BOP markets since the results reveal opportunities for inclusive business and market development, especially for social enterprises in the African fashion industry.

Further studies might build on the conceptual framework as developed in this research and enhance the findings by, amongst other ideas, incorporating additional material (e.g. personal interviews with the founders of the social enterprises analysed). In line with this, the theoretical-conceptual foundations of this study could be refined. In doing so, the trends and drivers as outlined by Todeschini et al. (2017) could be advanced by integrating further aspects that are pivotal for business model innovations for sustainability in the fashion industry or by more closely adapting them to the contextual peculiarities of Africa's fashion industry. This includes issues concerning political, legal, and regulatory developments as well as formal and informal institutional frameworks. In this vein, the results of the empirical analysis in this study could be further explored when reflecting them more strongly against the background of the fashion industries and their peculiar characteristics in each of the countries involved in the sample.

Literature streams relevant for addressing the present research could also be further investigated based on this study's findings. For example while this research has focused on characteristic impacts on components for business model innovations for sustainability, future studies might examine reasons and strategic choices for changes in business model components, thereby employing longitudinal research designs as well as dynamic perspectives on business model innovations. Next, follow-up research might investigate:

- negative externalities of social enterprises across Africa's fashion industry and the role of BOP customers in purchasing the enterprises' own products;
- tensions and paradoxes in social enterprises on BOP markets concerning the simultaneously aspired balancing and implementation of social, economic, and environmental sustainability objectives;
- the role of African- and Western-centric entrepreneurial mindsets, worldviews, and individual capabilities for the design and successful implementation of business model innovations for sustainability in the fashion industry (e.g. awareness and relevance of social values); or
- the transferability of the conceptual framework developed and employed in this study on the context of other textile market segments in Africa (e.g. home textiles) as well as other BOP contexts in or outside Africa (e.g. Northern Africa and Asian countries relevant for global fashion and textiles production).

Ultimately, the study offers some important practical and managerial implications. The analysis shows that – independent from the organizational form of a venture or company – business model innovations in the fashion industry should involve a holistic, systemic, and inclusive approach towards sustainability. Moreover, splitting the business model into different components of value proposition and profit equation in line with the triple bottom line concept of sustainability and including aspects concerning the organization, value constellation, and the target customer, allows companies to specifically newly design or realign their business models. This enables them to address systemic change and transformation towards a sustainable and socially responsible fashion sector in the African context. Given the interconnectedness of the fashion sector as well as its producing facilities in mainly developing and emerging countries with large BOP markets, the holistic incorporation of components of business model innovations for sustainability by fashion companies as suggested in this research could also support addressing global sustainability challenges such as poverty.

References

Abdelkafi, N., & Täuscher, K. (2016). Business models for sustainability from a system dynamics perspective. *Organization & Environment, 29*(1), 74–96. https://doi.org/10.1177/1086026615592930

Adams, K., Nayak, B. S., & Koukpaki, S. (2018). Critical perspectives on "manufactured" risks arising from Eurocentric business practices in Africa. *Critical Perspectives on International Business, 14*(2/3), 210–229. https://doi.org/10.1108/cpoib-11-2016-0058

Adams, R. J., Smart, P., & Huff, A. S. (2017). Shades of grey: Guidelines for working with the grey literature in systematic reviews for management and organizational studies. *International Journal of Management Reviews*, *19*(4), 432–454. https://doi.org/10.1111/ijmr.12102

Agarwal, N., Chakrabarti, R., Brem, A., & Bocken, N. (2018). Market driving at Bottom of the Pyramid (BOP): An analysis of social enterprises from the healthcare sector. *Journal of Business Research*, *86*, 234–244. https://doi.org/10.1016/j.jbusres.2017.07.001

Allianz Nachhaltige Universitäten in Österreich (2014). *Handbuch zur Erstellung von Nachhaltigkeitskonzepten für Universitäten*, 1–21.

Ansari, S., Munir, K., & Gregg, T. (2012). Impact at the 'Bottom of the Pyramid': The role of social capital in capability development and community empowerment. *Journal of Management Studies*, *49*(4), 813–842. https://doi.org/10.1111/j.1467-6486.2012.01042.x

Arnold, D. G., & Valentin, A. (2013). Corporate social responsibility at the Base of the Pyramid. *Journal of Business Research*, *66*(10), 1904–1914. https://doi.org/10.1016/j.jbusres.2013.02.012

Arnold, M. G. (2017). Inklusive wertschöpfung auf BOP märkten: Interdisziplinäre implikationen für nachhaltigkeitsmanagement in frugalen innovationskontexten. *UmweltWirtschaftsForum*, *25*, 25–32. https://doi.org/10.1007/s00550-017-0442-y

Arnold, M. G. (2018). Sustainability value creation in frugal contexts to foster Sustainable Development Goals. *Business Strategy & Development*, *1*(4), 265–275. https://doi.org/10.1002/bsd2.36

Asante, M. K. (2013). The Western media and the falsification of Africa: complications of value and evaluation. *China Media Research*, *9*(2), 64–70.

Ausrød, V. L., Sinha, V., & Widding, Ø. (2017). Business model design at the Base of the Pyramid. *Journal of Cleaner Production*, *162*, 982–996. https://doi.org/10.1016/j.jclepro.2017.06.014

Baden, S., & Barber, C. (2005). *The impact of the second-hand clothing trade on developing countries*. Retrieved from https://oxfamilibrary.openrepository.com/handle/10546/112464

Baffes, J. (2009). The 'full potential' of Uganda's cotton industry. *Development Policy Review*, *27*(1), 67–85. https://doi.org/10.1111/j.1467-7679.2009.00436.x

Bendul, J. C., Rosca, E., & Pivovarova, D. (2017). Sustainable supply chain models for Base of the Pyramid. *Journal of Cleaner Production*, *162*, S107-S120. https://doi.org/10.1016/j.jclepro.2016.11.001

Bidmon, C. M., & Knab, S. F. (2018). The three roles of business models in societal transitions: New linkages between business model and transition research. *Journal of Cleaner Production*, *178*, 903–916. https://doi.org/10.1016/j.jclepro.2017.12.198

Bittencourt Marconatto, D. A., Barin-Cruz, L., Pozzebon, M., & Poitras, J. E. (2016). Developing sustainable business models within BOP contexts: Mobilizing native capability to cope with government programs. *Journal of Cleaner Production*, *129*, 735–748. https://doi.org/10.1016/j.jclepro.2016.03.038

Bocken, N., Boons, F., & Baldassarre, B. (2019). Sustainable business model experimentation by understanding ecologies of business models. *Journal of Cleaner Production*, *208*, 1498–1512. https://doi.org/10.1016/j.jclepro.2018.10.159

Bocken, N., Miller, K., Weissbrod, I., Holgado, M., & Evans, S. (2017). Business model experimentation for circularity: driving sustainability in a large international clothing retailer. *Economics and Policy of Energy and the Environment (EPEE)*, *1*, 85–122. https://doi.org/10.3280/EFE2017-001006

Bocken, N., Short, S. W., Rana, P. & Evans, S. (2014). A literature and practice review to develop sustainable business model archetypes. *Journal of Cleaner Production*, *65*, 42–56. https://doi.org/10.1016/j.jclepro.2013.11.039

Brooks, A., & Simon, D. (2012). Unravelling the relationships between used-clothing imports and the decline of African clothing industries. *Development and Change*, *43*(6), 1265–1290. https://doi.org/10.1111/j.1467-7660.2012.01797.x

Bryman, A. (2015). *Social research methods* (5th ed.). Oxford: Oxford University Press.

Calvo, S., & Morales, A. (2016). Sink or swim: social enterprise as a panacea for non-profit organisations? *Journal of International Development*, *28*(7), 1170–1188. https://doi.org/10.1002/jid.3138

Cartier, M. (2017). The drive for ethical fashion boosts employment, raises standards. *International Trade Forum*, *3*, 8–9.

Cherrier, H., Goswami, P., & Ray, S. (2018). Social entrepreneurship: Creating value in the context of institutional complexity. *Journal of Business Research*, *86*, 245–258. https://doi.org/10.1016/j.jbusres.2017.10.056

Chikweche, T., & Fletcher, R. (2013). Customer relationship management at the Base of the Pyramid: Myth or reality? *Journal of Consumer Marketing*, *30*(3), 295–309. https://doi.org/10.1108/07363761311328964

Chmielewski, D. A., Dembek, K., & Beckett, J. R. (2018). 'Business unusual': Building BOP 3.0. *Journal of Business Ethics*, 1–19. https://doi.org/10.1007/s10551-018-3938-7

Cieslik, K. (2016). Moral economy meets social enterprise community-based green energy project in rural Burundi. *World Development*, *83*, 12–26. https://doi.org/10.1016/j.worlddev.2016.03.009

Corbett, J., Webster, J., & Jenkin, T. A. (2018). Unmasking corporate sustainability at the project level: Exploring the influence of institutional logics and individual agency. *Journal of Business Ethics*, *147*(2), 261–286. https://doi.org/10.1007/s10551-015-2945-1

Damoah, O. B. O. (2018). A critical incident analysis of the export behaviour of SMEs: Evidence from an emerging market. *Critical Perspectives on International Business*, *14*(2/3), 309–334. https://doi.org/10.1108/cpoib-11-2016-0061

Davies, I. A., & Torrents, A. (2017). Overcoming institutional voids in subsistence marketplaces: A Zimbabwean entrepreneurial case. *Journal of Macromarketing*, *37*(3), 255–267. https://doi.org/10.1177/0276146717698020

DeJaeghere, J., & Baxter, A. (2014). Entrepreneurship education for youth in sub-Saharan Africa: A capabilities approach as an alternative framework to neoliberalism's individualizing risks. *Progress in Development Studies*, *14*(1), 61–76. https://doi.org/10.1177/1464993413504353

Dembek, K., Sivasubramaniam, N., & Chmielewski, D. A. (2019). A systematic review of the Bottom/Base of the Pyramid literature: Cumulative evidence and future directions. *Journal of Business Ethics*, 1–18, https://doi.org/10.1007/s10551-019-04105-y

Dentchev, N., Rauter, R., Jóhannsdóttir, L., Snihur, Y., Rosano, M., & Baumgartner, R., ... Jonker, J. (2018). Embracing the variety of sustainable business models: a prolific field of research and a future research agenda. *Journal of Cleaner Production, 194*, 695–703. https://doi.org/10.1016/j.jclepro.2018.05.156

Dhahri, S., & Omri, A. (2018). Entrepreneurship contribution to the three pillars of sustainable development: what does the evidence really say? *World Development, 106*, 64–77. https://doi.org/10.1016/j.worlddev.2018.01.008

Douglas, K. (2016). *Fashionomics 101: An African industry that could be worth $15bn by 2021.* Retrieved from www.howwemadeitinafrica.com/fashionomics-101-african-industry-worth-15bn-2021/57043

Economic Commission for Africa (2015). *Is Africa moving towards a more inclusive development path?* Retrieved from www.uneca.org/publications/africa-moving-towards-more-inclusive-development-path

Eisenhardt, K. M. (1989). Building theories from case study research. *Academy of Management Review, 14*(4), 532–550. https://doi.org/10.5465/amr.1989.4308385

Essel, O. Q. (2017). Deconstructing the concept of 'African print' in the Ghanaian experience. *Journal of Pan African Studies, 11*(1), 37–52.

Fichter, K., & Tiemann, I. (2018). Factors influencing university support for sustainable entrepreneurship: Insights from explorative case studies. *Journal of Cleaner Production, 175*, 512–524. https://doi.org/10.1016/j.jclepro.2017.12.031

Five and Six Textiles. (2019). The Collective. Retrieved from www.fiveandsixtextiles.com/the-collective-1/

Frazer, G. (2008). Used-clothing donations and apparel production in Africa. *Economic Journal, 118*, 1764–1784. https://doi.org/10.1111/j.1468-0297.2008.02190.x

Gebauer, H., Haldimann, M., & Saul, C. J. (2017a). Business model innovations for overcoming barriers in the Base-of-the-Pyramid market. *Industry and Innovation, 24*(5), 543–568. https://doi.org/10.1080/13662716.2017.1310033

Gebauer, H., Saul, C. J., & Haldimann, M. (2017b). Business model innovation in base of the pyramid markets. *Journal of Business Strategy, 38*(4), 38–46. https://doi.org/10.1108/JBS-05-2016-0051

Geissdoerfer, M., Vladimirova, D., & Evans, S. (2018). Sustainable business model innovation: a review. *Journal of Cleaner Production, 198*, 401–416. https://doi.org/10.1016/j.jclepro.2018.06.240

George, G., Corbishley, C., Khayesi, J. N. O., Haas, M. R., & Tihanyi, L. (2016). Bringing Africa in: Promising directions for management research. *Academy of Management Journal, 59*(2), 377–393. https://doi.org/10.5465/amj.2016.4002

Gold, S., Hahn, R., & Seuring, S. (2013). Sustainable supply chain management in "Base of the Pyramid" food projects – a path to triple bottom line approaches for multinationals? *International Business Review, 22*(5), 784–799. https://doi.org/10.1016/j.ibusrev.2012.12.006

Goyal, S., Sergi, B. S., & Jaiswal, M. (2015). How to design and implement social business models for Base-of-the-Pyramid (BOP) markets? *European Journal of Development Research, 27*(5), 850–867. https://doi.org/10.1057/ejdr.2014.71

Grenier, E. (2019). Innovative designers challenge African fashion stereotypes. *Deutsche Welle.* Retrieved from www.dw.com/en/innovative-designers-challenge-african-fashion-stereotypes/a-50142773

Hahn, R., & Gold, S. (2014). Resources and governance in "Base of the Pyramid"-partnerships: Assessing collaborations between businesses and non-business actors. *Journal of Business Research, 67*(7), 1321–1333. https://doi.org/10.1016/j.jbusres.2013.09.002

Hill, R. P. (2016). Poverty as we never knew it: *THE* source of vulnerability for most of humankind. *Journal of Marketing Management, 32*(3–4), 365–370. https://doi.org/10.1080/0267257X.2015.1117519

Hlady-Rispal, M., & Servantie, V. (2016). Deconstructing the way in which value is created in the context of social entrepreneurship. *International Journal of Management Reviews, 20*(1), 62–80. https://doi.org/10.1111/ijmr.12113

Hodgson, A. (2017). *Africa's three largest BOP markets.* Retrieved from https://blog.euromonitor.com/three-largest-BOP-markets-africa/

Howell, R., van Beers, C., & Doorn, N. (2018). Value capture and value creation: The role of information technology in business models for frugal innovations in Africa. *Technological Forecasting & Social Change, 131*, 227–239. https://doi.org/10.1016/j.techfore.2017.09.030

Jackson, T. (2013). Reconstructing the indigenous in African management research. *Management International Review, 53*(1), 13–38. https://doi.org/10.1007/s11575-012-0161-0

Jamme, M. (2010). Negative perceptions slow Africa's development. *The Guardian,* Retrieved from www.theguardian.com/global-development/poverty-matters/2010/dec/10/africa-postcolonial-perceptions

Jose, P. D. (2008). Rethinking the BOP: New models for the new millennium – academic perspective. *IIMB Management Review, 20*(2), 198–202.

Juma, N. A., James, C. D., & Kwesiga, E. (2017). Sustainable entrepreneurship in sub-Saharan Africa: The collaborative multi-system model. *Journal of Small Business & Entrepreneurship, 29*(3), 211–235. https://doi.org/10.1080/08276331.2017.1293949

Kao, M. (2016). Lesotho's participation in apparel value chains: An opportunity for sustainable development? *Bridges Africa, 5*(9). Retrieved from www.ictsd.org/bridges-news/bridges-africa/news/lesotho%E2%80%99s-participation-in-apparel-value-chains-an-opportunity-for

Karanda, C. & Toledano, N. (2012). Social entrepreneurship in South Africa: A different narrative for a different context. *Social Enterprise Journal, 8*(3), 201–215. https://doi.org/10.1108/17508611211280755

Kirchgeorg, M., & Winn, M. I. (2006). Sustainability marketing for the poorest of the poor. *Business Strategy and the Environment, 15*(3), 171–184. https://doi.org/10.1002/bse.523

Kistruck, G. M., Webb, J. W., Sutter, C. J., & Bailey, A. V. (2015). The double-edged sword of legitimacy in Base-of-the-Pyramid markets. *Journal of Business Venturing, 30*(3), 436–451. https://doi.org/10.1016/j.jbusvent.2014.06.004

Kitenge. (2019). *Our story.* Retrieved from https://kitengestore.com/our-story/

Koistinen, K., Laukkanen, M., Mikkilä, M., Huiskonen, J., & Linnanen, L. (2018). Sustainable system value creation: Development of preliminary frameworks for a business model change within a systemic transition process. In L. Moratis, F. Melissen, & S. O. Idowu (Eds.), *Sustainable business models: Principles, promise, and practice* (pp. 105–127). Cham, Switzerland: Springer.

KoliKoWear. (2019). About Us. Retrieved from www.kolikowear.com/our%2520story. html

Kolk, A., & Rivera-Santos, M. (2018). The state of research on Africa in business and management: insights from a systematic review of key international journals. *Business & Society, 57*(3), 415–436. https://doi.org/10.1177/0007650316629129

Kühn, A. L., Stiglbauer, M., & Fifka, M. S. (2018). Contents and determinants of corporate social responsibility website reporting in sub-Saharan Africa: A seven-country study. *Business & Society, 57*(3), 437–480. https://doi.org/10.1177/0007650315614234

Langevang, T. (2016). *Fashioning the future: entrepreneuring in Africa's emerging fashion industry.* CBDS Working Paper Series, No. 25, 1–39.

Lawan, S. (2015). *An African take on the Sustainable Development Goals.* Retrieved from www.brookings.edu/blog/africa-in-focus/2015/10/13/an-african-take-on-the-sustainable-development-goals/

L'Huillier, B. M. (2016). Has globalization failed to alleviate poverty in sub-Saharan Africa? *Poverty & Public Policy, 8*(4), 368–386. https://doi.org/10.1002/pop4.158

Li, Y., Zhao, X., Shi, D., & Li, X. (2014). Governance of sustainable supply chains in the fast fashion industry. *European Management Journal, 32*(5), 823–836. https://doi.org/10.1016/j.emj.2014.03.001

Littlewood, D., & Holt, D. (2017). Social enterprise resilience in sub-Saharan Africa. *Business Strategy and Development, 1*, 53–63. https://doi.org/10.1002/bsd2.11

Littlewood, D., & Holt, D. (2018). Social entrepreneurship in South Africa: Exploring the influence of environment. *Business & Society, 57*(3), 525–561. https://doi.org/10.1177/0007650315613293

Lock, I., & Seele, P. (2015). Quantitative content analysis as a method for business ethics research. *Business Ethics: A European Review, 24*(1), 24–40. https://doi.org/10.1111/beer.12095

London, T., Anupindi, R., & Sheth, S. (2010). Creating mutual value: Lessons learned from ventures serving base of the pyramid producers. *Journal of Business Research, 63*(6), 582–594. https://doi.org/10.1016/j.jbusres.2009.04.025

Lüdeke-Freund, F., Gold, S., & Bocken, N. M. P. (2018). A review and typology of circular economy business model patterns. *Journal of Industrial Ecology, 23*, 36–61. https://doi.org/10.1111/jiec.12763

Luke, B., & Chu, V. (2013). Social enterprise versus social entrepreneurship: An examination of the 'why' and 'how' in pursuing change. *International Small Business Journal, 31*(7), 764–784. https://doi.org/10.1177/0266242612462598

Maji, I. K. (2019). Impact of clean energy and inclusive development on CO_2 emissions in sub-Saharan Africa. *Journal of Cleaner Production, 240*, 118–186. https://doi.org/10.1016/j.jclepro.2019.118186

Matinheikki, J., Rajala, R., & Peltokorpi, A. (2017). From the profit of one toward benefitting many – crafting a vision of shared value creation. *Journal of Cleaner Production, 162*, S83–S93. https://doi.org/10.1016/j.jclepro.2016.09.081

Matos, S., & Silvestre, B. S. (2013). Managing stakeholder relations when developing sustainable business models: the case of the Brazilian energy sector. *Journal of Cleaner Production, 45*, 61–73. https://doi.org/10.1016/j.jclepro.2012.04.023

Mayring, P. (2015). *Qualitative inhaltsanalyse. Grundlagen und techniken* (12th ed.). Weinheim, Germany: Beltz.

Mezzana, D. (2005). Represenations: A cancerous image. *African Societies.* Retrieved from https://cyber.harvard.edu/digitaldemocracy/mezzana.htm

Michelini, L., & Fiorentino, D. (2012). New business models for creating shared value. *Social Responsibility Journal, 8*(4), 561–577. https://doi.org/10.1108/17471111211272129

Mirvis, P., & Googins, B. (2018). Catalyzing social entrepreneurship in Africa: Roles for Western universities, NGOs and corporations. *Africa Journal of Management, 4*(1), 57–83. https://doi.org/10.1080/23322373.2018.1428020

Morgan, E. (2015). 'Plan A': Analysing business model innovation for sustainable consumption in mass-market clothes retailing. *Journal of Corporate Citizenship, 57*, 73–98. https://doi.org/10.9774/GLEAF.4700.2015.ma.00007

Morioka, S. N., & Carvalho, M. M. (2016). Measuring sustainability in practice: Exploring the inclusion of sustainability into corporate performance systems in Brazilian case studies. *Journal of Cleaner Production, 136*, 123–133. https://doi.org/10.1016/j.jclepro.2016.01.103

Morris, M., Schindehutte, M., & Allen, J. (2005). The entrepreneur's business model: Toward a unified perspective. *Journal of Business Research, 58*(6), 726–735. https://doi.org/10.1016/j.jbusres.2003.11.001

Morris, M., Staritz, C., & Plank, L. (2014). *Regionalism, end markets and ownership matter: Shifting dynamics in the apparel export industry in Sub Saharan Africa* (Working Paper No. 46). Austrian Foundation for Development Research (ÖFSE), Vienna.

Nørup, N., Pihl, K., Damgaard, A., & Scheutz, C. (2019). Replacement rates for second-hand clothing and household textiles – A survey study from Malawi, Mozambique and Angola. *Journal of Cleaner Production, 235*, 1026–1036. https://doi.org/10.1016/j.jclepro.2019.06.177

Nußholz, J. L. K. (2017). Circular business models: Defining a concept and framing an emerging research field. *Sustainability, 9*, 1810. https://doi.org/10.3390/su9101810

Onsongo, E. (2017). Institutional entrepreneurship and social innovation at the base of the pyramid: The case of M-Pesa in Kenya. *Industry and Innovation, 26*(4), 369–390. https://doi.org/10.1080/13662716.2017.1409104

Panum, K., Hansen, M. W., & Davy, E. (2018). The illusive nature of social enterprise at the base of the pyramid: Case studies of six Kenyan social enterprises. *Journal of Entrepreneurship in Emerging Economies, 10*(2), 249–276. https://doi.org/10.1108/JEEE-11-2016-0051

Patel, N. (2018). *Figure of the week: Understanding poverty in Africa.* Retrieved from www.brookings.edu/blog/africa-in-focus/2018/11/21/figure-of-the-week-understanding-poverty-in-africa

Poncian, J. (2015). The persistence of western negative perceptions about Africa: factoring in the role of Africans. *Journal of African Studies and Development, 7*(3), 72–80. https://doi.org/10.5897/JASD2014.0317

Qafa, M. F. (2017). Can degrowth rescue sub-Saharan Africa? *International Journal of Technology Management & Sustainable Development, 16*(2), 191–200. https://doi.org/10.1386/tmsd.16.2.191_1

Rahdari, A., Sepasi, S., & Moradi, M. (2016). Achieving sustainability through Schumpeterian social entrepreneurship: The role of social enterprises. *Journal of Cleaner Production, 137*, 347–360. https://doi.org/10.1016/j.jclepro.2016.06.159

Rauter, R., Jonker, J., & Baumgartner, R. J. (2017). Going one's own way: Drivers in developing business models for sustainability. *Journal of Cleaner Production, 140*, 144–154. https://doi.org/10.1016/j.jclepro.2015.04.104

Richardson, J. (2008). The business model: An integrative framework for strategy execution. *Strategic change, 17*(5–6), 133–144. https://doi.org/10.1002/jsc.821

Ritala, P., Huotari, P., Bocken, N., Albareda, L., & Puumalainen, K. (2018). Sustainable business model adoption among S&P 500 firms: A longitudinal content analysis study. *Journal of Cleaner Production, 170*, 216–226. https://doi.org/10.1016/j.jclepro.2017.09.159

Rivera-Santos, M., Holt, D., Littlewood, D., & Kolk, A. (2015). Social entrepreneurship in sub-Saharan Africa. *Academy of Management Perspectives, 29*(1), 72–91. https://doi.org/10.5465/amp.2013.0128

Rosca, E., Arnold, M., & Bendul, J. (2017). Business models for sustainable innovation – An empirical analysis of frugal products and services. *Journal of Cleaner Production, 162*, 133–145. https://doi.org/10.1016/j.jclepro.2016.02.050

Schaltegger, S., Lüdeke-Freund, F., & Hansen, E. G. (2012). Business cases for sustainability: The role of business model innovation for corporate sustainability. *International Journal of Innovation and Sustainable Development, 6*(2), 95–119. https://doi.org/10.1504/IJISD.2012.046944

Scott, M. (2009). Marginalized, negative or trivial? Coverage of Africa in the UK press. *Media, Culture & Society, 31*(4), 533–557. https://doi.org/10.1177/0163443709335179

Sierra, L. A., Yepes, V., & Pellicer, E. (2018). A review of multi-criteria assessment of the social sustainability of infrastructures. *Journal of Cleaner Production, 187*, 496–513. https://doi.org/10.1016/j.jclepro.2018.03.022

Sinkovics, N., Sinkovics, R. R., & Yamin, M. (2014). The role of social value creation in business model formulation at the bottom of the pyramid – Implications for MNEs? *International Business Review, 23*(4), 692–707. https://doi.org/10.1016/j.ibusrev.2013.12.004

Sneyd, A. (2015). The poverty of 'poverty reduction': The case of African cotton. *Third World Quarterly, 36*(1), 55–74. https://doi.org/10.1080/01436597.2015.976017

Stubbs, W., & Cocklin, C. (2008). Conceptualizing a "sustainability business model". *Organization & Environment, 21*(2), 103–127. https://doi.org/10.1177/1086026608318042

Swilling, M. (2013). Economic crisis, long waves and the sustainability transition: An African perspective. *Environmental Innovation and Societal Transitions, 6*, 96–115. https://doi.org/10.1016/j.eist.2012.11.001

Thomas, A., & Bendixen, M. (2000). The management implications of ethnicity in South Africa. *Journal of International Business Studies, 31*(3), 507–519. https://doi.org/10.1057/palgrave.jibs.8490919

Thorgren, S., & Omorede, A. (2015). Passionate leaders in social entrepreneurship: Exploring an African context. *Business & Society, 57*(3), 481–524. https://doi.org/10.1177/0007650315612070

Thorisdottir, T. S., & Johannsdottir, L. (2019). Sustainability within fashion business models: A systematic literature review. *Sustainability, 11*(8), 2233. https://doi.org/10.3390/su11082233

Todeschini, B. V., Cortimiglia, M. N., Callegaro-de-Menezes, D. & Ghezzi. A. (2017). Innovative and sustainable business models in the fashion industry: Entrepreneurial drivers, opportunities, and challenges. *Business Horizons, 60*, 759–770. https://doi.org/10.1016/j.bushor.2017.07.003

Tolkamp, J., Huijben, J. C. C. M., Mourik, R. M., Verbong, G. P. J., & Bouwknegt, R. (2018). User-centred sustainable business model design: The case of energy efficiency services in the Netherlands. *Journal of Cleaner Production, 182*, 755–764. https://doi.org/10.1016/j.jclepro.2018.02.032

Traub-Merz, R. (2006). The African textile and clothing industry: From import substitution to export orientation. In H. Jauch & R. Traub-Merz (Eds.), *The future of the clothing industry in Sub-Saharan Africa* (pp. 9–35). Bonn: Friedrich-Ebert-Stiftung.

United Nations Development Program (2014). *The role of the private sector in inclusive development: Barriers and opportunities at the Base of the Pyramid.* Retrieved from www. undp.org/content/undp/en/home/librarypage/poverty-reduction/private_sector/ barriers-and-the-opportunities-at-the-base-of-the-pyramid---the-.html

Urban, B. (2008). Social entrepreneurship in South Africa: Delineating the construct with associated skills. *International Journal of Entrepreneurial Behavior & Research, 14*(5), 346–364. https://doi.org/10.1108/13552550810897696

Utgård, J. (2018). Retail chains' corporate social responsibility communication. *Journal of Business Ethics, 147*(2), 385–400. https://doi.org/10.1007/s10551-015-2952-2

Valente, M., & Oliver, C. (2018). Meta-organization formation and sustainability in sub-Saharan Africa. *Organization Science, 29*(4), 678–701. https://doi.org/10.1287/ orsc.2017.1191

Van den Waeyenberg, S. & Hens, L. (2012). Overcoming institutional distance: expansion to base-of-the-pyramid markets. *Journal of Business Research, 65*(12), 1692–1699. https://doi.org/10.1016/j.jbusres.2012.02.010

Vlok, E. (2006). The textile and clothing industry in South Africa. In H. Jauch & R. Traub-Merz (Eds.), *The future of the clothing industry in Sub-Saharan Africa* (pp. 227–246). Bonn: Friedrich-Ebert-Stiftung.

Wrede, I. (2018). Der altkleider-wahnsinn: Mit spenden schlechtes tun. *Deutsche Welle.* Retrieved from www.dw.com/de/der-altkleider-wahnsinn-mit-spenden-schlechtes-tun/a-46450796

Xiaoyang, T. (2014). *The impact of Asian investment on Africa's textile industries.* Carnegie-Tsinghua Center for Global Policy. Retrieved from https://carnegieendowment. org/files/china_textile_investment.pdf

Yang, M., Evans, S., Vladimirova, D. & Rana, P. (2017). Value uncaptured perspective for sustainable business model innovation. *Journal of Cleaner Production, 140*, 1794–1804. https://doi.org/10.1016/j.jclepro.2016.07.102

Yevu Clothing. (2019). About Us. Retrieved from https://yevuclothing.com/pages/ about-us

Yunus, M., Moingeon, B., & Lehmann-Ortega, L. (2010). Building social business models: Lessons from the Grameen experience. *Long Range Planning, 43*(2–3), 308–325. https://doi.org/10.1016/j.lrp.2009.12.005

Zimmerling, E., Purtik, H., & Welpe, I.M. (2017). End-users as co-developers for novel green products and services – An exploratory case study analysis of the innovation process in incumbent firms. *Journal of Cleaner Production, 162*, S51-S58. https://doi. org/10.1016/j.jclepro.2016.05.160

Zoogah, D. B. (2008). African business research: A review of studies published in the *Journal of African Business* and a framework for enhancing future studies. *Journal of African Business, 9*(1), 219–255. https://doi.org/10.1080/15228910802053037

Appendix

Table 6.6 Entrepreneurial approaches in business model innovations for sustainability in the fashion industry★

Trends	Drivers	Brief description (stressed by the author)
Circular economy	Recycling	• Converting materials from existing products to create different products • Reducing new materials and natural resources consumption • Acquiring recycled materials
	Vegan	• Refraining from using raw materials of animal origin, thereby reducing overall energy consumption
	Upcycling	• Using waste materials to generate new goods of equal or higher perceived value, utility, and/or quality • Reusing materials that would be discarded as raw materials for new products
Corporate social responsibility	Sweatshop-free	• Transparency about working conditions in manufacturing firm • Opposition to the practice of outsourcing production to emerging countries • Addressing increasing consumer awareness about fair treatment
	Fair trade	• Offering a worthy wage for all workers involved, healthy workplace environments, and social investment for the communities • Adopting innovative customer relationship practices • Rethinking and adoption of innovative supply chain management procedures
	Locally sourced	• Prioritizing product manufacturing in regions geographically close to consumption • Reducing costs and environmental impact associated with transportation and stimulating local businesses • Improving employment in local communities
Sharing economy	Fashion library	• Subscription service for apparel • Fostering new way to engage customers and cross-upsell to them
	Second hand	• Selling or donating apparel no longer in use by consumers • Promoting reuse and reducing demand for new items and natural resources consumption

Table 6.6 Cont.

Trends	Drivers	Brief description (stressed by the author)
	Collaboration	• Adopting a collaborative mindset by all stakeholders involved in a sustainable value network • Creating supporting ecosystem for resource and knowledge sharing, diffusion of sustainable practices, and business model experimentation
Technological innovation	Sustainable raw materials	• Developing and adopting different types of environmentally-friendly raw materials (e.g. organic cotton) • Requiring (internal) technological development or external acquisition of technologies • Requiring reliable access to a source of materials and communication of brand commitment to sustainable practices
	Zero waste	• Minimizing material waste in apparel production • Reducing the use of raw materials through novel and more efficient production processes
	Wearables	• Incorporating electronic devices in fashion goods • Creating additional value through novelty, added functionalities, and exclusivity
Consumer awareness	Capsule wardrobe	• Committing to owning and using only a limited amount of clothes for a fixed period of time • Opposing compulsive consumption and fostering a minimalist conscience among consumers
	Lowsumerism	• Adopting a critical approach to consumption that prioritizes conscious and moderate buying • Opposing compulsive consumption and fostering a minimalist conscience among consumers
	Slow fashion	• Fashion production and commercialization practices that oppose the fast fashion paradigm • Orienting firms' offering toward increased perceived quality and authenticity • Orienting firms' offering toward addressing customer concerns in terms of environmental and social impacts

Source: adopted from Todeschini et al. (2017).

7 Women's economic empowerment and agricultural value chain development

Evidence from Mashonaland West Province in Zimbabwe

Evelyn Derera

Introduction

Women empowerment is widely acknowledged as an important goal for international development (Malapit & Quisumbing, 2015). Its significance is underscored by the inclusion of gender equality and women empowerment in the United Nations Sustainable Development Goals (SDGs) (United Nations, 2019; Malapit & Quisumbing, 2015). The fifth SDG, in particular, highlights the importance of "promoting gender equality and women empowerment" (United Nations, 2019: 20). This is necessary because women are generally marginalised in societies, yet they contribute significantly to global economic development (World Bank, 2012). Women constitute almost 66% of the global labour force and contribute 50% of global food production (World Bank, 2012). However, they earn only 10% of global income and own 1% of global property and assets (World Bank, 2012).

These figures demonstrate the existence of gender inequality, explaining why the majority of women are poor. Hence, poverty is "feminized" because women constitute approximately 70% of the 1.3 billion people living in extreme poverty (i.e. those who survive on less than $1.25 a day) (Women's Refugee Commission, 2015). Furthermore, poverty is extreme in the rural areas of Africa. Burney, Naylor, and Postel (2013) state that nearly 70% of Africa's poorest population live in rural areas and are primarily dependent on agriculture for their livelihoods. Women constitute the majority of the rural population in Africa and own less than 2% of the land (Applefield & Jun, 2014). Poverty eradication could undoubtedly be achieved when women own a significant share of the factors of production. It is therefore important to acknowledge the role of gender in hunger and poverty eradication by improving food security through sustainable agriculture in developing nations (Malapit & Quisumbing, 2015), in line with the first and second SDGs. Achieving women empowerment is centred around the development of sound policies, with a holistic approach to long-term sustainability that includes gender-specific interventions (OECD, 2012).

Within the Zimbabwean context, women constitute 52% of a population of approximately 16 million people (ZimStat, 2015). Like many other African countries, Zimbabwe is experiencing high levels of poverty. The poverty headcount ratio at the national poverty line constituted 72.3% of the population in 2011 (World Bank, 2014), and females make up the majority of those living in poverty (World Bank, 2012). Furthermore, the majority of the population in Zimbabwe resides in rural areas, where livelihoods are largely dependent on subsistence farming (World Food Programme, 2014; Ministry of Lands and Rural Resettlement, 2015).

Given that so many women are impoverished, there is a tendency for them to operate at the Base or Bottom of the Pyramid (BOP) market as both buyers and sellers, where marginalisation is experienced in a variety of ways. BOP markets are composed of people who live on less than two dollars per day (Kistruck, Beamish, Qureshi & Sutter, 2013). For example smallholder farmers sell their produce at low prices due to a lack of resources for value addition. Understanding value chain development, especially for women participating in smallholder farming, is crucial in order to improve returns on farm produce and would lead to increased profit margins. Value chain development is a framework that creates opportunities for smallholder farmers to participate in competitive and profitable value chain activities in agriculture. Therefore, research in agriculture is a strategic tool to inform policies on poverty alleviation and the overall economic development of poor countries like Zimbabwe.

Limited research has been conducted on women's economic empowerment in agriculture and value chain development. Although some scholars have paid attention to the economic empowerment of women in agriculture (e.g. Applefield & Jun, 2014; Jayne, Mather & Mghenyi, 2010; Derera, 2015), little is known about the challenges hindering their participation in agriculture value chains. These are mainly rooted in value chain systems. Previous research on value chain development has focused on definitional issues of how value chain analysis differs from value chain addition (e.g. Donovan, Franzel, Cunha, Gyau & Mithöfer, 2015; Kolavalli, Mensah-Bonsu & Zaman, 2015). Some authors (e.g. Louw & Jordaan, 2016; Negi & Anand, 2015; Göbel, Langen, Blumenthal, Teitscheid & Ritter, 2015) explored the obstacles associated with value chain development. However, these challenges were not explored from a gender perspective, leaving an incomplete picture and a chasm in this area of research. This study aimed to fill this research gap by examining the challenges hindering women's empowerment in value chain development from a gender perspective, focusing on the BOP of a selected rural agricultural setting. Against this backdrop, it examined the bottlenecks that hamper women economic empowerment in agriculture, focusing on value chain development in women agro-businesses in Mashonaland West Province of Zimbabwe. The three research objectives were to:

• analyse the pre-production obstacles hindering women's economic empowerment in value chain development;

- investigate the post-production obstacles hindering women's economic empowerment in value chain development; and
- examine how socio-cultural factors influence women's economic empowerment in value chain development.

The chapter responds to a call for new thinking on how women could benefit as actors, co-creators, and consumers of BOP markets if all key stakeholders commit to their advancement and economic empowerment in agriculture. It explores how this could lead to poverty reduction. The study was conducted in one of the ten provinces in Zimbabwe, namely Mashonaland West, using non-probability sampling techniques to identify the respondents. Because of this, the findings cannot be generalised to all provinces in Zimbabwe. Nonetheless, the study contributes to the body of knowledge on women empowerment and value chain development in developing countries. The findings are expected to assist key stakeholders, development practitioners, and the private sector in developing sustainable support mechanisms to advance value chain development for women-run agro-based businesses with a focus on developing nations.

The chapter follows the format of first introducing the literature on women's economic empowerment. This is followed by a review of extant literature on value chain development and women in agribusiness, with particular focus on the challenges affecting agro-based businesses in developing nations, while also situating the study and its contributions, giving context to the discourse. The chapter continues with a reflection on research methodology and how it relates to a feminist research paradigm. The results of the study are discussed, beginning with a summary of the demographic profiles of the respondents, followed by a discussion on the study objectives. The chapter concludes with implications, limitations, and directions for future research.

Women's economic empowerment

Women empowerment occurs in different domains, which are economic, socio-cultural, interpersonal, legal, political, and psychological. Empowerment is a socio-political concept that includes cognitive, psychological, economic, and political constructs (Mosedale, 2005). Empowerment in one domain may not necessarily result in positive change in another dimension (Mosedale, 2005). For example economically empowered women may suffer physical and psychological abuse from their spouses. Nonetheless, economic empowerment of women is central to realising women's rights and gender equality (UN Women, 2019). It is important to continue advancing economic empowerment for women in spheres where they are largely represented, such as agriculture. The benefits of women's economic empowerment are well documented in the development literature (Slegh, Barker, Kimonyo, Ndolimana & Bannerman, 2013). Investing in women's economic empowerment charts a direct path towards gender equality, poverty eradication, and inclusive economic growth (United Nations Women, 2015). Similarly, investing in women benefits not only them, but also their families, and boosts the welfare of the broader society (Golla, Malhotra, Nanda & Mehra, 2011). Empowered women are more likely than men to spend their income on the well-being of the family, such as purchasing nutritious food, paying school fees, and attending to the health care needs of their children (Mehra & Hill Rojas, 2008).

Value chain development and women in agro-businesses

The concepts of value chain and value chain development

The concepts of value chain and value chain development (VCD) are widely debated in business management, sociology, and development studies (Donovan, Franzel, Cunha, Gyau & Mithöfer, 2015; Devaux, Torero, Donovan & Horton, 2018; Clay & Feeney, 2019). Consensus has yet to be reached on the definitions of these concepts (Donovan et al., 2015; Devaux et al., 2018; Clay & Feeney, 2019). Value chain analysis and value chain development are widely applied in pro-poor economic development (Coles & Mitchell, 2011; Devaux et al., 2018; Orr, Donovan & Stoian, 2018; Tobin & Glenna, 2019) for two reasons. First, it promotes economic viability and sustainability along the value chain process, resulting in win-win outcomes for participants (Coles & Mitchell, 2011; Devaux et al., 2018). Second, it is a solid qualitative diagnostic tool that is used to identify key issues and blockages along the value chain system for specific target groups with the aim of developing robust policies and strategies to create an efficient and effective value addition system (Coles & Mitchell, 2011; Devaux et al., 2018; Orr et al., 2018). However, the success of the diagnostic tool depends on commitment, proper planning, and implementation by all stakeholders including government, development agencies, the private sector, and all the human capital involved in value chain development (Coles & Mitchell, 2011; Devaux et al., 2018; Orr et al., 2018).

The value chain examines the range of value adding activities required to transform raw materials into finished products or services (Donovan et al., 2015; Devaux et al., 2018; Clay & Feeney, 2019; Tobin & Glenna, 2019). It is also defined as connected actors participating in a chain process of producing, transforming, and bringing goods and services to end-consumers through a sequential set of activities (Donovan et al., 2015; Devaux et al., 2018; Tobin & Glenna, 2019). The value of the product increases at each stage of the value chain, and the product becomes more available and attractive to the consumer (KIT, Agri-ProFocus & IIRR, 2012). Correspondingly, the cost of developing the product increases as it progresses along the value addition process (KIT, Agri-ProFocus & IIRR, 2012).

Value chain development is rooted in value chains and relates more to value addition activities in agriculture (Kolavalli, Mensah-Bonsu & Zaman, 2015; Devaux et al., 2018; Park, Jung & Kim, 2019; Tobin & Glenna, 2019). It is also defined as a strategic framework that creates opportunities for smallholder farmers to participate in competitive and profitable business activities (Coles

& Mitchell, 2011; KIT, Agri-ProFocus & IIRR, 2012; Kolavalli, et al., 2015; Devaux et al., 2018; Tobin & Glenna, 2019). The concept focuses on improving the efficacy of production processes, logistics, and the regulatory framework (Donovan et al., 2015; Devaux et al., 2018; Orr et al., 2018). Donovan et al. (2015) further argue that a focus on all stages or the full range of activities of the value chain is likely to open opportunities to participate in international markets, as most interventions rarely extend beyond the national borders of countries where primary production takes place. The full range of the activities of a value chain involves bringing a product or service from conception, through the different phases of production (involving a combination of physical transformation and the input of various producer services), delivery to final consumers, and final disposal after use (Kaplinsky & Morris, 2016).

Actors, supporters, and the context of value chain development

Within the value chain process, a series of actors are linked by the flow of products, finance, information, and other related services (KIT, Agri-ProFocus & IIRR, 2012; Donovan et al., 2015). They include, among others, farmers, traders, processors, retailers, and consumers (KIT, Agri-ProFocus & IIRR, 2012; Donovan et al., 2015). These actors perform specific functions within the value chain process known as functional nodes. Functional nodes are defined by Mitchell and Coles (2011) "as a collection of value chain actors or firms who perform similar activities" (p. xxi). Examples include input supply nodes, production nodes, and processing nodes.

Along the chain process are chain supporters who are individuals and organizations that support the actors (KIT, Agri-ProFocus & IIRR, 2012; Donovan et al., 2015). Examples include financial institutions, suppliers, transporters, business services, and certification agents (KIT, Agri-ProFocus & IIRR, 2012; Donovan et al., 2015).

Value chain actors and supporters operate within a specific context, which differs across nations (KIT, Agri-ProFocus & IIRR, 2012; Donovan et al., 2015). The context is made up of various factors that include the physical environment, the weather, currency exchange rates, the economic environment, government's economic and political policies, tax regulation, and the nation's regulatory and legal framework (KIT, Agri-ProFocus & IIRR, 2012; Donovan et al., 2015). All these factors can either promote or hinder value addition along the production process (KIT, Agri-ProFocus & IIRR, 2012; Donovan et al., 2015).

Gender and value chain development

Barriers to entry exist at different stages of value chain development (Coles & Mitchell, 2011). Higher barriers to entry correspond to greater returns and more control of chain management functions (Coles & Mitchell, 2011). Mitchell and Coles (2011) state that shifting from low markets to high level markets is based on economies of scale which could increase rewards and reduce risks. The level of participation in the value chain pipeline is shaped by gender, making it particularly difficult for women (Coles & Mitchell, 2011), who tend to experience more barriers to entry than men (Laven & Verhart, 2011). Furthermore, women have access to fewer support services than their male counterparts (Laven & Verhart, 2011). As a result, men dominate and influence the value production flow process (Coles & Mitchell, 2011), while most women participate in the least valued parts of value chain development (Tallontire, 2005; Laven & Verhart 2011; Mitchell & Coles, 2011; Pyburn & Terrillon, 2013). Gender is thus an important aspect of value chain development that is often overlooked (Barrientos, 2001; Stoian, Donovan, Elias & Blare, 2018).

Gender-specific patterns of access to key functions of the value chain (e.g. processing, marketing, etc.) are influenced by societal norms and the patriarchal hierarchy linked to household functions (Coles & Mitchell, 2011; Stoian et al., 2018), which negatively affect the income received by women in value chain addition (Negi & Anand, 2015). The potential for increased profit margins achieved by different actors in the value chain system depends on the scale and efficiency of value addition in the roll out phase of the process.

Women are the most invisible actors in value chains, yet they do most of the work (Laven & Verhart 2011). Gendered divisions of labour, decision making, and access to resources also exist along the value chain (Coles & Mitchell, 2011; Apotheker, Laven & Verhart, 2014; Stoian et al., 2018). Productive work is a serious burden for women who are also tasked with domestic responsibilities (Tallontire, 2005; Mitchell & Coles, 2011; KIT, Agri-ProFocus & IIRR, 2012; Stoian et al., 2018). Unpaid responsibilities include, among others, reproductive duties and taking care of the family, including cooking, cleaning, and fetching water and firewood (KIT, Agri-ProFocus & IIRR, 2012). The opportunity cost of an increased domestic workload equates to a loss of other income-generating activities (Mitchell & Coles, 2011; KIT, Agri-ProFocus & IIRR, 2012; Stoian et al., 2018). Furthermore, tensions may arise within the household in cases where married women try to exert greater bargaining power over family resources (KIT, Agri-ProFocus & IIRR, 2012).

Gender differences in literacy rates also place women at a serious disadvantage. Lack of education implies that women occupy roles that require lower skills sets within value chains (Shackleton, Paumgarten, Kassa, Husselman & Zida, 2011). As a result, their ability to participate effectively in value addition is reduced (Coles & Mitchell, 2011). In most cases, people with limited education lack the confidence to negotiate with buyers and suppliers, resulting in reduced bargaining power (Coles & Mitchell, 2011). This limits the role that women could potentially play in value chain addition. Understanding gender roles assist in identifying bottlenecks that require attention and support for the economic empowerment of women along VCD.

Researchers from different disciplines have developed several models to understand value chain systems. However, there is consensus on the components that make up the value chain. The model developed for this study (see Figure 7.1)

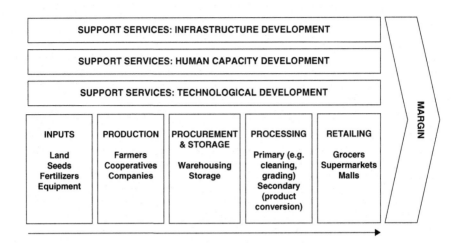

Figure 7.1 Value chain development model.

Source: adapted from various authors (e.g. Gereffi and Frederick, 2010; Gereffi and Fernandez-Stark, 2011; African Development Bank, 2014; Stoian et al., 2018; Park et al., 2019).

was adopted from several researchers (e.g. Gereffi & Frederick, 2010; Gereffi & Fernandez-Stark, 2011; African Development Bank, 2014; Park et al., 2019).

Figure 7.1 shows five stages of value chain development, namely: inputs, production, procurement and storage, processing, and retailing. The five stages are supported by technological development, human capacity development, and infrastructure support. The aim of value addition is to improve profit margins through increased product competitiveness, efficiency, and quality through differentiation (Başer & Bozoğlu, 2018).

Inputs: Inputs relate to what is added in a production process. Inputs into the agricultural value chain include factors of production such as land, access to human resources, and access to capital for purchasing key resources such as seeds, fertilizers, and farming equipment. Unfortunately, gender disparity is embedded in access to value chain inputs. Coles and Mitchell (2011) state that men and women have unequal access to property and capital. Land ownership, businesses, and property arrangements favour men over women (Coles & Mitchell, 2011; Trienekens, 2011; Apotheker et al., 2014; Devaux et al., 2018). The situation is exacerbated in developing countries where women's exclusion from land ownership is widespread (Coles & Mitchell, 2011; Apotheker et al., 2014). Cultural traditions in developing countries dictate that land ownership is the prerogative of men (Gobezie, 2013; Apotheker et al., 2014). If a parent (father) dies, the land is usually inherited by a son and not a daughter.

Land ownership presents a stepping stone to acquire physical assets and leverage access to services such as funding opportunities (Coles & Mitchell,

2011; Stoian et al., 2018; Devaux et al., 2018; Park et al., 2019). To illustrate the severity of the obstacles faced by women, Applefield and Jun (2014) note that only 10% of bank loans are extended to women in sub-Saharan Africa. Funding for women enterprises is referred to as "micro loans" by some researchers (e.g. Trienekens, 2011; Gobezie, 2013; Applefield & Jun, 2014; Ghosh & Vinod, 2017). This is tantamount to gender insensitivity because the nature of funding restricts women's potential to the micro level, yet on the ground, they are at the forefront of food production.

Importantly, gender inequality also emerges in power imbalances relating to the decision making process around inputs. In most cases, decisions on acquisitions are made by men. Gobezie (2013) states that once a man pays the bride price, the woman becomes his "property", and it is her duty to be subservient to her husband. This means that she has limited, if any, control over household decisions. The notion that women are secondary earners who rely on the earnings of men to buffer them against the risk of economic insecurity also negatively affects their decision making power (Tallontire, 2005). Apotheker et al. (2014) state that with limited economic resources and little control over household income, it is often difficult for women to secure key resources for value chain systems such as fertilizer, pesticides, and equipment. Even in situations where traditional farming methods are utilised for farming, such as a cattle drawn plough, women still do not own family resources, as these belong to the husband.

Production: This is the process of combining factors of production and inputs in order to create the desired output of goods or services (Shephard, 2015). Women are generally at the front lines of production of agricultural goods, but rarely participate in activities beyond this (Laven & Verhart, 2011). As a result, they miss out on empowering value addition opportunities with better profit margins that exist beyond the point of growing crops and vegetables. They have little involvement in marketing and distribution of products to retailers (Laven & Verhart, 2011). Participation in activities beyond production contributes to women's empowerment and poverty alleviation (Laven & Verhart, 2011). Chain empowerment requires producers to manage the chain process; thus, women, and rural women in particular, are left out of potentially lucrative opportunities (Laven & Verhart, 2011).

Agricultural production is executed using different forms. It can be executed at an individual level, cooperative level, or on a commercial farming basis. The form of agricultural production influences the type of opportunities available along the value chain. The intensity of linkages and integration, knowledge, and awareness of value addition processes favours large-scale farmers (Göbel et al., 2015). Commercial farmers are better able to access key resources and marketing opportunities than smallholder farmers. Large-scale farmers also benefit from increased bargaining power because they can afford to purchase inputs in bulk. Post-harvest risks are also lower for commercial farmers (Coles & Mitchell, 2011). The aforementioned opportunities tend to favour large-scale farmers at the expense of smallholder farmers. The dynamics are further complicated by gender disparity, as women have limited access to these opportunities (Pyburn & Terrillon, 2013), with most of them participating at the level of smallholder farming (Weng, Boedhihartono, Dirks, Dixon, Lubis & Sayer, 2013).

Procurement and storage: Access to adequate procurement and storage facilities offers significant opportunities for value add-ons. Obstacles to maximising these include a lack of access to warehousing and a lack of cold storage facilities for farm produce (Louw & Jordaan, 2016; Negi & Anand, 2015). Ultimately, losses are incurred through the wastage of perishable products, crippling growth and the development of value addition (Maheshwar & Chanakwa, 2006; Reddy et al., 2010). Ownership and control of procurement and storage facilities is dominated by men, making it difficult for women to participate meaningfully along the value chain.

Processing: Processing is divided into two categories, namely, primary and secondary processing. Primary processing involves cleaning and grading agricultural produce (Göbel et al., 2015). Barrientos (2001) postulates that women are preferred in the processing of agricultural products because of the perception that they have "nimble fingers" and are better able to handle the more delicate labour-intensive work involved in export production processes. Generally, women tend to pay finer attention to detail, which is pivotal in value addition (Barrientos, 2001). Secondary processing involves the transformation of agricultural produce (Göbel et al., 2015). Value is added when goods are transformed in part or completely, with value appreciating at the various levels of transformation. For example milk can be processed into long-life pasteurised milk and other related dairy products, including cheese and yoghurt. Other value addition processes include reducing the fat content of milk products on different scales. Value addition creates opportunities for new markets and greater opportunity for higher profit margins as products begin to appeal to niche markets. Again, gender disparity in access to resources, education, and training development plays a significant role in disadvantaging women in the acquisition of skills to contribute to value chain development. Researchers (e.g. Louw & Jordaan, 2016; Negi & Anand, 2015) suggest that a lack of appropriate packaging resources for perishable goods compromises shelf life, quality, and the price of the product. This is evident in the informal markets of developing countries where vegetables are sold with inappropriate or no packaging. This mainly affects women.

Retailing: Retailing challenges relate to access to lucrative markets, including those at local, regional, and international levels (Trienekens, 2011). Trienekens (2011) categorizes these markets into three systems, namely, A-system, B-system, and C-system. The A-system is characterised by local low-income value chain markets, which are made up of a large number of small-scale producers who depend on traditional farming and production methods. The value chain system is relatively inefficient. The small producers generally have limited information about the end-user market, leading to oversupply of goods and reduced selling prices.

The value chain system serving the A-system markets is characterised by a large number of actors, and the value chain is supported by an inefficient transport system (Trienekens, 2011). The volume of agricultural production is high, but low value is generated (Trienekens, 2011).

The B-system consists of local middle to high-income value chains (Trienekens, 2011). Producers are subcontracted by supermarkets to deliver according to consumers' specifications and needs (Trienekens, 2011). A large share of the volume is delivered by small and medium producers (Trienekens, 2011). Although the production volume is smaller, the value generated is higher than in the A-system (Trienekens, 2011). The value addition process is governed by retail quality and safety standards (Trienekens, 2011), which are stringent and strongly enforced. Most women participate in A and B-systems, where they experience low profit margins. Apotheker et al. (2014) argue that women often have difficulties in selling their produce to favourable markets. They typically do not belong to producer organizations that assist and support with marketing activities. This reduces their reach to potentially profitable markets (Apotheker et al., 2014). In cases where women belong to producer groups, these tend to be less structured and powerful than male-dominated producer groups. While some women producer groups have made considerable progress in improving their members' income, access to markets, and other services, many have not succeeded (Shiferaw, Hellin & Muricho, 2016). Women can organize themselves into groups where they pool their resources to access more favourable markets (Apotheker et al., 2014).

The C-system is characterised by the export value chain. Products perceived as being low quality or rejected products can still be sold on national markets (Trienekens, 2011). Export value chains tend to be more integrated and consist of fewer actors (Trienekens, 2011). Tallontire, Dolan, Smith, and Barrientos (2005) note that more than 80% of export-quality vegetables from Zambia are sold to UK retailers through importers who mediate and facilitate their relationship with the supermarkets. Similar market arrangements existed in Zimbabwe before the introduction of targeted economic sanctions. Such functional nodes of the value chain are dominated by men (Tallontire et al., 2005). The volumes of products are small compared to local markets, but the value addition process is relatively high, generating higher profit margins than A and B market systems (Trienekens, 2011).

The value addition process influences access to lucrative markets, and it depends on what, when, how, and where value addition takes place (Louw & Jordaan, 2016). For perishable products such as vegetables, key timing of harvesting, cleaning, packaging, and the quality of packaging influence where, how, when, and to whom the products are sold. Coles and Mitchell (2011) state that women are disproportionately represented at low levels of value chains that correspond with considerably low functional nodes that limit marketing opportunities. In contrast, high value chain functional nodes, characterised by globalised marketing opportunities and lucrative returns, are mainly occupied by men (Coles & Mitchell, 2011).

Support services: Support services for infrastructure, technology, and human capacity development are essential in building efficient and successful value chain systems (Trienekens, 2011; Negi & Anand, 2015). Poor infrastructure hampers the efficient flow of products to markets and also disturbs the exchange of market information in value chains (Trienekens, 2011; Park et al., 2019). Wide coverage of efficient technology systems enhances the value chain development process (Trienekens, 2011). The use of cell phones by producers in developing countries is enabling the transfer of market supply and demand information in real time (Trienekens, 2011).

Weak institutional support structures, such as government tailored support programmes, unbalanced trade relationships, and unfavourable social and political conditions, lead to increased business risk and hinder the growth of value chain development (Reddy, Murthy & Meena, 2010; Trienekens, 2011). Infrastructure development is generally the responsibility of the government, while technology and human capacity development can be supported by government, development agencies, and the private sector.

Input supplies, such as energy and water, can hinder or support value chain development (Trienekens, 2011). The relatively high energy costs in developing countries restrict growth possibilities for actors in the value chains (Trienekens, 2011). High energy costs affect all actors in this chain regardless of gender.

Access to agricultural support services (e.g. agriculture extension advice) is more biased towards men (Apotheker et al., 2014). Applefield and Jun (2014) observe that only 5% of women benefit from the services of agricultural extension officers in sub-Saharan Africa. It is estimated that, if women were to receive high-quality extension services that provide technical training, productivity could increase by up to 4% (Applefield & Jun, 2014). Furthermore, access to technology, training, and development favours men. Due to time constraints associated with domestic responsibilities, women often miss out on training and development opportunities (Mitchell & Coles, 2011; Apotheker et al., 2014).

Research methodology

The study adopted a pragmatic research philosophy in line with feminist research methodologies, which advocate for mixed methods where multiple data sources are used for data collection. Feminist research focuses on sets of traditions that prioritise women's issues, voices, and their lived experiences (Hesse-Biber, 2013).

Data were gathered from women participating in agro-based enterprises in Mashonaland West Province in Zimbabwe. The target population consisted of 965 women farmers registered on the provincial agriculture database. A sample size of 275 respondents was drawn from the target population using the Krejcie and Morgan (1970) sample calculator. The database comprised of different farming models, namely communal or irrigation, A1 and A2. A1 is a resettlement model representing communal village or self-contained subsistence farming (Gwate, 2015). A2 is a commercial farming model with different variants of small, medium, large, and peri-urban farms (Gwate, 2015). The aim of including these types of farming activities was to gather deeper, wider, and varied perspectives on the challenges hindering value chain development in women's agro-based enterprises.

The respondents were identified using the purposive sampling technique. Primary data collection was conducted in three stages: focus groups, surveys, and in-depth interviews. As an initial point of departure, focus group interviews were conducted with two groups of women with the aim of gaining insights into the specific challenges hindering empowerment along value chain development. The two groups consisted of 14 women in total, divided into groups of six and eight. The interviews were conducted at two institutions that support farmers in Zimbabwe, the Zimbabwe Farmers Union (ZFU) and Zimbabwe Indigenous Women Farmers Association Trust. The ZFU was established with the objective of supporting large-scale indigenous commercial farmers after Zimbabwe gained independence in 1980. The Zimbabwe Indigenous Women Farmers Association Trust was established to support indigenous women farmers. Both focus group interviews took approximately 45 minutes to one hour. Challenges raised included the rising cost of agricultural inputs, access to farming loans, and the inadequate supply of farming inputs on the local markets.

Insights from the focus group interviews were used to develop the quantitative questionnaire for the second phase of data collection. The challenges were ranked on a 5-point Likert scale ranging from Strongly Disagree (1) to Strongly Agree (5). The researcher distributed the questionnaires with the help of two research assistants who received training before embarking on the data collection process. A pilot test was conducted using four questionnaires, which were excluded from the data analysis process. The questionnaire items for pre-production, post-production, and socio-cultural factors were subjected to Cronbach's Alpha statistic. The results were 0.595, 0.798, and 0.948, respectively.

The last stage involved one-on-one interviews with ten women identified during the first two stages of data collection. In-depth interviews were conducted for approximately 45 minutes. Principal Component Analysis, a multivariate statistical technique that is used to reduce the number of dimensions or variables while retaining data variation, was applied for quantitative data analysis (Härdle & Simar, 2012). In interpreting the mean scores of the challenges, a score of 3 was interpreted as neutral, while a score of above 3 suggested that the respondents agreed that the highlighted construct is indeed labelled as a challenge. For challenges with a mean score of below 3, it meant that the respondents did not agree or perceive the construct as a severe challenge affecting them in value chain development. The qualitative data was analysed using content analysis. Self-reflection formed part of qualitative data analysis to minimise the researcher's bias in the research process. This ensured the rigour, credibility, and trustworthiness of the empirical data (Bengtsson, 2016).

Demographic profile of respondents

The study achieved a response rate of 90.18% (i.e. the 248 total respondents included the 14 women who participated in the focus group interviews and

Table 7.1 Demographic profile of focus group respondents

Participant	Age	Marital status	No. of children	Level of education	Type of farming scheme
1	45	Married	4	Ordinary level	A1
2	50	Married	5	Ordinary level	AI
3	62	Married	6	Teaching diploma	A2
4	46	Widow	4	Bachelor's degree	AI
5	43	Married	3	Ordinary level	A1
6	39	Married	2	Advanced level	A1
7	55	Widow	4	Below Ordinary level	A1
8	42	Married	2	Ordinary level	AI
9	48	Married	5	Ordinary level	A1
10	58	Married	6	Below Ordinary level	A2
11	57	Married	7	Nursing diploma	A1
12	40	Married	4	Teaching diploma	AI
13	38	Married	3	Ordinary level	AI
14	45	Married	4	Master's degree	AI

Source: author's own compilation.

234 who participated in the survey). The ten women who participated in one-on-one in-depth interviews were drawn from the survey sample. This section starts by describing the demographic profile of the women in the following order: focus group respondents, survey participants, and interview respondents. The demographic profile of focus group respondents is presented in Table 7.1.

The women's ages ranged from 38 to 62 years. Two were widowed, while the rest were married. Their number of children ranged from two to seven. The plurality (42.86%) of the women had an Ordinary Level certificate. Zimbabwe follows a British education system that is made up of (1) two years of Pre-primary school or Early Childhood Development (ECD) for pupils between the ages of 3 and 5/6 years; (2) seven years of Primary school (i.e. Grades 1–7), (3) four years of Secondary school (i.e. Forms 1–4); and (5) two years of High school (i.e. Forms 5 and 6). The exit qualification for secondary school is called the Ordinary, or "O", Level certificate, while that for high school is the Advanced, or "A", Level certificate. The majority (85.71%) of the women had A1 farms, while two women had A2 farms.

Demographic profile of questionnaire survey respondents

Table 7.2 presents the demographic details of the women who participated in the survey.

Age: The plurality (30.34%) of the women were aged between 40 and 49 years. The 50–59 and 30–39 age categories had 20.94% and 19.23%

Table 7.2 Demographic profile of survey respondents

Demographic Details	Category	Frequency	Percentage	Demographic Details	Category	Frequency	Percentage
Age	0–29 years	19	8.12	**Number of children**	2 children and below	42	17.75
	30–39 years	45	19.23		3–4 children	100	42.86
	40–49 years	71	30.34		5–6 children	63	26.84
	50–59 years	49	20.94		7–8 children	23	9.96
	60–69 years	39	16.67		Above 7 children	6	2.60
	Above 70 years	11	4.70	**Level of Education**	Below Ordinary level	150	64.10
Marital status	Married	130	55.56		Ordinary level	31	13.20
	Divorced	12	5.13		Advanced level	33	14.10
	Widowed	84	35.90		Diploma	15	6.40
	Never married	8	3.42		Bachelor's degree	2	0.90
Age at marriage	Below 16 years	27	11.40		Master's degree	2	0.90
	17–19 years	85	36.40		Doctorate	1	0.40
	20–24 years	105	44.74	**Professional Status**	Professionals	69	29.50
	25–30 years	17	7.46		Non-professional, self-employed	165	70.50
Total		**234**		**Total**		**234**	

Source: author's own compilation.

representation, respectively. The other age categories were 60–69 (16.67%) and 0–29 (8.12%). The age category with the fewest (4.70%) respondents was 70 and above.

Marital status: The majority (55.56%) of the women were married, while 35.90% were widowed. Divorced women and women who never married constituted 5.13% and 3.42% of the sample, respectively.

Age at marriage: The plurality (44.74%) of the women married at the age of 20–24 years, whilst 36.40% married at the age of 17–19. Women who married at the age of 25–30 and below the age of 16 constituted 7.46% and 11.40% of the sample, respectively.

Number of children: The plurality (42.86%) of the women had 3–4 children, while 26.84% had between 5 and 6 children, and 17.75% had two children or fewer. A small minority (2.60%) had more than seven children.

Level of education: Most women (64.1%) did not achieve an Ordinary Level certificate, reflecting gender discrimination in attaining formal education for "the girl child". The women who achieved Advanced Level and Ordinary Level certificates constituted 14.1% and 13.2% of the sample, respectively. The women with a bachelor's and a master's degree represented 1.8% of the sample. Only one (0.4%) woman graduated with a doctoral degree.

Professional status: The majority (70.5%) of the women were self-employed, and 29.5% were in teaching and nursing professions.

Demographic profile of in-depth interview respondents

The excerpts below give an indication of the demographic profile of the women who participated in the interviews.

> *I am 55 years old and I am married with five children. Unfortunately, I dropped out of school in Form 3 due to financial hardships. I ended up getting married at the age of 17 years.*

(A1 farmer)

> *I am a 65-year-old widow, and I have five children. I never went to school, instead my parents sent my brothers to school (Irrigation scheme member).*

(A2 farmer)

> *I am a 45-year-old widow and I have five daughters. I have a master's degree in Agricultural Economics.*

(A2 farmer)

> *I am 38 years old, married, with two children and four dependents. I am a school teacher, and I have a diploma in Education.*

(A2 farmer)

The first quote indicates the challenges facing "the girl child" in securing formal education. Due to poverty (i.e. financial hardships), the girl child is forced to marry at the young age of 17, before reaching the age of 18, which is considered to be the entry into adulthood. The second quote reflects elements of deeply rooted gender discrimination imbedded within the culture. The woman was never exposed to formal education simply because she was a girl; her brothers received formal education instead. Lack of education negatively affects the value chain process and forces women to participate in low skilled functions of this process. This perpetuates poverty, as opportunities are generally limited for people with no formal education (Coles & Mitchell, 2011). The last two quotes show fairly educated women who are participating in commercial farming (A2). Exposure to formal education could have contributed to their participation in large-scale farming.

Background on farming activities

The women participated in various farming activities. Some engaged in market gardening, focusing on the following vegetables: cabbages, peas, potatoes, tomatoes, green mealies, onions, and butternut. Market gardening "is the commercial production of vegetables, fruits, flowers and other plants on a scale larger than a home garden, yet small enough that many of the principles of gardening are applicable" (Bachmann, 2002, p. 1). The goal is to run the operation as a business and to make a profit (Bachmann, 2002). A1 and A2 farmers were mainly participating in livestock farming (beef and poultry) and crop production (tobacco, maize, and soybeans). Below are extracts from the women explaining some of their farming activities.

> *We are members of an irrigation scheme. We are able to do farming throughout the year. We grow maize, sweet potatoes, vegetables, potatoes, groundnuts, pumpkins, and tomatoes. We focus on vegetables recommended by the Agricultural Extension Officer.*
> (Communal/irrigation scheme member)

> *We are involved in both crop and livestock production. For crop production, we grow maize, tobacco, and other crops for family consumption, e.g., potatoes, beans and vegetables. For livestock production, we do beef and poultry farming.*
> (A2 farmer)

In these quotes, the plural "we" is used instead of the singular "I", indicating the sense of community rooted within the Shona culture. The excerpts also provide evidence of how women are contributing to food production in communities. Applefield and Jun (2014) state that women are at the forefront of food production in Africa.

Results

The analysis of the challenges experienced by the women along the value chain system is divided into pre-production, post-production, and socio-cultural challenges.

Pre-production challenges

The analysis of input and pre-production challenges is displayed in Table 7.3.

Table 7.3 shows that the majority (89.7%) of the women are overwhelmed by the rising costs of agricultural inputs. The mean score for this challenge is 4. The other challenges with a mean score of above 3 are lack of farming loans (79.9%) and lack of supply of farming inputs and equipment to the local market (53.0%). The remainder of the challenges have a mean score of less than 3 and a percentage of less than 50. These include a lack of irrigation facilities, poorly resourced agriculture extension officers, lack of agricultural training, poor infrastructure such as road networks, and the low ratio of agriculture extension officers to farmers. An overall measure of agricultural production challenges was calculated as a summary of the eight items presented in Table 7.3. The summary variable (ChallengePreprodn) was calculated using principal components (or latent factors). The weighting of the variables is presented in the last column. The item with the highest (0.813) weighting is "low ratio of agriculture extension officers to farmers", indicating that it is the most important pre-production challenge. The other critical challenges are poorly resourced agriculture extension officers (0.714), lack of agricultural training (0.811), and poor infrastructure (0.729).

Post-production challenges

Table 7.4 presents an analysis of post-production challenges.

The challenges presented in this table negatively affect women in agribusiness, as evidenced by a mean score of above 3 for all the challenges. The majority of the women identified the lack of disposable income (82.5%), lack of lucrative markets for agricultural produce (72.6%), high transportation costs (70.5%), oversupply of agricultural produce to the market (63.7%), lack of training on value addition (e.g. food processing; 57.7%), and a lack of business management training (53.1%) as critical post-production challenges. The summary variable representing post-production challenges (ChallengePostproduction) generated using Principal Component Analysis shows that the lack of vending shades at marketplaces was a major (0.924) contributing challenge. The other major contributors are lack of infrastructure (0.903), high licensing costs (0.895), and a lack of refrigeration facilities at marketplaces (0.871).

Effect of education on pre-production and post-production challenges

Table 7.5 presents the effect of education on the challenges facing women in their agro enterprises. The data originated from the women who participated in the survey.

The results in Table 7.5 indicate that education has a significant effect on pre-production (F = 2.504, df1 = 6, df2 = 227, p-value = 0.023); and post-production challenges (F = 3.618, df1 = 6, df2 = 227, p-value = 0.002). It is

Table 7.3 Pre-production challenges

Pre-production challenges (Challenge Preprodn)		Frequency distribution						Descriptive statistics		Latent factor (Principal Component)
		Strongly disagree (1)	Disagree (2)	Neutral (3)	Agree (4)	Strongly agree (5)	% Agree / Strongly disagree	Mean	Std dev	Coefficient
Rising costs of agriculture inputs	Count	16	0	8	171	39	89.7%	4.00	0.69	−0.372
	%	6.8%	0.0%	3.4%	73.1%	16.7%				
Lack of farming loans	Count	18	0	29	157	30	79.9%	3.85	0.73	−0.116
	%	7.7%	0.0%	12.4%	67.1%	12.8%				
Lack of supply of farming inputs and equipment to the local market	Count	77	0	33	119	5	53.0%	3.22	0.94	0.205
	%	32.9%	0.0%	14.1%	50.9%	2.1%				
Lack of irrigation facilities	Count	6	105	19	95	9	44.4%	2.98	1.06	0.398
	%	2.6%	44.9%	8.1%	40.6%	3.8%				
Poor infrastructure (e.g. roads)	Count	15	141	31	46	1	20.1%	2.47	0.89	0.729
	%	6.4%	60.3%	13.2%	19.7%	0.4%				
Low ratio of extension officers to farmers	Count	16	120	55	42	1	18.4%	2.54	0.88	0.813
	%	6.8%	51.3%	23.5%	17.9%	0.4%				
Poorly resourced extension officers (e.g. lack of transport to visit farmers)	Count	15	93	49	74	3	32.9%	2.82	1.00	0.714
	%	6.4%	39.7%	20.9%	31.6	1.3%				
Lack of agricultural training	Count	15	86	60	70	3	31.2%	2.83	0.97	0.811
	%	6.4%	36.8%	25.6%	29.9%	1.3%				
	Cronbach's Alpha							0.595		
	% of total variation accounted for by latent factor							33.88%		

Source: author's own compilation.

Table 7.4 Post-production challenges

Post-production challenges (Challenge Postproduction)		Frequency distribution						% Agree/ Strongly disagree	Descriptive statistics		Latent factor (Principal Component)
		Strongly disagree (1)	Disagree (2)	Neutral (3)	Agree (4)	Strongly agree (5)			Mean	Std dev	Coefficient
Lack of lucrative markets for livestock and agricultural produce	Count	3	43	18	160	10		72.6%	3.56	0.88	0.306
	%	1.3%	18.4%	7.7%	68.4%	4.3%					
Lack of refrigerated storage facilities for agricultural fresh produce	Count	4	81	55	84	10		40.2%	3.06	0.97	0.871
	%	1.7%	34.6%	23.5%	35.9%	4.3%					
High transportation costs to the markets	Count	1	37	31	153	12		70.5%	3.59	0.83	0.612
	%	0.4%	15.8%	13.2%	65.4%	5.1%					
High licensing cost for securing selling space	Count	3	75	67	82	7		38.0%	3.06	0.92	0.895
	%	1.3%	32.1%	28.6%	35.0%	3.0%					
Lack of basic infrastructure at marketplaces (e.g. ablution facilities)	Count	1	78	66	82	7		38.0%	3.07	0.91	0.903
	%	0.4%	33.3%	28.2%	35.0%	3.0%					
Lack of vending shades at markets	Count	1	80	66	83	4		37.2%	3.04	0.89	0.924
	%	0.4%	34.2%	28.2%	35.5%	1.7%					
Over-flooding of agricultural produce on the market	Count	0	43	42	110	39		63.7%	3.62	0.97	0.631
	%	0.0%	18.4%	17.9%	47.0%	16.7%					
Lack of disposable income	Count	0	14	27	176	17		82.5%	3.84	0.63	0.376
	%	0.0%	6.0%	11.5%	75.2%	7.3%					
Lack of business management training	Count	5	45	64	120	0		51.3%	3.28	0.85	0.105
	%	2.1%	19.2%	27.4%	51.3%	0.0%					
Lack of training in value addition activities (e.g. food processing skills)	Count	3	34	62	118	17		57.7%	3.48	0.88	0.142
	%	1.3%	14.5%	26.5%	50.4%	7.3%					
Cronbach's Alpha									0.798		
% of total variation accounted for by latent factor									42.68%		

Source: author's own compilation.

Table 7.5 Effects of education on challenges (ANOVA)

		N	Mean	Std dev	F	ANOVA Tests			Comment
						DF1, DF2	p-value		
Pre-production challenges	Below Ordinary level	150	3.07	0.46	2.507	6 227	0.0.23		Significant
	Ordinary level	31	3.03	0.49					
	Advanced level	33	3.16	0.36					
	Diploma	15	3.36	0.47					
	Bachelor's degree	2	2.94	0.27					
	Master's degree	2	2.19	0.09					
	Doctorate	1	3.00						
Post-production challenges	Below "O" level	150	3.36	0.49	3.618	6 227	0.002		Significant
	Ordinary level	31	3.32	0.57					
	Advanced level	33	3.48	0.50					
	Diploma	15	3.44	0.53					
	Bachelor's degree	2	2.30	0.14					
	Master's degree	2	2.30	0.14					
	Doctorate	1	4.00	–					

Source: author's own compilation.

clear that the negative impact of these challenges is more severe among women with lower education levels. This is indicated by high mean scores of above 3 for women with a diploma certificate and lower, compared to a mean score of below 3 for women with a bachelor's degree and above. It is important to note that only one respondent had a doctoral degree, which is an outlier. These findings concur with the literature which states that lack of education exacerbates the severity of challenges hindering women's participation in value chain development (Coles & Mitchell, 2011; Shackleton et al., 2011).

Socio-cultural challenges

The socio-cultural challenges are presented in Table 7.6.

The majority of the women agreed that socio-cultural factors are affecting their agro-businesses, as indicated by a mean score of above 3 for all challenges. A summary variable representing all socio-cultural factors (SocioCultFactors) was generated using Principal Component Analysis to create a latent factor for socio-cultural factors based on the ten questionnaire items. The question with the highest weighting (0.902) relates to society believing that a woman's success is linked to and belongs to the husband, demonstrating that it is the most important socio-cultural factor.

Qualitative insights on the challenges

The excerpts below highlight some of the qualitative insights gathered during focus group and in-depth interviews.

> *Our main challenge is that the Grain Marketing Board (GMB) has not paid us for the maize they purchased from us. Low tobacco prices and theft by employees are also some of the challenges we are experiencing. Male employees generally under-mine women when we give them instructions at the farm. . . . Ways of dealing with some of these challenges is to grow irrigated tobacco to improve quality, selling maize to the informal sector, and scaling down operations.*
>
> (A2 farmer)

> *Our main challenge is finance to purchase seeds and other farming equipment. We also struggle to sell our crops. "Tinogara tichitaura nemudhumeni kuti atitsvagire kwekutengesera" (translated as: We are continuously pleading with the Agricultural Extension Officer to help us source buyers for our produce).*
>
> (Communal/Irrigation scheme member)

> *I only receive support from my children. "Hama dzemurume dzandirasa pakafa murume wangu" (translated as: My husband's family and relatives turned their back on me when my husband died). . . . My community assists me a lot with farming advice and clothes.*
>
> (Irrigation scheme member)

Table 7.6 Socio-cultural factors

Socio-Cultural Factors (SocioCultFactors)		Frequency distribution					% Agree / Strongly disagree	Descriptive statistics		Latent factor (Principal Component)
		Strongly disagree (1)	Disagree (2)	Neutral (3)	Agree (4)	Strongly agree (5)		Mean	Std dev	Coefficient
Society believes that a woman's place is in the kitchen	Count	9	45	22	142	16	67.5%	3.47	1.00	0.833
	%	3.8%	19.2%	9.4%	60.7%	6.8%				
Society believes that a woman's role is to bear children and support her husband	Count	11	42	19	151	11	69.2%	3.47	0.99	0.855
	%	4.7%	17.9%	8.1%	64.5%	4.7%				
Society believes that the husband is the head of the house and has total control of household decisions	Count	7	34	20	156	17	73.9%	3.61	0.93	0.868
	%	3.0%	14.5%	8.5%	66.7%	7.3%				
Society believes that the success of the woman is linked to the husband	Count	10	31	26	157	10	71.4%	3.54	0.93	0.902
	%	4.3%	13.2%	11.1%	67.1%	4.3%				
Society believes that women are not capable of achieving anything in life without help from men	Count	12	27	20	167	8	74.8%	3.56	0.93	0.891
	%	5.1%	11.5%	8.5%	71.4%	3.4%				
Society believes that women are inferior to men, and therefore, must not own property (e.g. land)	Count	12	31	22	156	13	72.2%	3.54	0.97	0.863
	%	5.1%	13.2%	9.4%	66.7%	5.6%				
Society believes that a woman cannot make sound decisions on her own	Count	7	34	21	163	9	73.5%	3.57	0.89	0.897
	%	3.0%	14.5%	9.0%	69.7%	3.8%				
Society is not supportive of women who work hard because they are seen to be competing with men	Count	11	51	25	132	15	62.8%	3.38	1.04	0.685
	%	4.7%	21.8%	10.7%	56.4%	6.4%				
Society believes that women who are successful in business are not "straight forward"	Count	9	28	20	146	31	75.6%	3.69	0.98	0.740
	%	3.8%	12.0%	8.5%	62.4%	13.2%				
Society believes that certain farming activities are performed by a particular gender	Count	10	24	27	149	24	73.9%	3.65	0.95	0.753
	%	4.3%	10.3%	11.5%	63.7%	10.3%				
	Cronbach's Alpha								0.948	
	% of total variation accounted for by latent factor								69.20%	

Source: author's own compilation.

Our main challenge is high transport costs to the markets. The cost of farming inputs is also very high. What we have resorted to do is buying farming inputs collectively, so we can increase our bargaining power. Because of this, we also save on transport costs because we share the costs.

(A1 farmer)

The cost of electricity and water is very high. Our electricity was cut off at some point, our seedlings dried up, and we were not able to continue with farming operations. The government should assist us.

(Communal/Irrigation scheme member)

Our biggest challenge is that there are so many of us producing the same crops, so we end up selling our produce at low prices. We want the officers to advise us on the crops we can grow on the farm to avoid repeating the same mistakes.

(A1 farmer)

I received overwhelming support from my family. I am respected by women from my community. "Vanoshora havashaike kana madzimai ave kugona kuzvimiririra" (translated as: There are always people who despise and criticise women when they become financially independent). I don't listen to such people.

(A1 farmer)

I am very much respected in my community. A lot of women consult me on various farming issues. . . . I once faced resistance from my community, especially from my relatives who thought farming activities will come to a halt when my husband died. Right now, some relatives and community members are accusing me of causing my husband's death so I will be in charge of the farming activities. I work even harder than my late husband. I have positive support from workmates and friends, especially my boss who is also a woman.

(A2 farmer)

The above quotes emphasise the challenges hindering women's growth in agribusiness. They support the quantitative data represented in Tables 7.3, 7.4, 7.5, and 7.6. Additional challenges emanating from the quotes are: (1) failure to process payment on time on the part of the GMB (a state-owned commodity trading enterprise responsible for ensuring national food security through production, procurement, and management of cereal crops in Zimbabwe), (2) theft of farm produce and equipment, (3) the high cost of electricity and water, (4) and cash flow problems. The quotes also indicate gender-specific challenges, such as: (1) women being undermined by male farm workers; (2) lack of support from family and the community, especially when the spouse dies; (3) society despising women who are financially independent; and (4) women being accused of causing the death of their spouse. The qualitative insights also reveal the strategies devised by the women to overcome some of the challenges.

They include: (1) installation of irrigating equipment to enhance the quality of farm produce, (2) avoiding selling cereal crops to the GMB, (3) selling farm produce to informal markets, (4) buying inputs in bulk, and (5) sharing transportation costs.

Discussion of results

Pre-production challenges and value chain development

The results indicate that women experience numerous pre-production related challenges along the value chain (see Table 7.3). These include, among others, the rising cost of agricultural inputs, lack of availability of farming loans, and inadequate supply of farming inputs and equipment on the local market. The mean scores for these challenges are above 3. The qualitative insights also highlight and support some of these challenges. These findings agree with extant literature, which states that women encounter numerous challenges in value chain development (Tallontire, 2005; Coles & Mitchell, 2011; Laven & Verhart, 2011; Mitchell & Coles, 2011; Gobezie, 2013; Apotheker et al., 2014; Negi & Anand, 2015).

In contrast, the respondents did not agree that lack of irrigation facilities, poor infrastructure, the low ratio of extension officers to farmers, and poorly resourced extension officers are severe challenges that affect value chain development (see Table 7.3). The mean scores of these challenges are less than 3. These findings contradict extant literature (Apotheker et al., 2014; Applefield & Jun, 2014). While the challenge of poor infrastructure is applicable to other developing countries, it appears that it is not prevalent in the Zimbabwean context. This is because Zimbabwe generally has good infrastructure inherited in the 1980s from the colonial government but which subsequent governments have unfortunately not maintained well. Furthermore, Mashonaland West Province was previously considered as the breadbasket of Africa (Mupedziswa, 2011). It thus makes sense that it will have good infrastructure systems.

The results also indicate that the percentage of total variation accounted for by latent factors for pre-production challenges is low (33.88%). This implies that the pre-production challenges that are affecting women empowerment in agriculture need to be explored further, to identify other challenges that may have been omitted in this study. A low Cronbach Alpha statistic of 0.595 supports this.

Post-production challenges and value chain development

The results indicate that women encounter numerous post-production challenges relating to value chains as indicated by mean scores of above 3 for all the issues raised (see Table 7.4). The qualitative insights also highlight and support some of these issues. Similar to pre-production challenges, the results correlate with extant literature (e.g. Barrientos, 2001; Maheshwar & Chanakwa,

2006; Reddy et al., 2010; Coles & Mitchell, 2011; Laven & Verhart, 2011; Mitchell & Coles, 2011; Trienekens, 2011; Pyburn & Terrillon, 2013; Apotheker et al., 2014; Göbel et al., 2015; Negi & Anand, 2015; Louw & Jordaan, 2016).

A key issue that emerged from the interviews was the fact that the GMB was failing to pay farmers on time for agricultural produce. This has negatively affected the success of agribusinesses in Zimbabwe, especially considering the lack of farming loans, as it causes cash flow challenges. The issues raised not only heighten the risk of food insecurity in Zimbabwe, but also considerably reduce farmers' contribution to overall agricultural production in the country (UNDP, 2012). Providing women with essential tools and resources has a significant impact on agricultural productivity, especially with respect to value chain development. Such measures require buy-in and commitment for positive change to be affected. Paying farmers on time motivates them to increase production.

The low percentage of total variation (42.68%) accounted for by the latent factors for post-production challenges implies that the challenges need to be explored further to understand the core issues affecting women. However, these results are still more influential than pre-production challenges (33.88%).

Socio-cultural factors and value chain development

The results show that socio-cultural factors hinder women's participation in value chain development, as indicated by a mean score of 3 for all factors (see Table 7.6). The qualitative quotes also provide a detailed perspective on these challenges. These findings are in agreement with extant literature on how deeply rooted social norms hinder value chain development (Barrientos, 2001; Tallontire, 2005; Coles & Mitchell, 2011; Laven & Verhart, 2011; Mitchell & Coles, 2011; Shackleton et al., 2011; KIT, Agri-ProFocus & IIRR, 2012; Gobezie, 2013; Pyburn & Terrillon, 2013; Apotheker et al., 2014; Göbel et al., 2015; Negi & Anand, 2015).

Women in agro-businesses and implications for value chain development

The results point to the need for a concerted effort by all stakeholders to find solutions to the challenges that hinder women's participation in agriculture value chain development. The stakeholders should include all actors in the value chain, the government, development practitioners, the private sector, and the community. Women should play an integral role in developing solutions because, in most cases, such forums are dominated by men who do not really understand the influence of gender inequality in the value chains. The government should (1) invest more resources in infrastructure and technology development, (2) provide resources and agriculture support services (e.g. agriculture extension officers) to enable them to perform their duties effectively, (3) pay farmers on time, and (4) support land ownership for women. The government should also adopt and implement policies that support economic growth (e.g. favourable export incentives) and enhance citizens' buying power. Finally, the government should ensure that there is ongoing debate around gender inequality as a way of educating its citizens. More importantly, it should invest additional resources in educating the girl child and in education in general.

The private sector, especially agro-based organizations, should invest in resources (e.g. financial, training, and skills development) through Corporate Social Investment (CSI) to support women in agro-businesses. One such initiative would be establishing schemes to support women to acquire inputs for production. Equipping women with skills to participate in global markets would increase their profit margins, and the private sector would benefit through increased sales. There is also a need to develop innovative financial solutions to support women in agro-businesses. Value co-creation with rural women is one of the viable options for sustainable development, especially with regard to organic farming, which provides healthier alternatives for poor communities. Supporting women in value chain development improves food security, alleviates poverty, and promotes rural economic development.

Conclusion

This chapter explored the challenges hindering women's economic empowerment in value chain development. It showed that women encounter various challenges in the value chain development process that negatively affect their earnings. These challenges are deeply rooted in socio-cultural factors that perpetuate gender inequality in value chain development. They include lack of access to resources and support services, such as financial and agricultural extension services and agricultural information and training; poor infrastructure; low levels of access to technology; and a lack of access to lucrative markets. All stakeholders in value chain development should thus direct more attention to developing strategies to solve these challenges, and women should play an integral part in coming up with solutions.

The government needs to create a conducive and enabling environment that fosters economic development by implementing policies that ease the process of registering businesses, offering guarantees for agribusiness loans, and opening up export opportunities for women in agro-businesses. There is also a need for innovative financial solutions to support women-run agro-businesses by formalising their saving clubs. The private sector, especially firms within the agricultural sector, should invest resources through Corporate Social Responsibility to support value chain development. The initiatives could include bespoke training in business management skills and marketing of their products. The training programmes should be supported by provision of finance, farming inputs, leasing of shared equipment, and improved hybrid seeds for better yields.

Technology is key in creating a competitive advantage for women agribusinesses. Computer application programmes that link producers and the rest of the value chain system, such as consumers, the services of agriculture extension officers, and financial institutions, would go a long way in increasing efficiency along the value chain. This is key to improving communication in value chain development. The importance of investing more resources in quality education for the girl child cannot be overemphasized, as it is the foundation for a better life and sustainable development. Provision of quality education opens up opportunities for women in every sphere of their lives.

The study suffered two limitations. First, it was conducted in one of the ten provinces in Zimbabwe, namely Mashonaland West. Secondly, non-probability sampling techniques were utilised to identify the respondents. As a result, the findings cannot be generalised to all provinces in Zimbabwe. However, the study contributes to the debate on the economic empowerment of women in agro-businesses and value chain development. Future studies could explore and unpack these challenges further. The most appropriate means to promote value addition in agro-businesses could be examined in more depth and detail, incorporating men to form control groups. Many other areas could be explored in relation to this subject. They include the role of education, training, government and private sector support in value chain development, as well as how women could benefit from organic farming and accessing export markets. Such research could be useful in informing the formulation of policies to foster sustainable economic development and poverty eradication.

References

African Development Bank. (2014). Economic empowerment of African women through equitable participation in agricultural value chains, 1–148. Retrieved from www.afdb.org/fileadmin/uploads/afdb/Documents/Publications/Economic_Empowerment_of_African_Women_through_Equitable_Participation_in___Agricultural_Value_Chains.pdf

Apotheker, R., Laven, A., & Verhart, N. (2014). The gender and cocoa livelihoods toolbox: A practical guide for business to work on gender in the cocoa livelihood program matching grants. World Cocoa Foundation, 1–150. Retrieved from www.worldcocoafoundation.org/wp-content/uploads/files_mf/1476298058TheGenderandCocoaLivelihoodToolboxDecember2014.pdf

Applefield, A., & Jun, J. (2014). Working with women: An essential component of global food security and agricultural development. *Fletcher F. World Aff., 38*(2), 185–192. Retrieved from www.fletcherforum.org/wp-content/uploads/2014/09/Applefield-Jun_Vol38No2.pdf

Bachmann, J. (2002). *Market gardening: A start-up guide.* ATTRA. Retrieved from https://douglas.extension.wisc.edu/files/2010/05/Market-Gardening-Getting-Started-ATTRA.pdf

Barrientos, S. (2001). Gender, flexibility and global value chains. *IDS bulletin, 32*(3), 83–93.

Başer, U., & Bozoğlu, M. (2018). Determination of value-creating activities in the agricultural value chain. *Turkish Journal of Agriculture-Food Science and Technology, 6*(8), 1002–1007.

Bengtsson, M. (2016). How to plan and perform a qualitative study using content analysis. *NursingPlus Open, 2*, 8–14.

Burney, J. A., Naylor, R. L., & Postel, S. L. (2013). The case for distributed irrigation as a development priority in sub-Saharan Africa. *Proceedings of the National Academy of Sciences, 110*(31), 12513–12517.

Clay, P. M., & Feeney, R. (2019). Analyzing agribusiness value chains: A literature review. *International Food and Agribusiness Management Review, 22*(1), 31–46.

Coles, C., & Mitchell, J. (2011). *Gender and agricultural value chains: A review of current knowledge and practice and their policy implications* (ESA Working Paper No. 11–05).

Derera, E. (2015). *Women's economic empowerment and entrepreneurship in agriculture: A case of Mashonaland West Province in Zimbabwe* (Unpublished doctoral dissertation, University of KwaZulu-Natal, South Africa).

Devaux, A., Torero, M., Donovan, J., & Horton, D. (2018). Agricultural innovation and inclusive value-chain development: A review. *Journal of Agribusiness in Developing and Emerging Economies, 8*(1), 99–123.

Donovan, J., Franzel, S., Cunha, M., Gyau, A., & Mithöfer, D. (2015). Guides for value chain development: A comparative review. *Journal of Agribusiness in Developing and Emerging Economies, 5*(1), 2–23.

Food and Agriculture Organization (2011). The state of food and agriculture (2010–2011). *Women in agriculture: Closing the gender gap for development*, 1–160. Retrieved from www.fao.org/docrep/013/i2050e/i2050e.pdf

Gereffi, G., & Fernandez-Stark, K. (2011). *Global value chain analysis: A primer*. Durham, NC: Center on Globalization, Governance and Competitiveness (CGGC), Duke University.

Gereffi, G., & Frederick, S. (2010). *The global apparel value chain, trade and the crisis: challenges and opportunities for developing countries*. The World Bank.

Ghosh, S., & Vinod, D. (2017). What constrains financial inclusion for women? Evidence from Indian micro data. *World Development, 92*, 60–81.

Göbel, C., Langen, N., Blumenthal, A., Teitscheid, P., & Ritter, G. (2015). Cutting food waste through cooperation along the food supply chain. *Sustainability, 7*(2), 1429–1445.

Gobezie, G. (2013). Promoting empowerment of women and gender equality through integrated microfinance, value-chain support and gender capacity building: The case of Bukonzo Joint Cooperative Microfinance Service Ltd (Uganda), 1–24. Retrieved from www.findevgateway.org/case-study/2013/02/promoting-empowerment-women-and-gender-equality-through-integrated-microfinance

Golla, A. M., Malhotra, A., Nanda, P., & Mehra, R. (2011). Understanding and measuring women's economic empowerment. *Definition, framework, indicators*. Washington DC: International Centre for Research on Women. Retrieved from www.icrw.org/sites/default/files/publications/Understanding-measuring-womens-economic-empowerment.pdf

Gwate, O. (2015). Presence and functionality of rangeland management institutions: The case of Insindi smallholder resettlement in Gwanda, Zimbabwe. *Global Journal of Human-Social Science Research, 14*(8), 1–8.

Härdle, W. K., & Simar, L. (2012). Canonical correlation analysis. In W. K. Härdle & L. Simar, *Applied Multivariate Statistical Analysis* (pp. 385–395). Berlin: Springer.

Hesse-Biber, S. N. (Ed.). (2013). *Feminist research practice: A primer*. Thousand Oaks, CA: Sage Publications.

Jayne, T. S., Mather, D., & Mghenyi, E. (2010). Principal challenges confronting small-holder agriculture in sub-Saharan Africa. *World Development, 38*(10), 1384–1398.

Juma, C. (2015). *The new harvest: Agricultural innovation in Africa.* Oxford: Oxford University Press.

Kaplinsky, R., & Morris, M. (2016). Thinning and thickening: Productive sector policies in the era of global value chains. *The European Journal of Development Research, 28*(4), 625–645.

Kistruck, G. M., Beamish, P. W., Qureshi, I., & Sutter, C. J. (2013). Social intermediation in base-of-the-pyramid markets. *Journal of Management Studies, 50*(1), 31–66.

KIT, Agri-ProFocus, & IIRR. 2012. *Challenging chains to change: Gender equity in agricultural value chain development.* Amsterdam: KIT Publishers.

Kolavalli, S., Mensah-Bonsu, A., & Zaman, S. (2015). Agricultural value chain development in practice: Private sector-led smallholder development (IFPRI Discussion Paper No. 1460), 1–36.

Krejcie, R. V., & Morgan, D. W. (1970). Determining sample size for research activities. *Educational and psychological measurement, 30*(3), 607–610.

Lagarde, C. (2013). A new global economy for a new generation. A speech delivered at introduction: Priorities for 2013. Davos, Switzerland: International Monteary Fund. Retrieved from www.imf.org/external/np/speeches/2013/012313.htm.

Laven, A., & Verhart, N. (2011). Addressing gender equality in agricultural value chains: Sharing work in progress. *Nijmegen, The Netherlands*, 1–17.

Louw, A., & Jordaan, D. (2016). Supply chain risks and smallholder fresh produce farmers in the Gauteng province of South Africa. *Southern African Business Review, 20*(1), 286–312.

Maheshwar, C., & Chanakwa, T. S. (2006). Postharvest losses due to gaps in cold chain in India-a solution. *IV international conference on managing quality in chains: The integrated view on fruits and vegetables quality, 712*, 777–784.

Malapit, H. J. L., & Quisumbing, A. R. (2015). What dimensions of women's empowerment in agriculture matter for nutrition in Ghana? *Food Policy, 52*, 54–63.

Mehra, R., & Hill Rojas, M. (2008). Women, food security and agriculture in a global marketplace. *International Center for Research on Women (ICRW)*, 1–20. Retrieved from www.icrw.org/files/publications/A-Significant-Shift-Women-Food%20Security-and-Agriculture-in-a-Global-Marketplace.pdf

Ministry of Lands and Rural Resettlement (2015). About the Ministry. Retrieved from www.lands.gov.zw/home/about-the-ministry

Mitchell, J., & Coles, C. (Eds.). (2011). *Markets and rural poverty: Upgrading in value chains.* Ottawa, Canada: IDRC.

Mosedale, S. (2005). Assessing women's empowerment: Towards a conceptual framework. *Journal of International Development, 17*(2), 243–257.

Mupedziswa, R. (2011). Climate change and its effect on urban housing and liveable cities: the case of Harare, Zimbabwe. In B. Yuen, & A. Kumssa (Eds.), *Climate Change and Sustainable Urban Development in Africa and Asia* (pp. 243–262). Dordrecht, the Netherlands: Springer.

Negi, S., & Anand, N. (2015). Issues and challenges in the supply chain of fruits and vegetables sector in India: a review. *International Journal of Managing Value and Supply Chains, 6*(2), 47–62.

OECD (2012). Women's economic empowerment. *The OECD DAC Network on Gender Equality (GENDERNET)*, 1–29. Retrieved from www.oecd.org/dac/povertyreduction/50157530.pdf

Orr, A., Donovan, J., & Stoian, D. (2018). Smallholder value chains as complex adaptive systems: A conceptual framework. *Journal of Agribusiness in Developing and Emerging Economies*, *8*(1), 14–33.

Park, Y. H., Jung, J. W., & Kim, Y. (2019). An analysis of Africa's agricultural value chain and lessons from Korea's agricultural development policies. *World Economy Brief*, *19*(9), 1–10.

Pyburn, R., & Terrillon, J. (2013). Achieving gender equity in agricultural value chains. New Agriculturist. Retrieved from www.new-ag.info/en/focus/focusItem.php?a=2923

Reddy, G. P., Murthy, M. R. K., & Meena, P. C. (2010). Value chains and retailing of fresh vegetables and fruits, Andhra Pradesh. *Agricultural Economics Research Review*, *23*, 455–460.

Shackleton, S., Paumgarten, F., Kassa, H., Husselman, M., & Zida, M. (2011). Opportunities for enhancing poor women's socioeconomic empowerment in the value chains of three African non-timber forest products (NTFPs). *International Forestry Review*, *13*(2), 136–152.

Shephard, R. W. (2015). *Theory of cost and production functions*. Princeton, NJ: Princeton University Press.

Shiferaw, B., Hellin, J., & Muricho, G. (2016). Markets access and agricultural productivity growth in developing countries: Challenges and opportunities for producer organizations. In J. Bijman, R. Muradian, & J. Schuurman (Eds.), *Cooperatives, Economic Democratization and Rural Development*, (pp. 103–122). Cheltenham, UK: Edward Elgar.

Slegh, H., Barker, G., Kimonyo, A., Ndolimana, P., & Bannerman, M. (2013). 'I can do women's work': Reflections on engaging men as allies in women's economic empowerment in Rwanda. *Gender and Development*, *21*(1), 15–30.

Stoian, D., Donovan, J., Elias, M., & Blare, T. (2018). Fit for purpose? A review of guides for gender-equitable value chain development. *Development in Practice*, *28*(4), 494–509.

Tallontire, A., Dolan, C., Smith, S., & Barrientos, S. (2005). Reaching the marginalised? Gender value chains and ethical trade in African horticulture. *Development in Practice*, *15*(3–4), 559–571.

Tobin, D., & Glenna, L. (2019). Value chain development and the agrarian question: Actor perspectives on native potato production in the highlands of Peru. *Rural Sociology*, *84*(3), 541–568.

Trienekens, J. H. (2011). Agricultural value chains in developing countries a framework for analysis. *International Food and Agribusiness Management Review*, *14*(2), 51–82.

Tripathi, R., Chung, Y. B., Deering, K., Saracini, N., Willoughby, R., Wills, O., & Churm, M. (2012). What works for women: Proven approaches for empowering women smallholders and achieving food security. *Oxfam Policy and Practice: Agriculture, Food and Land*, *12*(1), 113–140.

United Nations. (2019). *Transforming our world: The 2030 agenda for sustainable development*. Retrieved from https://sustainabledevelopment.un.org/content/documents/21252030%20Agenda%20for%20Sustainable%20Development%20web.pdf

United Nations Development Programme (UNDP). (2012). *Gender, agriculture and food security.* Retrieved from www.undp.org/content/dam/undp/library/gender/Gender%20and%20Environment/TM4_Africa_Gender-ClimateChange-and-Food-Security.pdf

United Nations Women (2015). *Annual Report 2015–2016.* Retrieved from www.unwomen.org/-/media/annual%20report/attachments/sections/library/un-women-annual-report-2015-2016-en.pdf?la=en&vs=3016

United Nations Women (2019). *Facts and Figures: Economic Empowerment.* Retrieved from www.unwomen.org/en/what-we-do/economic-empowerment/facts-and-figures

Weng, L., Boedhihartono, A. K., Dirks, P. H., Dixon, J., Lubis, M. I., & Sayer, J. A. (2013). Mineral industries, growth corridors and agricultural development in Africa. *Global Food Security, 2*(3), 195–202.

Women's Refugee Commission (2015). *Engaging men.* Retrieved from https://womensrefugeecommission.org/about/board/50-protection/gender/75-gender

World Bank (2012). Women's business and the law: Removing barriers to economic inclusion. *The World Bank and the International Finance Corporation,* 1–167. Retrieved from http://wbl.worldbank.org/~/media/FPDKM/WBL/Documents/Reports/2012/Women-Business-and-the-Law-2012.pdf

World Bank (2014). *Brief on the World Bank group's work on land and food security.* Retrieved from www.worldbank.org/en/topic/agriculture/brief/land-and-food-security

World Food Programme (2014). *WFP in Zimbabwe: 2014 in review.* Retrieved from www.wfp.org/sites/default/files/Zimbabwe%20Annual%20Report%202014.pdf

ZimStat (2015). Zimbabwe National Statistics Agency. *Zimbabwe National Statistics Agency,* p. 1–134.

Part IV

Design, integration, innovation, and change of BOP markets

8 Building and scaling social enterprise business models for BOP markets in Kenya

Giacomo Ciambotti, David Littlewood, Andrea Sottini, and Esther Nkatha M'ithiria

Introduction

The term Base of the Pyramid (BOP) describes the estimated 4.5 billion people globally living on less than US $8 per day (BOP Innovation Center, 2019). Despite this population's limited income, and its hitherto constrained access to products and services, it has been suggested that it represent a major opportunity for business (Prahalad & Hammond, 2002; Prahalad, 2009). Proponents of BOP strategies argue that if businesses can address the various unmet needs of this population, for instance in the supply of food, education, energy, and healthcare, that there is a "fortune" to be made, whilst doing so will also positively impact society (Prahalad, 2009). Growing interest in opportunities in BOP markets has led to the emergence of so-called "BOPreneurs" (Mohr, Sengupta, & Slater, 2012), amongst whom are social entrepreneurs launching ventures with an embedded social and/or environmental mission. These ventures are typically known as social enterprises, and they combine the goals and processes of the for-profit and non-profit sectors (Battilana & Lee, 2014; Ciambotti & Pedrini, 2019).

This chapter focuses on such BOP social enterprises. It examines BOP social enterprises in African markets, generally, and in Kenya more specifically, and how they build and scale their business models. To do so, it draws upon empirical qualitative case study research with 12 BOP social enterprises in Kenya, many of which also operate internationally across multiple African countries. This research entailed key informant interviews, which were undertaken in 2017 and 2018. We were guided by the following research questions: (1) how do social enterprises build their business models for BOP markets in Kenya?; (2) how do social enterprises scale their business models to serve BOP markets in Kenya?; and (3) what challenges do social enterprises in Kenya face when building and scaling their business models for BOP markets, and how do they overcome them?

Literature on venturing in BOP markets has blossomed over the last twenty years (for recent reviews, see Kolk, Rivera-Santos, & Rufin, 2014; Nahi, 2016; Dembek, Sivasubramaniam, & Chmielewski, 2019). Nevertheless, there remains much scope for further inquiry. One area identified as requiring further examination is the role of actors other than multinational enterprises in the BOP. Recent reviews by Kolk et al. (2014) and Dembek et al. (2019) specifically call for more research on the work of social entrepreneurs and social enterprises in the BOP. Our chapter is a response to these calls. Kolk et al. (2014) furthermore identify that Africa remains underrepresented as a context for BOP studies. They suggest that a "broadening of the empirical base, particularly to Africa, seems necessary, paralleling recent calls for more research on this continent" (p. 360). This chapter, and the empirical research in Africa it draws upon, contribute to such a project. It is further the case that whilst business model perspectives have been widely deployed in extant BOP scholarship, the business models of BOP social enterprises are less well understood. This reflects the general paucity of research specifically on BOP social enterprises. Thus, our study of the way BOP social enterprises build and scale their business models in Kenya represents a valuable contribution. Finally, Kolk et al. (2014) call for deeper analysis of BOP business models and greater understanding of their variation. Our chapter contributes towards developing such understanding.

Social enterprises in BOP markets focus on selling basic goods and services at affordable prices. In so doing, they aim to contribute to poverty eradication through pursuit of a business opportunity (Yunus, Moingeon, & Lehmann-Ortega, 2010; Bocken, Fil, & Prabhu, 2016). However, whilst low-income people in the BOP may be customers of social enterprises, they may also interact with them in other ways, for instance as suppliers, producers, employees, entrepreneurs, owners/shareholders, etc. (Littlewood & Holt, 2014). Indeed, recent iterations of BOP approaches, so-called BOP 2.0, 3.0, and beyond (Simanis, 2012; Cañeque & Hart, 2015; Nahi, 2016), stress the importance of value co-creation and the involvement of the poor as venture partners rather than just consumers. BOP scholars now advocate creating a fortune with the BOP rather than just in it (London & Hart, 2011), and this is something we are cognisant of in this chapter.

The chapter is structured as follows. We first outline the study's theoretical background, introducing the key concept of business models and reviewing extant work on their building and scaling for BOP markets. We also position our research in relation to extant literature and introduce significant works by Anderson and Billou (2007) on criteria for success in BOP markets, and Ansoff and McDonnell (1988) and Bocken et al. (2016) on scaling strategies. These works frame our later analysis and discussions. Next, we explain and justify our methodology and introduce the cases. Our findings on how Kenyan BOP social enterprises build and scale their business models, and the challenges they face in doing so, are then presented and considered in relation to extant literature. The chapter concludes with a discussion of its academic contributions, implications for practice, and future research directions and opportunities.

Theoretical background

Building social enterprise business models for BOP markets in Africa

The business model concept describes how organizations create, deliver, and capture value. Business models comprise three key components: value proposition, value delivery, and value capture (Amit & Zott, 2001; Teece, 2018). The value proposition is the firm or, in this case, the social enterprise's offering to address customers' needs or wants. Value delivery concerns the activities and networked relationships with partners and suppliers through which organizations deliver value (Amit & Zott, 2001; Seelos & Mair, 2005). This equates somewhat with an organization's internal and external value chains (Yunus et al., 2010). The value capture component describes how value is captured from revenues and how costs are managed during value creation and delivery (Hahn, Spieth, & Ince, 2018).

Designing these components and building business models for BOP markets in Kenya or elsewhere is not, however, straightforward (Seelos & Mair, 2005; Hahn et al., 2018). Anderson and Billou (2007) propose the four A's framework, identifying key criteria of affordability, availability, awareness, and acceptability, which they suggest need to be achieved to sell successfully in BOP markets. This framework is comprehensive, widely cited, and has been drawn upon in BOP studies across geographical and organizational contexts. It highlights some key challenges those venturing in BOP markets face, as they strive to deliver social impact and achieve financial objectives. This framework is elaborated below and is deployed in this chapter to analyse how our social enterprise case studies build their business models.

According to Anderson and Billou (2007), in the design of the value proposition component of BOP business models there is need to ensure affordability of the offering (see also Bowen, Morara, & Mureithi, 2009). BOP customers have low and often irregular incomes, so business models for BOP markets need to be appropriate for this cash flow and budgetary situation. Anderson and Billou (2007) argue, second, that there is a need to ensure the availability of products and services for individuals in BOP markets. Distribution channels should reach the BOP; there may even be a need to design alternative distribution strategies to deliver offerings to particularly isolated communities. Third, it is suggested that awareness is important. Those building business models for BOP markets need to ensure customers are aware of their products and services, and they can do this by establishing strong relationships with customers to grow demand for their offering (Bowen et al., 2009; London, Anupindi, & Sheth, 2010). Finally, when building business models for BOP markets, Anderson and Billou (2007) suggest that it is important to understand and factor in local needs, and to align with the heterogeneous cultures of BOP communities. Therefore, products or services should be designed and adapted for local cultures, tastes, or socio-economic conditions to ensure acceptability. Gaining acceptability makes customers more willing to buy products or services, and to distribute or sell them on behalf of ventures, including social enterprises.

In addition to the difficulty of achieving Anderson and Billou's (2007) four A's, BOP ventures in Africa, including social enterprises, face various market related challenges limiting the potential for business growth (London et al., 2010; Ciambotti & Pedrini, 2019). The first of these relates to infrastructural limitations and a potential lack of suitable distribution channels (Anderson &

Billou, 2007; Rivera-Santos, Holt, Littlewood, & Kolk, 2015). Across Africa, transport links remain underdeveloped. Rail services are slow and infrequent, whilst roads may be badly maintained and impassable during certain times of the year. This increases travel times and makes some journeys impossible. Rural villages, and BOP customers, distributors, and producers living there, are thus isolated and unable to access or supply products and services. Setting up an entirely new distribution channel is also costly (Katz, Koh, & Karamchandani, 2012), especially for resource-constrained social enterprises. Additionally, in African BOP markets there are often few established formal economy distributors, and those that exist may lack sufficient warehousing or cold storage. This can reduce the geographical range of product distribution and limit the sale of some perishable products (e.g. yoghurt). Furthermore, BOP markets are fragmented. Customers are often geographically dispersed, increasing the costs of reaching them (Manning, Kannothra, & Wissman-Weber, 2017). This also creates challenges for the provision of after-sale services.

As identified earlier, BOP social enterprises in Africa face challenges relating to the limited and irregular income of their customers (Goyal, Sergi, & Kapoor, 2017; Ciambotti, Sottini, & Sydow, 2019b). People in the BOP are frequently either unemployed, precariously or vulnerably employed in the informal economy – perhaps as casual or seasonal workers – or they follow subsistence livelihoods (International Labour Organization, 2019). These constrained financial circumstances of customers challenge BOP social enterprises and wider ventures, as the price of the products and services offered may be too high for low-income individuals and households. Additional complexity and costs ensue where customers are not able to pay for products in full at the time of purchase. These challenges of cost and pricing pressurise social enterprise profit margins, and cash flows, when working in BOP markets (Desa & Koch, 2014).

A further challenge for BOP social enterprises, and wider ventures, is the often limited education, literacy, and numeracy levels of individuals in the BOP (Simanis, 2012). Such individuals may also be unfamiliar with the products or services social enterprises are selling, which have hitherto not been part of local consumption cultures. Indeed, literature has suggested that individuals in the BOP may lack "cultural competence" in product consumption (Simanis, 2012). Awareness of the potential benefits of using certain products or services may also be lacking, meaning demand is low; examples include insurance and sanitary products (Anderson & Billou, 2007). Furthermore, in Africa, building awareness and loyalty amongst customers is challenging where they may not be accessible using conventional advertising and media channels, and where informal purchasing is strong (Zoogah, Peng, & Woldu, 2015; Manning et al., 2017; Lashitew, Bals, & van Tulder, 2018).

A final challenge relates to BOP customer heterogeneity, reflecting cultural diversity across Africa (Rivera-Santos et al., 2015). Customer needs and preferences may vary significantly across the continent and even within countries, and social enterprises may lack sufficient cultural knowledge and the capabilities to respond to local particularities (Rivera-Santos et al., 2015; Zoogah et al., 2015). If social enterprises offer products that do not meet local cultures and tastes, they may struggle to gain acceptability (Anderson & Billou, 2007), which can be a significant barrier to market penetration.

To summarise, in this section we have introduced the business model concept and discussed work on BOP business models, including those established by social enterprises. We have also identified key criteria for success and explained Anderson and Billou's (2007) four A's framework. We have further discussed challenges to be surmounted when developing BOP business models, particularly in African contexts (Seelos & Mair, 2005; Davies, Haugh, & Chambers, 2018). From our review, it is clear that more research is needed specifically on how social enterprises can overcome such challenges to develop BOP business models in Africa. In this chapter, we shed light on this, drawing upon our empirical case study research.

Scaling social enterprise business models for BOP markets in Africa

In the social entrepreneurship field, "scaling" is used to describe processes whereby social enterprises improve their financial performance and social impacts (Davies et al., 2018). Authors have identified that scaling social impact may encompass strategies of "scaling up", where more impact is delivered to the same beneficiary groups, as well as "scaling out", where the number of beneficiaries served is expanded (Lyon & Fernandez, 2012; Davies et al., 2018). Other scholars conceptualise them somewhat differently. For instance, Moore, Riddell, and Vocisano (2015) suggest that scaling up refers to impacts on laws and institutions, and scaling out to impacts on greater numbers of beneficiaries. Interestingly, Moore et al. (2015) also introduce the notion of "scaling deep" to refer to impact on cultural roots and informal institutions. Clearly, there remains debate on the meaning and forms that social enterprise scaling can take; nevertheless, there is broad agreement that it encompasses an expansion of financial performance and social impact, and that scaling is different in social enterprises compared to more traditional business ventures (Austin, Stevenson, & Wei-Skillern, 2006; Davies et al., 2018).

Scaling a solution can increase the social impact of a social venture and its contribution to addressing previously unmet social and/or environmental needs (Seelos & Mair, 2005). Financial dimensions of scaling enhance a social enterprise's sustainability, which is crucial to sustain any social impact (Katz et al., 2012; Bocken et al., 2016; Davies et al., 2018). Some social entrepreneurship scholars examining scaling processes focus on the role of social entrepreneurs (Bloom & Smith, 2010; Smith, Kistruck, & Cannatelli, 2016), while others adopt a more organizational perspective (Bocken et al., 2016; Davies et al., 2018). Recent work has started to examine business model scaling in BOP social enterprises (Gebauer, Haldimann, & Saul, 2017a; Gebauer, Saul, & Haldimann 2017b; Ciambotti et al., 2019b). Gebauer et al. (2017a) suggest that social enterprises may need to innovate and reconfigure their business models when scaling to overcome barriers of operating in the BOP, including incorporating local knowledge. They further identify modification and experimentation as important activities. Despite this emerging work, there remain limits to the depth of our understanding of scaling by BOP social enterprises (Bocken et al., 2016; British Council, 2017; Davies et al., 2018). Examination of this subject in African contexts also remains limited. The research presented in this chapter therefore provides further insights on this understudied topic.

There are particularities of scaling in social enterprises, especially when serving BOP markets. However, extant literature suggests that at least some notions of how scaling works in traditional businesses can be translated to social enterprise contexts, and that social enterprises may select scaling strategies similar to those adopted by for-profit ventures. For example, Bocken et al. (2016) identify that social enterprises may scale their businesses through four main strategies: market penetration, market development, product development, and diversification (after Ansoff & McDonnell, 1988). Bocken et al. (2016) unpack these scaling strategies for a social enterprise context suggesting two further activities important in supporting scaling: (1) diversifying revenue streams and (2) increasing revenues per stream. In our analysis of business model scaling in social enterprises in this chapter, we draw upon this recent work of Bocken et al. (2016), which is grounded in the well-known and widely applied framing of Ansoff and McDonnell (1988).

Scaling remains challenging for social enterprises, including, if not especially, those working in BOP markets. For instance, Katz et al. (2012) examined a sample of 439 social enterprise inclusive business ventures and found that only 32% were commercially viable and had the potential to scale, whilst just 13% were actually operating at scale. Extant research suggests that in social enterprises, the scaling process often fails because of challenges in balancing financial and social impact scale up (Dees, Anderson, & Wei-Skillern, 2002).

One of the reasons for this difficulty relates to access to financial resources and the fact that grants and wider external funding often focuses on supporting innovative "breakthrough" ideas and early-stage ventures rather than the scaling up of existing ones (Desa & Koch, 2014). A specific challenge for scaling BOP social enterprises is that of gaining additional revenues from low-income BOP customers (Santos, Pache, & Birkholz, 2015). This is both a practical challenge, as these customers inherently have little money, and can also raise ethical dilemmas for mission-driven social enterprises around potential exploitation of the poor. Those operating in BOP markets in Africa also often have to cope with underdeveloped infrastructure as well as the existence of institutional voids in BOP markets, which represent a further difficulty and source of complexity when scaling (Bowen et al., 2009; Yunus et al., 2010)

To conclude, whilst we understand some of the challenges BOP social enterprises face when scaling their business models, there remains room for further inquiry. Research is needed addressing business model scaling by BOP social enterprises in African contexts and examining how BOP social enterprise business models are dynamically reconfigured during scaling, all of which are covered in this chapter. Furthermore, there is a need to identify key factors for success in BOP social enterprise scaling and to provide insights for practice (Dees et al., 2002; Bocken et al., 2016; Davies et al., 2018).

Methodology

Research setting

This research aims to shed light on how social enterprises build and scale business models to serve BOP markets in Kenya. It considers the challenges such ventures face in doing so, offering implications for practice. Due to the understudied nature of this topic, we adopted an exploratory, qualitative approach that entailed multiple-case study research (Eisenhardt, 1989) and used a purposeful sampling logic (Patton, 1990; Gehman, Glaser, Eisenhardt, Gioia, Langley, & Corley, 2018). The qualitative approach adopted is particularly suited to researching questions of "why" and "how", to researching new and emerging topic areas (Yin, 1984; Eisenhardt & Graebner, 2007), and when collecting data in complex institutional environments like those found in Kenya, and Africa more widely (Ghauri, 2004).

Scholars have identified that Africa represents a rich setting for further social entrepreneurship research (Rivera-Santos et al., 2015; Kolk & Rivera-Santos, 2018). Amongst African countries, Kenya has been a regional hub for the establishment of social enterprises, including those targeting the BOP (Zoogah et al., 2015; British Council, 2017). This made it ideal as the setting for our study. Numerous social enterprises operate in Kenya, across various industries, and at different life stages. However, whilst Kenya has witnessed a blossoming of social entrepreneurial activity, it remains quite a challenging place to do business – for both social and more traditional business ventures. For instance, although Kenya now ranks 61st globally on the World Bank's Ease of Doing Business Index 2019, its performance on important metrics around starting a business (126th), registering property (122nd), or paying taxes (91st) is lower (World Bank, 2019a). There is also no legislation expressly relating to social enterprises in Kenya, and government engagement with the sector remains nascent (British Council, 2017). These formal institutional challenges are furthermore accompanied by limitations in physical infrastructure and market architecture. Conversely, and from a more positive perspective, Kenya's GDP grew by 6.32% in 2018 (World Bank, 2019b). It also has one of the largest BOP markets in Africa in terms of BOP household expenditure (Euromonitor International, 2019), which accounts for an estimated 84% of national yearly household consumption (Business Call to Action, 2019). Kenya has also been at the forefront of technological advances in East Africa and the continent more widely. There are therefore substantial opportunities for BOP social enterprises operating in Kenya.

Data collection

Data collection occurred in August 2017 and November 2018. Desk-based research was first undertaken analysing reports from international and local organizations and institutions (e.g. E4Impact Foundation, World Bank, GrowthAfrica, etc.). We used these to identify interesting and relevant cases that were then contacted to participate. We adopted a theoretical sampling approach (Eisenhardt & Graebner, 2007) with the aim of illuminating and extending our understanding and theorising about how BOP social enterprises in Kenya build and scale their business models. Our cases were social enterprises – they were trading for social and/or environmental social purposes – and all had operated for at least two years. They all also sold products and/or services in BOP markets in Kenya. These core criteria framed our case selection; beyond them, however, we tried to identify Kenyan BOP social enterprises selling various kinds of products and services to gain richer, more varied empirical evidence and to, thus, develop a more comprehensive understanding of the phenomenon (Gehman et al., 2018).

We carried out a first round of interviews with six cases in August 2017 in Nairobi. The interview protocol was revised following insights from these initial interviews (Gehman et al., 2018). Another 12 interviews were undertaken in November 2018. In total, 18 semi-structured interviews were completed across 12 cases. Whilst the interview protocol was adapted after the initial interviews, overall, across the 18 interviews, it covered four key topics aligned with the study's research questions. These were: (1) general history of the social enterprise; (2) the social business model; (3) challenges faced and how these were overcome; and (4) scaling strategies and pathway to growth. Interviews were mostly conducted with founder social entrepreneurs or senior leaders. They lasted one hour on average, with almost 18 hours of interviews in total. They were recorded and subsequently transcribed verbatim.

Table 8.1 provides a summary of each case, including a description of the social enterprise and information on its age, sector, and who and how many people were interviewed. From these interviews, plus analysis of wider company documentation, we identified the main characteristics of the BOP social enterprises' business models, how they developed, what challenges they faced, and their approach to and experiences of scaling.

Data analysis

Data analysis first entailed within-case analysis drawing upon the transcribed interviews and our notes, and using tables and matrices. For each case, we inductively identified initial codes linked to our research questions (Miles & Huberman, 1994). In this way, we were able to develop an understanding of each case's business model, how it was built, their scaling activities, and the challenges they faced. Cross-case analysis was then undertaken in which similarities and differences between cases and their associated codes were identified, following Eisenhardt (1989) and Gehman et al. (2018). This enabled us to find common patterns and, through a refinement process, consolidate to identify higher-level codes and constructs (Eisenhardt & Graebner, 2007). These higher-level codes and constructs were then more deductively assessed,

Table 8.1 Case study BOP social enterprises in Kenya

#	Name	Sector	Social enterprise description	Year of start-up	No. of interviews	Role
1	Innovation Eye Centre (IEC)	Healthcare	Health social enterprise offering high-quality, affordable, and accessible comprehensive eye care services to communities in Kenya's southwestern region.	2013	2	CEO & Co-Founder
2	Totohealth	ICT / Healthcare	Social enterprise that utilises mobile technology to allow parents from marginalized communities to monitor their pregnancies and children, as well as empowering them with vital health information.	2014	2	CEO & Founder
3	M-Kopa	Energy	Social enterprise that provides a solar-powered system (with a home kit) offering a more cost-effective energy solution to rural Kenyans.	2011	1	COO
4	Strauss Energy	Energy	Social enterprise that provides integrated photovoltaic roofing materials to produce sustainable clean energy, contribute to addressing the energy gap in Kenya, and address sustainability in BOP/middle-class households.	2008	2	CEO & Co-Founder
5	Bio Afriq Energy	Briquettes & cooking stoves	Social enterprise that manufactures and sells pellet fuels from no-fodder biomass waste. These fuels are used in conjunction with a cook stove, which is provided and installed for free.	2018	1	CEO & Founder
6	Ecotact	Services	Social enterprise that provides sanitation services to the BOP, making access to a decent bathroom affordable for every citizen.	2006	1	CEO & Founder
7	Africaqua	Water supply	Social enterprise that provides affordable, safe drinking water to customers in semi-arid areas of Kenya.	2016	1	CEO & Founder

(continued)

Table 8.1 Cont.

#	Name	Sector	Social enterprise description	Year of start-up	No. of interviews	Role
8	M-Paya	Financial services	A financial technology social venture that enables small, informal traders to accept mobile and digital money as a form of payment. It also offers micro–credit.	2015	2	CEO & Founder
9	Reliance Chama	Financial services	Social enterprise that aims to empower the poor and micro–enterprises to start or expand their businesses by offering flexible, convenient, and affordable financial services.	2014	1	CEO
10	Daisy Girl	Consumer goods	Social enterprise that designs and builds sustainable houses in rural areas and manufactures and sells washable pants and pads for women.	2015	1	CEO & Founder
11	Bubayi	Agro business	Social enterprise supplying improved, treated, and certified high-quality seeds to small farmers in Western Kenya. The venture contributes to sustainable farming practices and food security.	1963	2	Managing Director
12	Bidhaa Sasa	Durable goods	Social enterprise that distributes various kinds of goods to improve the lives of people in rural areas (i.e. solar panels, cookstoves, etc.). Also offers consumer credit to purchase those products.	2015	2	CEO

Source: authors' own data.

honed, and positioned in relation to extant literature, and particularly our theoretical framework comprising the four A's (Anderson & Billou, 2007), and the growth strategies of Ansoff and McDonnell (1988). Through this multi-step process, we developed and structured our findings, with different members of the research team performing sense checking of identified codes and constructs as part of the analysis.

Findings

How social enterprises build business models for BOP markets in Kenya

The case studies were (deliberately) quite varied, reflecting our aim to better understand how BOP social enterprises in Kenya build and scale their business models and the challenges they face in doing so. Turning first to how social enterprises in Kenya build business models for BOP markets, we gained fine-grained insights in relation to their development of each of the business model components: value proposition, value delivery, and value capture. As discussed previously, we furthermore analysed the actions they take when building business models through the lens of Anderson and Billou's (2007) four A's – awareness, acceptability, availability, and affordability – framework. Key findings are summarised in Table 8.2 and discussed in detail below.

Awareness

When building social enterprise business models to operate in Kenyan BOP markets, it is important to design a viable and clear value proposition and to make customers aware of products and/or services. The value proposition should reflect the social enterprise's social mission, with a clear link between the issues customers face and the venture's solution. Across our cases we observed the importance of a concrete value proposition to customers, with customers made aware of this through demonstrations and practical experiences of products and services. For instance, Bidhaa Sasa increased awareness by showcasing its offering (solar panels and cooking stoves) directly to customers in villages, who were able to try the product before they bought it.

Educational programmes may be required for BOP customers to become aware of and understand a social enterprise's products or services. Educating customers may include explaining to them the benefits of a product or service. For example, Innovation Eye Centre (IEC) delivers a customer education programme (Outreach Programme) to promote its product and sensitise customers on the importance of preventative healthcare and its positive implications for their daily lives. Similarly, Reliance Chama organized training sessions for customers who hitherto relied on informal credit-lenders who charge high interest rates.

Social enterprises need to be configured to deliver their value propositions. Our research found that, to deliver value, it can be important for social

Table 8.2 Key findings on building business models for Kenyan BOP markets and the four A's

Four A's	Value proposition	Value delivery	Value capture
Awareness	• Make the value proposition as simple and comprehensible as possible to show a clear relationship with customer needs. • Make the value proposition concrete, by demonstrating and providing experiences of the product/service.	• Increase customer knowledge of the benefits provided by the product/service through education (IEC, Totohealth, M-Kopa, Daisy Girl, Reliance Chama). • Build a field presence to spread knowledge of the value proposition through employees (M-Kopa, Strauss Energy, Reliance Chama). • Engage influential customers in the community who will become first promoters of the product/services (Bidhaa Sasa, Daisy Girl). • Co-promote the value proposition with NGOs, churches, schools, community groups, etc. (Africaqua, Bubayi, Bio Afriq Energy, Daisy Girl).	• Provide clear payment terms and methods using SMS (Totohealth, M-Paya, M-Kopa) or offline advertisement (Bidhaa Sasa, Ecotact). • Price the products and services to align with the price customers are already paying for equivalents (M-Kopa, Strauss Energy, Bio Afriq Energy, Bidhaa Sasa, Bubayi).
Acceptability	• Embed the value proposition in the local community to avoid perceptions of strangeness and raise acceptability. • Match the value proposition to local culture, tastes, languages, and customer education levels.	• Leverage social recognition of local influencers in the community to raise acceptability to other customers (Bidhaa Sasa, Totohealth). • Engage and integrate local micro-entrepreneurs (so-called village level entrepreneurs, VLEs) as touchpoints to embed in local community and facilitate acceptance (Africaqua, Bidhaa Sasa). • Partner with highly legitimate, recognised institutions and NGOs to increase own legitimacy with customers (Bubayi, Totohealth). • Use local vernacular in SMS to reach people of different ethnic groups and education levels (Totohealth, M-Paya, Reliance Chama).	• Improve brand image, communicate product and service quality and safety (Ecotact, Strauss Energy, Africaqua, Daisy Girl). • Make price transparent to increase customer trust (Bubayi, Reliance Chama). • Align payment methods to customer needs, e.g. mobile payments (Bidhaa Sasa, Totohealth, Strauss Energy, M-Kopa).

Availability	• Make the value proposition fill an infrastructure gap. Ensure closeness to customers, be able to "reach the last mile", and ensure fast delivery.	• Adopt a capillary distribution network using existing local distributors when skill and knowledge requirements are low (Africaqua, Bubayi, Bio Afriq Energy, Daisy Girl). • Create own distribution network when delivery requires high-level skills, or products/services are difficult to install (M-Kopa, Strauss Energy, Reliance Chama, Bidhaa Sasa). • Meet customers by organizing visits to the field or creating networking events for customers (IEC, Bubayi). • Leverage ICT to cover some infrastructure deficiencies: to achieve fast delivery (M-Kopa, Strauss Energy, Bidhaa Sasa, Reliance Chama); gaining and sharing information with customers (Totohealth, Ecotact); managing money transfer and payments (M-Paya, M-Kopa, Reliance Chama, Totohealth, Bubayi).	• Use of ICT (e.g. mobile payment) to unlock payments from customers, and 'reach the last mile' (M-Kopa, Totohealth, Bidhaa Sasa).
Affordability	• Match the value proposition to the (low) income of customers. • Match the value proposition to customers' variable cash flows.	• Provide close, easy access to products/services, reducing travelling costs for customers (IEC, Ecotact, M-Kopa). • Outsource production to local (M-Kopa, Ecotact) and/or foreign suppliers (Bidhaa Sasa, Strauss Energy, Bio Afriq Energy, Totohealth) to reduce production costs and rapidly reach economies of scale. • Reduce costs of marketing and promotion through partnership with NGOs and public institutions (Ecotact, Bubayi, Totohealth, Daisy Girl).	• Match customers' low income by cross-subsidizing, or reducing prices and/or mark-ups (IEC). • Match customers' variable cash flow by using pay-as-you-go (M-Kopa, Ecotact) or leasing methods with upfront fees and fixed repayments (Bidhaa Sasa, Strauss Energy). • Match customers' cash flows through customer financing, allowing them to buy the product and service whenever they need it (Bubayi, Bio Afriq Energy, Bidhaa Sasa).

Source: authors' own data.

enterprises to establish a field presence close to customers. For instance, M-Kopa developed a network of sales representatives close to customers and local communities, especially in rural areas. These sales agents explained the benefits of using solar energy versus traditional energy sources like wood or charcoal. Reliance Chama, meanwhile, positioned their offices close to two large slums, and the biggest retail market in Nairobi, allowing customers to meet their team whenever needed.

Another important aspect of value delivery relates to engaging customers as first promoters. Bidhaa Sasa uses women as first promoters for their products. They interact with them as "educated customers" willing to promote their products in the community and highlight their positive development impacts. This is detailed in the following quotation:

> *We exploit the power of the ladies who do the marketing themselves, also for nothing. . . . The reason is that they benefit from it. It improves their image because they want to help the people . . . it increases trust in them, and so they will have more opportunities in the future.*

(Interview Bidhaa Sasa)

Delivering value propositions may also entail social enterprises working in partnerships. Partnerships can include co-promotion to extend awareness. For example, IEC delivered its Outreach Programme in partnership with local health centres, schools, and churches. Meanwhile, Bubayi collaborated with Agri Experience, a consulting company supporting the development of farmers and seed companies. This partnership enables Bubayi to access a large network of small farmers for promotion and sensitization campaigns, including how its improved seeds can enhance crop yields.

Turning lastly to value capture, social enterprises operating in Kenyan BOP markets should clearly present their payment terms and methods. Enterprises may communicate this directly on product labels. Ecotact, for example, wrote on the entrance to its Eco-toilets the price and the time that customers can spend inside. This writing is easily understood, especially if translated into local languages. ICT also plays a critical role in communicating payment terms to customers. M-Paya and Totohealth use SMS technology to make customers aware of payment frequency, amount, and the account into which money should be paid. These SMS messages also include a payment deadline reminder. Finally, prices should reflect and be presented in relation to current customer costs for a product or service. For example, M-Kopa estimated that householders in Kenya are currently paying KSh 50 (around US $0.50) daily for kerosene. Consequently, they decided on a fixed daily payment of the same amount for their solar panels.

Acceptability

When devising value propositions, BOP social enterprises must also consider acceptability to customers. In gaining such acceptability, the embeddedness of a social enterprise within local communities was found to be important, so that customers feel close to the enterprise and don't perceive it as strange or foreign. For example, Daisy Girl provides sanitary pants and pads and, to be closer to customers, has partnered with community-based organizations and churches. To be accepted by customers, social enterprise value propositions should also be adapted to local cultures, tastes, languages, and education levels.

Additionally, acceptability must be considered in value delivery by social enterprises. For example, Totohealth faced a challenge when serving poorly educated, sometimes illiterate, and non-English speaking users. In response, Totohealth translated SMS content into different local languages and dialects, and they even converted some SMS messages into voice messages for the completely illiterate.

To ensure acceptability during value delivery, social enterprises may also leverage the social recognition of influential people in target communities, including engaging with village level entrepreneurs (VLEs). For instance, Bidhaa Sasa did this by leveraging the embeddedness of local women. Africaqua, meanwhile, partnered with VLEs to sell water in communities. These vendors act as a "touch point" between businesses and local customers, enabling enterprises to embed and, thus, increase acceptability.

Partnerships with local organizations may also enhance the acceptability of the social enterprise and its products. The venture Bubayi gained acceptability through a partnership with Kenya Agricultural and Livestock Research Organization (KALRO). KALRO is highly recognised and considered legitimate amongst local farmers, and this legitimacy then extended to Bubayi. Totohealth used similar strategies, co-promoting its services with high-legitimacy local hospitals and NGOs.

To capture value in BOP markets in Kenya, social enterprises need to gain and maintain customer acceptability. We observed that organizations enhanced their acceptability through improving their reputations. For instance, Africaqua invested in its brand, including strengthening the association of its light-blue and white coloured logo with safe, high-quality drinking water. The following quotation explains this approach:

> *I want to distinguish Africaqua from other vendors who sell dirty water to the community . . . I built a unique brand image with light-blue colours. People recognise my water as good and of safe quality!*

> (Africaqua)

Ecotact, meanwhile, initially faced mistrust of its products and was not accepted by communities. Consumers did not accept paying for toilet services, viewing that they should be free, even if the only ones available in slums were low-quality. Ecotact recruited the locally famous Miss Kenya to enhance acceptability of paying for Eco-toilets. Miss Kenya promoted the Eco-toilets in slums, showing that even famous people would use and pay for them. A final component of acceptability concerns payment method. Our cases (Totohealth,

Strauss Energy, and M-Kopa) highlight the importance of aligning payment method with customer preferences. All these enterprises used mobile payment platforms. By doing so, customers further accepted the products and services provided, enabling the ventures to capture value.

Availability

Kenya faces infrastructure challenges. This issue negatively affects the operations of BOP social enterprises that need to consider how to configure their value propositions to mitigate and even address this issue. Our cases show the importance of creating a value proposition that reflects closeness with customers and includes a direct presence in the field.

To deliver value in a way that ensures availability, social enterprises can build their operations close to customers. Reliance Chama, for example, placed its offices close to slums to facilitate one-to-one meetings with customers, as well as run educational programmes. Similarly, Bidhaa Sasa placed several of its offices in target communities, giving customers easy access to its personnel to arrange payments. Finally, IEC placed its hospital on the outskirts of Kisii town (a town in southwestern Kenya) to improve access for rural patients. Nevertheless, some patients still faced challenges going to the hospital, for instance due to disabilities, and IEC implemented its Eye Camp Initiative consisting of eye interventions delivered by doctors directly in rural and isolated parts of the county. This latter case shows the importance of social enterprises also sometimes going to customers.

To make products and services available to BOP customers, social enterprises can also utilise existing local informal distribution channels. For example, Africaqua delivers its water products to remote areas through a network of informal "Tuk-Tuk" (local small vehicle) drivers. This strategy is explained in the following quotation:

> Here in Kenya we have really good means of deliveries named tuk-tuk . . . they bring the water directly to the households. They are very fast and efficient; a tuk-tuk has a capacity of 30 jerry cans, and it is able to drive for around four to seven laps a day!
>
> (Africaqua)

Likewise, Daisy Girl exploited existing informal distributors to deliver sanitary pants and pads to women in rural areas, usually through "Boda Boda" (motorbike taxi) riders. A further possibility is for social enterprises to create their own distribution networks. In our cases we found this to be more likely when product or service delivery required advanced skills. For instance, M-Kopa requires its own sales agents to deliver and install solar panels and TV components to households in rural areas, as residents are unable to complete the installations themselves.

Finally, our cases show how the use of ICT may help to overcome a lack of distribution channels. Totohealth, which provides health information to pregnant women, uses SMS technology to do this. It works across Africa and fills infrastructure and service delivery gaps in rural areas through providing remote healthcare information, monitoring, and follow-up, at low cost. Mobile money technologies are also being used to increase the availability of financial services in African BOP markets. The M-Paya case uses this technology to lend money to rural and urban customers. Technological developments are also playing a crucial role in making energy available to BOP customers in Kenya. M-Kopa delivers energy through an off-grid solar panel system, with the energy flow able to be switched on and off remotely through mobile technology, based on customer demand. Finally, BOP customers, especially in rural areas, often live far from each other, thus receiving payments from them can be expensive for firms. We observed that ICT plays a critical role in value capture, helping social enterprises to unlock payments and reduce costs of delivery to the BOP. Social enterprises were using mobile apps to receive payments from customers; for instance, M-Kopa and Strauss Energy both partnered with M-Pesa (a Kenyan mobile money transfer system). When using such apps, transaction costs are minimised, the apps are readily available, and transferring money is quick, reliable, and safe.

Affordability

When developing value propositions for BOP markets, social enterprises also need to consider issues of affordability. Our research highlights that value propositions should align with the low incomes of BOP customers. However, there is a need to also be sensitive to their often irregular cash flows. For instance, such individuals may have seasonal incomes or rely on casual informal work that does not assure them of a consistent fixed wage.

To deliver value whilst ensuring affordability for BOP customers, social enterprises in Kenya can act in various ways. First, many BOP customers struggle to travel long distances to access products or services because of lack of funds or infrastructure and transportation limitations, which also make travel expensive. Social enterprises can develop business models to deliver products and provide services directly where BOP customers live, reducing travel costs for them. An example of this is the previously discussed Eye Camp Initiative by IEC. This initiative enabled customers to avoid accruing travel costs, making access to the service more affordable. In another example, Ecotact distributed its Eco-toilets across slums and especially at transit meeting points. Ecotact also designed a movable Eco-toilet which can be repositioned to populous and busy areas or where events, such as commemorations or electoral rallies, are occurring. This again saves consumers costs, making the product or service more affordable.

Production is another important aspect of value delivery and one where affordability needs to be considered. Outsourcing of production to specialised local or international suppliers can reduce costs and facilitate the achievement of economies of scale. In fact, organic growth typically requires, but can also be held back by, the need for expensive investments in machines and equipment.

Our cases avoided this through outsourcing. Building partnerships with local and international organizations like NGOs, churches, and community groups can also enable social enterprises to reduce costs of training, marketing, and promotion. For instance, Bubayi partnered with KALRO, which supplies basic seeds to famers. Bubayi exploited the channels KALRO had already established, avoiding the cost of creating its own distribution network. KALRO also promoted Bubayi's products to their network.

Affordability also impacts the design of products and services. Products and services for the BOP may be simply designed, with few extra features, to keep costs low, or they may be innovative low-cost solutions compared to traditional products and services. Social enterprises may also be more willing to accept slimmer margins on their products and services than are more commercial firms. Social enterprises can further achieve affordability through offering more flexible payment terms to customers. This latter approach was evident in the cases of Totohealth, Ecotact, and Africaqua, who all assisted customers with payments. Likewise, IEC assisted its customers with payment through a cross-subsidising approach. The enterprise offered the same quality service – eye surgery and eye health services – to all customers, with payment based on income. Revenue from high-paying patients subsidised costs for low-income patients.

Payment assistance may also be used to enable BOP consumers to purchase larger, more expensive goods and costly services. Bidhaa Sasa and Bio Afriq Energy opted for lease-to-own models. They divided payment for cookstoves into multiple small payments linked to the purchasing of biomass pellets. Ownership was transferred upon full payment for the product. Strauss Energy and M-Kopa, meanwhile, installed solar panels asking for a low upfront fee, and customers pay for energy through a "pay-as-you-go" approach. This enabled customers to make small payments when they desired and to utilise the product's benefits for a set amount of time. This action is explained in the following quotation:

> *Building a payment method close to the customers is very important to make the service affordable. Our beneficiaries have low income and irregular cash flows. . . . We helped people that could never afford any service through a repayment model that is working for them!*

(Strauss Energy)

Finally, some social enterprises offered finance to consumers to buy products or services and help them manage their cash flows. For example, Bubayi provided bean seeds for free; after the beans had grown, it purchased beans from them, reducing their credit balance.

In this section, we have explored how social enterprises build their business models for BOP markets in Kenya, achieving the four A's of awareness, acceptability, availability, and affordability. Next, we examine how they scale them.

How social enterprise scale business models for BOP markets in Kenya

Drawing upon the work of Ansoff and McDonnell (1988) and authors like Bocken et al. (2016), four principal scaling strategies for BOP social enterprises in Kenya are identified: market penetration, market development, product development, and diversification. For each scaling strategy, we discuss its implications for the different business model components – value proposition, value delivery, and value capture. Discussions draw upon our various case studies. Table 8.3 provides a summary of key findings.

Market penetration

One way BOP social enterprises in Kenya may scale is through market penetration – selling more of their existing products or services in current markets. In our research, we discovered that to penetrate Kenyan BOP markets, social enterprises should leverage their value propositions and promote their businesses to increase their customer base. For instance, the case study IEC uses social marketing to educate and raise customer awareness of its products and services through its Outreach Programme. This initiative helps IEC connect with customers, even in remote rural areas, who would otherwise be unaware of its services.

To penetrate BOP markets, social enterprises can also adjust their prices to better align with customers' willingness and ability to pay. An example of this is provided by Totohealth when it launched its "Newborn kit" (this provides basic health products, such as sanitary pads, thermometer, Vaseline, etc.). The product's price point was initially set too high and was unaffordable for BOP customers. In response, Totohealth found ways to reduce its costs and lower its price. Undertaking thorough customer analysis can also help to increase a social enterprise's customer base. Such customer analysis enables social enterprises to differentiate their products or services based on local preferences, thus attracting more local customers. Totohealth again illustrates this point. They initially targeted pregnant women and mothers with children up to 5 years old but did not sufficiently factor in different needs based on the age of the child. Through customer analysis they realised their mistake, gained understanding of different preferences, and adapted their products to suit different customer segments.

Distribution channels are another important consideration when seeking to penetrate BOP markets. Effective distribution channels enable social enterprises to reach more customers, even those in rural areas. To penetrate such markets, some social enterprises partner with organizations that already distribute in such areas. Examples from the cases include Totohealth, which partnered with local NGOs already running healthcare programmes in rural Kenya, while, as discussed previously, Africaqua established a partnership with local "Tuk-Tuk" drivers already making deliveries in rural and semi-urban areas.

Table 8.3 Scaling strategies of social enterprise business models in BOP markets in Kenya

Scaling strategy	Value proposition	Value delivery	Value capture	Examples
Market penetration	• Leverage the original value proposition by deepening impact on the original group of customers.	• Increase promotion through social marketing and education. • Adjust product's price based on customers' willingness to pay. • Adapt technical design of products based on environmental conditions. • Segment properly to satisfy more customers' needs. • Create own and/or exploit existing distribution channels. • Create payment assistance and finance the consumer to increase their willingness to pay.	• Increase income per stream of revenue. • Reduce production cost per unit.	• IEC • Totohealth • Africaqua • Daisy Girl • Bidhaa Sasa
Market development	• Export the original value proposition, by proposing the original products and services to a new customer target.	• New strategic partners to gain knowledge on local rules, laws, etc. • New distribution network to reach new customers with products or services. • New communication channels to establish a relationship with new customers.	• Increase income per stream of revenue. • Reduce production cost per unit.	• Totohealth • M-Kopa
Product development	• Extend the value proposition by addressing additional needs of the original customers.	• Create suppliers' networks to get raw materials to build the new product/service. • Implement new activities to support the delivery and sales of new products (e.g. specific marketing events, etc.).	• Add revenue streams from the new product/services. • Add cost streams, especially upstream.	• M-Paya • IEC • Totohealth • Bidhaa Sasa
Diversification	• Build a new value proposition by complementing the original one with a new offer to address completely new customers' needs.	• Create new partnerships to supply and produce additional products/services. • Implement completely new activities to create multi-industry business. • Exploit downstream channels to sell and distribute products/services to customers.	• Diversify revenue streams. • Add cost streams, both upstream and downstream.	• Ecotact • M-Kopa • Bio Afriq Energy • Bubayi

Source: authors' own data

Innovations in payment and consumer financing also enable social enterprises in Kenya to penetrate BOP markets, thus helping to solve challenges of low and volatile incomes amongst BOP customers. Customer financing means products and services are sold with an "affordable" upfront fee, with the remainder paid as a fixed daily or monthly payment. Examples of this include Bio Afriq Energy and M-Kopa, which used consumer financing to match the cash flows of low-income customers, making their products and services more affordable. Specifically, in the case of M-Kopa, they sold thousands of solar home kits to BOP customers who only initially paid around US $35. The remainder was paid in daily instalments of US $0.50, the same amount rural households pay daily for kerosene. However, it is important that such consumer financing approaches do not exploit vulnerable BOP customers by costing more than they can afford, and more than traditional approaches, including through excessive interest. This is documented in the following quotation:

> *I noticed that only few customers could afford the full price of our products, so I thought to sell the product with an affordable upfront fee and then charge a very low daily instalment. . . . So now, our sales are increased.*

(M-Kopa)

Market development

A second scaling strategy that social enterprises in the BOP in Kenya can adopt is market development. In this strategy, existing products are sold in new domestic and international markets. We find that when adopting this strategy for scaling, BOP social enterprises often transplant their original business models – with varying degrees of adaptation – into these new markets. Amongst our cases, Totohealth and M-Kopa internationalised, entering new markets in other African countries. Their business models were already well tested in their home country (Kenya), with proven financial sustainability and social impact, so they were largely replicated in the target countries.

Replication of BOP social enterprise business models, and their different components, often occurs through strategic partnerships with local organizations. Such partner organizations enable BOP social enterprises to become more rapidly embedded within local environments and networks and to gain knowledge about the characteristics of local markets, local legislation, informal rules and cultures, etc., based upon which business model adaptation may occur. Lack of local responsiveness, as well as limited embeddedness, acceptance, and legitimacy, are challenges that can constrain or undermine internationalisation efforts by BOP social enterprises. Moreover, local partners can support social enterprises in building new distribution networks and establishing the necessary communication channels to develop relationships with customers and deliver services or products. This is what Totohealth and M-Kopa did when internationalising. They targeted the same customers and beneficiaries in target countries, exporting their value proposition and market offering – with only limited adjustments. The following quotation explains this strategy clearly:

> *I met a guy from Tanzania who was impressed by Totohealth . . . he asked me to start the business in Tanzania together with him, as he knew very well the local market and legislation, and it worked very well!*

(Totohealth)

Product development

We turn next to product development scaling strategies, where BOP social enterprises in Kenya introduce new products and services to their existing customer base. Viewed through the lens of business model components, we observed that BOP social enterprises in Kenya adopting this strategy "extend" their value proposition, as they add more products and services to it. This extension also involves social enterprises targeting new unmet needs of their customers or beneficiaries. In so doing, social enterprises may expand their social missions. Product development strategies often involve a reconfiguring and/or expansion of value delivery activities to support the new products and services. BOP social enterprises must also devise ways to capture value from them.

An example from amongst our cases of a BOP social enterprise adopting a product development strategy is IEC, which began offering additional products and services to its patients. The core service of IEC is eye care prevention and surgery. It engaged in product development by selling spectacles and lenses to patients, adding a social benefit of reducing future eye sight deterioration. Totohealth is another example of utilising a product development strategy to scale. It launched the previously discussed Newborn Kit in 2017 as an addition to its pregnancy and health information services. Launching this new product extended its value proposition. This launch was predicated on the understanding that parents were missing many basic tools to clean and care for their babies after birth. Totohealth designed the product, including baby clothes, nappies, sanitary pads, a thermometer, and other items. This product development strategy is documented in the following quotation:

> *We discovered that when mothers go to the hospital to deliver the baby, miss items to handle the newborn, such as clothes for changing, no baby wipes, no diapers. Based on this need, we launched our Newborn Kit to provide products for mothers and baby after the delivery.*

(Totohealth)

When developing and delivering new products and services, BOP social enterprises may need to outsource this activity or undertake it through partnerships. This is especially the case where the value chains needed to design and deliver new products and services are quite different from the social enterprise's original value chain. In the case of IEC's provision of affordable spectacles and lenses, it partnered with Vision Spring, another social venture. Totohealth meanwhile outsourced the manufacturing of its Newborn Kit.

Diversification scaling strategies

Diversification is entry into a new market with new products or services. From a business model perspective, it means creating a new value proposition, with new strategies for value delivery and capture. Analysis of our cases reveals that the unmet needs of Kenyan BOP customers provide many opportunities for social enterprises (Ciambotti et al., 2019b). Accordingly, once social enterprises have satisfied existing customer needs in one domain, they may diversify into new BOP consumer markets with new products and services. M-Kopa provides an example of scaling through diversification. This social enterprise initially focused on providing Kenyans with access to clean energy through selling solar panels. However, several years after start-up it began to supply solar-powered FM radios, small solar-charged TVs, as well as micro-loans. M-Kopa now sells its products in Kenya, Tanzania, and Uganda.

We observed that when scaling through diversification, social enterprises may create a varied portfolio of different activities for different markets. Nevertheless, they cannot disregard their core social or environmental mission. This original core mission may be addressed through the provision of core products or services, which in turn enable other social needs to be targeted (Ciambotti, Sydow, & Sottini, 2019a). In the case of Ecotact, it engaged in related diversification of its business of providing Eco-toilets in slums by giving micro-businesses the opportunity to advertise on the wall of Eco-toilets. Moreover, Ecotact built kiosks close to its Eco-toilets to provide other community services. This quotation explains Ecotact's diversification strategy:

> *We realised that many people queued for a long time before they get into the Eco-toilets, so I thought to create spaces close to the Eco-toilets where micro-businesses could sell their products or service, like shoeshines!*
>
> (Ecotact)

With time, many local entrepreneurs decided to rent these kiosks to sell shoes, snacks and drinks, or provide basic financial services, such as insurance. A diversification strategy can enable social enterprises to diversify their revenues streams. However, it also brings additional costs and complexity, for instance in product supply and recruitment of personnel to handle new activities and product lines.

In this section, we have explored four strategies for social enterprise scaling as well as unpacking current practices and identifying issues faced and how these can be overcome. We have further provided insights on some important characteristics social enterprise business models need to successfully scale in Kenyan BOP markets.

Discussion and conclusions

This chapter contributes to our understanding of how social enterprises build and scale business models for BOP markets in Kenya. With respect to social enterprises building business models for the BOP, our work supports previous studies highlighting the importance, and difficulty, of balancing financial sustainability and social value creation (Yunus et al., 2010; Bocken et al., 2016). The research presented in this chapter also sheds light on some further challenges BOP social enterprises in Kenya, and beyond, face when building business models and how these can be overcome, offering implications for practice (Seelos & Mair, 2005; Gebauer et al., 2017a; Davies et al., 2018; Ciambotti & Pedrini, 2019). Anderson and Billou (2007) introduced the four A's framework describing key characteristics (awareness, accessibility, affordability and acceptability) that ventures – including social enterprises – doing business in the BOP must achieve to be successful. However, to date there has been limited examination of how business models can be developed to fulfil these characteristics, especially in social enterprises, and in African country contexts (Lashitew et al., 2018). Our work provides fine-grained, empirically grounded insights on this, drawing upon novel case study research. Zooming out, to date, much of the literature on building business models for the BOP has focused on large, often multinational corporations (Bocken et al., 2016; Kolk et al., 2014; Seelos & Mair, 2005). Less research has examined other actors serving the BOP, including social enterprises, which are the focus of this chapter.

Our chapter next examined how BOP social enterprises in Kenya scale their business models. Extant literature on this topic has often focused on the role of entrepreneurial capabilities in scaling (Dees et al., 2002; Bloom & Smith, 2010), with some limited investigation of challenges to scaling (Desa & Koch, 2014; Bocken et al., 2016). Nevertheless, there remains room for more detailed examinations of scaling in BOP markets, by social enterprises, and especially in African country contexts. Our work contributes towards addressing these limitations. Existing research on scaling strategies for BOP markets has deployed the work of Ansoff and McDonnell (1988), who identify four strategies of market penetration, product development, market development, and diversification (Bocken et al., 2016). In our chapter, we similarly deploy Ansoff and McDonnell's (1988) framework and reveal key considerations and issues for BOP social enterprises adopting these different scaling strategies. For instance, we find that if social enterprises are seeking to penetrate BOP markets, they should refine their promotion strategies, ensure the technical design of their products is suitable for BOP environments, and also properly segment the market to satisfy customer needs (Seelos & Mair, 2005; Ciambotti et al., 2019a). In relation to market development scaling strategies, which often involve internationalisation, we have demonstrated the significance of networks and partnerships with actors in target markets to increase knowledge, local responsiveness and suitability, and to build distribution networks and a customer base (Lashitew et al., 2018). In summary, our research provides in-depth insights on the processes and particularities of social enterprise scaling for BOP markets in Kenya, adding to the hitherto limited research in this area.

In addition to its academic contributions, this chapter has important implications for practice. Its discussions may assist social entrepreneurs and social enterprise managers, in Kenya and beyond, as they work to build business models for the BOP – for instance, by offering suggestions on how to achieve the four A's. It also highlights some of the challenges they might face when doing so and how they can be overcome. This chapter has further implications for those looking to scale social enterprise business models for the BOP. It outlines four strategies and offers broader reflections about issues in BOP social enterprise scaling and how to address them.

There are limitations to our research, but these may provide opportunities for further study. First, our research is restricted to social enterprises in one African country – Kenya. To assess the generalisability of our findings, further work is needed in other African countries. This would enable cross-country comparison and the identification of country-specific particularities linked to the environment. Second, we have considered four scaling strategies informed by extant literature, but there may be further strategies for scaling BOP social enterprises in Kenya, and Africa more widely, that may be considered. Third, our data collection occurred during a relatively short window of time and relies on informant recollection to explain how business models were built, challenges faced and overcome, etc. A longitudinal research design would provide real-time and more accurate insights on processes of business model building and scaling and offer a more dynamic perspective on the phenomena. Finally, whilst our work adds to the understanding of how BOP social enterprises in Kenya build and scale business models, our contributions to theory building are more modest. Such theory building is therefore an important next step for scholars working in this area.

In addition to the above, future research might examine the role of resources and capabilities, including dynamic capabilities, in building and scaling social enterprise business models for BOP markets. Alternate theoretical perspectives could also be applied to examine processes of business model building and scaling by BOP social enterprises, for instance network theories, institutional theory, and resource-based perspectives. Business model building and scaling by BOP social enterprises might also be compared with other types of ventures. There is, furthermore, a need for research examining this topic in social enterprises addressing social or environmental needs different from those of our case studies. Finally, and with respect to scaling particularly, future studies could assess the impact of scaling on social enterprise financial sustainability and social performance.

To conclude, this chapter has aimed to advance our understanding of how social enterprises build and scale business models for BOP markets in Kenya. We have further aimed to stimulate dialogue amongst and between academics and practitioners. Our chapter focuses particularly on Kenya, but is of relevance to those interested and working in BOP social enterprises across Africa. Indeed, we hope it provides wider useful insights for understanding the phenomenon of business model building and scaling by BOP social enterprises globally.

References

Amit, R., & Zott, C. (2001). Value creation in e-business. *Strategic Management Journal*, *22*(6/7), 493–520.

Anderson, J., & Billou, N. (2007). Serving the world's poor: Innovation at the base of the economic pyramid. *Journal of Business Strategy*, *28*(2), 14–21.

Ansoff, H. I., & McDonnell, E. J. (1988). *The new corporate strategy*. New York: J. Wiley.

Austin, J., Stevenson, H., & Wei-Skillern, J. (2006). Social and Commercial Entrepreneurship: Same, Different, or Both? *En/trepreneurship Theory and Practice*, *30*(1), 1–22.

Battilana, J., & Lee, M. (2014). Advancing research on hybrid organizing–Insights from the study of social enterprises. *Academy of Management Annals*, *8*(1), 397–441.

Bloom, P. N., & Smith, B. R. (2010). Identifying the drivers of social entrepreneurial impact: Theoretical development and an exploratory empirical test of SCALERS. *Journal of Social Entrepreneurship*, *1*(1), 126–145.

Bocken, N.M., Fil, A., & Prabhu J. (2016). Scaling up social business in developing markets. *Journal of Cleaner Production*, *139*, 295–308.

BOP Innovation Center (2019). *Base of the Pyramid*. Retrieved from http://BOPinnovationcenter.com/what-we-do/base-of-the-pyramid

Bowen, M., Morara, M., & Mureithi, M. (2009). Management of business challenges among small and micro enterprises in Nairobi-Kenya. *KCA Journal of Business Management*, *2*(1).

British Council. (2017). *The state of social enterprise in Kenya*. Retrieved from www.britishcouncil.org/sites/default/files/state_of_social_enterprise_in_kenya_british_council_final.pdf

Business Call to Action (2019). Businesses breaking the cycle of poverty in Kenya. Retrieved from www.businesscalltoaction.org/news/businesses-breaking-cycle-poverty-kenya

Cañeque, F. C., & Hart, S. L. (Eds.). (2017). *Base of the Pyramid 3.0: Sustainable development through innovation and entrepreneurship*. London: Routledge.

Ciambotti, G., & Pedrini, M. (2019). Hybrid harvesting strategies to overcome resource constraints: Evidence from social enterprises in Kenya. *Journal of Business Ethics*, 1–20.

Ciambotti, G., Sydow, A., & Sottini, A. (2019a). *The Strauss energy business model: Affordable technology innovation to empower Kenya and light up the world*. Thousand Oaks, CA: SAGE Business Cases Originals.

Ciambotti, G., Sottini, A., & Sydow, A. (2019b). *Scaling strategies of social enterprises in fair-trade markets: Meru herbs in Kenya*. Thousand Oaks, CA: SAGE Business Cases Originals.

Davies, I. A., Haugh, H., & Chambers, L. (2018). Barriers to social enterprise growth. *Journal of Small Business Management*, *57*(4), 1616–1636.

Dees, J. G., Anderson, B. B., & Wei-Skillern, J. (2002). *Pathways to social impact: Strategies for scaling out successful social innovations*. Boston: Harvard Business School.

Dembek, K., Sivasubramaniam, N. & Chmielewski, D.A. (2019). A systematic review of the bottom/base of the pyramid literature review: Cumulative evidence and future directions. *Journal of Business Ethics*, 1–18.

Desa, G., & Koch, J. L. (2014). Scaling social impact: Building sustainable social ventures at the base-of the-pyramid. *Journal of Social Entrepreneurship*, 5(2), 146–174.

Eisenhardt, K. M. (1989). Building theories from case study research. *Academy of Management Review*, 14(4), 532–550.

Eisenhardt, K. M., & Graebner, M. E. (2007). Theory building from cases: Opportunities and challenges. *Academy of Management Journal*, 50(1), 25–32.

Euromonitor International (2019). *Africa's three largest BOP markets*. Retrieved from https://blog.euromonitor.com/three-largest-BOP-markets-africa/

Gebauer, H., Haldimann, M., & Saul, C. J. (2017a). Business model innovations for overcoming barriers in the base-of-the-pyramid market. *Industry and Innovation*, 24(5), 543–568.

Gebauer, H., Saul, C. J., & Haldimann, M. (2017b). Business model innovation in base of the pyramid markets. *Journal of Business Strategy*, 38(4), 38–46.

Gehman, J., Glaser, V. L., Eisenhardt, K. M., Gioia, D., Langley, A., & Corley, K. G. (2018). Finding theory–method fit: A comparison of three qualitative approaches to theory building. *Journal of Management Inquiry*, 27(3), 284–300.

Ghauri, P. (2004). *Designing and conducting case studies in international business research. Handbook of qualitative research methods for international business.* Cheltenham, UK: Edward Elgar.

Goyal, S., Sergi, B. S., & Kapoor, A. (2017). Emerging role of for-profit social enterprises at the base of the pyramid: The case of Selco. *Journal of Management Development*, 36(1), 97–108.

Hahn, R., Spieth, P., & Ince, I. (2018). Business model design in sustainable entrepreneurship: Illuminating the commercial logic of hybrid businesses. *Journal of Cleaner Production*, 176, 439–451.

International Labour Organization (2019). *Five facts about informal economy in Africa*. Retrieved from www.ilo.org/addisababa/whats-new/WCMS_377286/lang--en/index.htm

Katz, R., Koh, H., & Karamchandani, A. (2012). *From blueprint to scale: The case for philanthropy in impact investing*. Monitor Group.

Kolk, A., & Rivera-Santos, M. (2018). The state of research on Africa in business and management: Insights from a systematic review of key international journals. *Business & Society*, 57(3), 415–436.

Kolk, A., Rivera-Santos, M., & Rufin, C. (2014). Reviewing a decade of research on the "base/bottom of the pyramid" (BOP) concept. *Business & Society*, 53(3), 338–377.

Lashitew, A. A., Bals, L., & van Tulder, R. (2018). Inclusive business at the base of the pyramid: The role of embeddedness for enabling social innovations. *Journal of Business Ethics*, 1–28.

Littlewood, D., & Holt, D. (2014). Addressing rural social exclusion in the developing world: Exploring the role of African social purpose ventures. In C. Henry & G. Mcelwee (Eds.), *Exploring rural enterprise: new perspectives on research, policy & practice*, (pp. 105–131). Bingley, UK: Emerald Group Publishing Limited.

London, T., Anupindi, R., & Sheth, S. (2010). Creating mutual value: Lessons learned from ventures serving base of the pyramid producers. *Journal of Business Research*, *63*(6), 582–594.

London, T., & Hart, S. L. (2011). Creating a fortune with the base of the pyramid. In T. London, & S. L. Hart (Eds.), *Next Generation Business Strategies for the Base of the Pyramid*, (pp. 1–18). Upper Saddle River, NJ: FT Press.

Lyon, F., & Fernandez, H. (2012). Strategies for scaling up social enterprise: Lessons from early years providers. *Social Enterprise Journal*, *8*(1), 63–77.

Manning, S., Kannothra, C. G., & Wissman-Weber, N. K. (2017). The strategic potential of community-based hybrid models: The case of global business services in Africa. *Global Strategy Journal*, *7*(1), 125–149.

Miles, M. B., & Huberman, A. M. (1994). *Qualitative data analysis: An expanded sourcebook* (2nd ed.). Thousand Oaks, CA: Sage.

Mohr, J. J., Sengupta, S., & Slater, S. F. (2012). Serving base-of-the-pyramid markets: Meeting real needs through a customized approach. *Journal of Business Strategy*, *33*(6), 4–14.

Moore, M. L., Riddell, D., & Vocisano, D. (2015). Scaling out, scaling up, scaling deep: strategies of non-profits in advancing systemic social innovation. *Journal of Corporate Citizenship*, *58*, 67–84.

Nahi, T. (2016). Cocreation at the base of the pyramid: Reviewing and organizing the diverse conceptualizations. *Organization & Environment*, *29*, 416–437.

Patton, M. (1990). *Qualitative evaluation and research methods*. Thousand Oaks, CA: Sage.

Prahalad, C. K. (2009). *The fortune at the bottom of the pyramid: Eradicating poverty through profits* (5th anniversary ed.). Upper Saddle River, NJ: Pearson FT Press.

Prahalad, C. K., & Hammond, S. L., (2002). Serving the world's poor, profitability. *Harvard Business Review*, *80*(9), 48–57.

Rivera-Santos, M., Holt, D., Littlewood, D., & Kolk, A. (2015). Social entrepreneurship in sub-Saharan Africa. *Academy of Management Perspectives*, *29*(1), 72–91.

Santos, F., Pache, A. C., & Birkholz, C. (2015). Making hybrids work: Aligning business models and organizational design for social enterprises. *California Management Review*, *57*(3), 36–58.

Seelos, C., & Mair, J. (2005). Social entrepreneurship: Creating new business models to serve the poor. *Business Horizons*, *48*(3), 241–246.

Simanis, E. (2012). Reality check at the bottom of the pyramid. *Harvard Business Review*, (June), 120–125.

Smith, B. R., Kistruck, G. M., & Cannatelli, B. (2016). The impact of moral intensity and desire for control on scaling decisions in social entrepreneurship. *Journal of Business Ethics*, *133*(4), 677–689.

Teece, D. J. (2018). Business models and dynamic capabilities. *Long Range Planning*, *51*(1), 40–49.

World Bank (2019a). *Doing business, measuring business regulations*. Retrieved from www.doingbusiness.org/en/rankings

World Bank (2019b). *World Bank national accounts data, and OECD National Accounts data Kenya*. Retrieved from https://data.worldbank.org/indicator/NY.GDP.MKTP.KD.ZG?locations=KE

Yin, R. K. (1984). *Case study research: Design and methods.* Thousand Oaks, CA: Sage.

Yunus, M., Moingeon, B., & Lehmann-Ortega, L. (2010). Building social business models: Lessons from the Grameen experience. *Long Range Planning, 43*(2/3), 308–325.

Zoogah, D. B., Peng, M. W., & Woldu, H. (2015). Institutions, resources, and organizational effectiveness in Africa. *Academy of Management Perspectives, 29*(1), 7–31.

9 From informal to formal and back

Theoretical reflections on the formal – informal divide in the Base of the Pyramid markets

Elena Vallino, Cecilia Navarra,[1] and Cristiano Lanzano[2]

Introduction

In understanding the nature and the dynamics of poverty in African societies, and their interplay with the creation of sustainable development paths, we argue that a deep understanding of the processes of the so-called informal economy is necessary. The informal economy is not a static concept that describes an isolated sector of the society, but it has complex and fluctuating relations with the so-called formal sector (Guha-Khasnobis, Kanbur, & Ostrom, 2006; Holt & Littlewood, 2014; Kanbur, 2009; Portes, Castells, & Benton, 1989). The interplay between the formal and informal dimensions has consequences at different levels, such as the labour market, product development, outcomes in terms of income diversification, and food security. Such reflection would benefit from the simultaneous consideration of theoretical contributions from different disciplines, such as economics, economic sociology, and anthropology (see, among others, Biggeri, 2004; De Soto, 1989; Hart, 2009; La Porta & Shleifer, 2014; Loayza & Rigolini, 2011; Meagher, 2018; Portes & Haller, 2005).

Among the many definitions of informality, we consider a broad one for which the informal economy is the sum of production and distribution activities of goods and services that are excluded from the national accounting (Portes & Haller, 2005). We recall that Chen (2012, 8) identifies two sub-groups of entities within this broad definition. The first is the informal sector, represented by "the production and employment that takes place in unincorporated small or unregistered enterprises", while the second is the informal employment, which refers to "employment without legal and social protection – both inside and outside the informal sector".

The debate on the relationships between formal and informal sectors has the potential to inform fruitfully the Bottom of the Pyramid (BOP) narrative for different reasons. First, a significant BOP feature is the strong role played by the informal sector and by the informal employment opportunities for livelihood and income generation (Hammond et al., 2008). Second, according to many scholars, successful development of BOP markets is dependent on strategic and effective interactions between stakeholders from the informal domain and actors of the formal sphere, who are mainly represented by private enterprises of different sizes. Third, the BOP narrative builds partly on the idea about a natural tendency of small informal actors to innovate as a means of escaping poverty (Anderson et al., 2010; Linna, 2012; Meagher, 2018). Consequently, a more specific (and critical) understanding of this idealised "natural" innovation process can improve the BOP narrative.

The first wave of the BOP literature was more focused on considering low income individuals as potential customers of the formal economy (Hammond & Prahalad, 2004; Karamchandani, Kubzansky, & Lalwani, 2011). Subsequently, the BOP debate turned to see the poor, often engaged in informal economic activities, as potential entrepreneurs, given their supposed "natural" tendency to innovate in order to improve life conditions (Linna, 2012). We aim to contribute mainly with this second aspect of the discourse. However, a placement of the BOP scholarly discussion within the wider debate on the informal economy and its interconnectedness with the formal sector, beyond the managerial approach, is still missing, and it is this gap that we aim to fill.

We argue that the distinctive elements that lead to an enthusiastic consideration of BOP market opportunities, such as tendency to innovate, strong networks, and knowledge of the territory (Anderson et al., 2010; Meagher, 2018), are in reality part of the dense interactions between the wider formal and informal sectors in a complex economy. Therefore, it is the modality by which the BOP environment is inserted in the formal economy that determines its dynamics and results. The unavoidable connection of the informal economy with formal companies, regulations, and markets influences why and how individuals enter the informal BOP sphere, and whether they are able, or willing, to escape it. In this chapter, we investigate whether a deeper analysis of specific informal settings and their relation with the formal domain improves the understanding of the actual impact of this interaction on the BOP environment. In order to do so, we start by classifying theoretical contributions on informality into categories. Furthermore, we apply these frameworks to two cases that have been extensively studied in the literature. For each case, we consider the peculiar features of the formal – informal interaction, and we wonder which are the actual positive and negative consequences for the BOP stakeholders.

Methodologically, we provide a review of the empirical literature on two African case studies that represent examples of the different approaches used for interpreting the formal – informal interaction. In reviewing some theories on the formal – informal relations, we focus on the interdependence of the two domains and, more particularly, we highlight two approaches. The first considers such interactions as structural in contexts where the two domains have undefined boundaries; they are typical of complex economies in which articulated value chains of production and distribution are present (Chen, 2012; Portes et al., 1989). The second interprets formal – informal interactions as the result of individual strategies in dealing with both domains separately, according to their needs and opportunities (Banerjee & Duflo, 2011; Biggeri, 2004; Toulabor, 2012; UNCTAD, 2015).

We review the empirical literature on two case studies that illustrate the two theoretical perspectives mentioned above. The first case deals with the emergence of the mobile money market in Kenya (Iazzolino, 2017; Maurer, 2012; Meagher, 2018). It shows how large formal companies commercially exploited the opportunities offered by informal networks, knowledge, and practices, and created a system in which BOP informal actors are at the same time consumers and co-creators of innovation. The related literature presents successes and contradictions of these systems in which, despite the undeniable overall achievements, the large formal actors benefit the most, and the profit margin for the BOP stakeholders diminishes. The second case focuses on Ethiopia and investigates the relationship between the formal labour market and BOP small-scale entrepreneurship (Bigsten, Kebede, & Shimeles, 2005; Blattman & Dercon, 2017; Chinigò & Navarra, 2017; Rossetti, Chinigò, Navarra, & Argaw, 2015). In this case, formal and informal sectors are both active but coexist on parallel routes, and both are used in complex livelihood strategies; workers seem to enter the self-employment sphere as a reaction to the imperfections of the formal labour market, and this process produces a path of informalisation and an enlargement of the BOP sphere. This path contradicts the expected formalisation dynamics that should come along with economic development.

The two cases are comparable in the sense that both show how the informal sphere remains strongly present, even in the case of important economic and societal changes in African countries, and how this sphere remains populated by BOP stakeholders. Moreover, in both cases, the informal domain is not insulated but strongly interacts with the formal one. The cases differ in the way in which interdependencies between the two sectors are articulated.

Section 2 presents the theoretical background on the formal – informal divide, first in a historical perspective and then focusing on each of the two selected theoretical approaches: structural relations between the formal and the informal sector and the individual agency perspective. Sections 3 and 4 present the empirical literature on, respectively, the development of mobile money in Kenya and the relationship between micro and small enterprises and the formal labour market in Ethiopia. In Section 5 we conclude the chapter by highlighting the implication of these reflections for future research streams and decision-making.

A theoretical framework on the formal/informal divide

The idea of informality in an historical view

In Holt and Littlewood's definition, a significant feature of the BOP is a prevailing reliance on the informal sector and on informal employment opportunities (Holt & Littlewood, 2014). More generally, informality is assumed to be an essential aspect of African economies where wage employment provided by the public sector or by the formal private sector is relatively marginal. A recent study by the International Labour Organization (ILO, 2018) estimates that around 85% of non-agricultural employment in Africa is informal, compared with around 68% in Asia and the Pacific, 68% in the Arab states, 40% in the Americas, and 25% in Europe and Central Asia. Therefore, one may consider the African continent, by and large, the most informalised area in the world.

Indeed, the concept of informal economy, today extensively used both in policy circles and in academic debates, presents an interesting historical evolution. It made its first appearances in the early 1970s, precisely in reference to the newly independent African states and to the challenges they were facing in terms of macroeconomic development and urban (un)employment. In 1973, the British social anthropologist Keith Hart published an article where he reflected on the occupational status of recent immigrants from the rural areas to the cities. He built on his ethnographic work in an informal neighbourhood in Accra, the rapidly expanding capital of Ghana. Fearing the risk of nourishing an unemployment bulge, the new urbanites mostly survived through unstable jobs in unregistered businesses, but they occasionally generated wealth that could even be reinvested later in the formal economy. In the previous year, the ILO had published a study based on similar concerns, describing urbanisation in Kenya and the associated challenges for the government to create employment opportunities and keep demographic change under control (ILO, 1972). Both texts, although with different emphases on scholarly or political questions, underlined the importance of the informal economy for the livelihood of recently urbanised populations, and highlighted the need of analytical tools both for understanding economic change in development contexts, and for elaborating realistic and effective employment policies.

Informal workers, and their more or less successful livelihood strategies, defied some consolidated assumptions of modernisation theory and the macroeconomic models associated with it, such as Arthur Lewis's dual sector model (1954) and others reviewed in Biggeri (2004). These were people who had – often only recently – left (supposedly) traditional social contexts and subsistence-oriented economies; however, they did not seem to benefit from the opportunities offered by the modern and regulated economy commonly associated with urban life. Instead, they survived by mobilising resources and navigating networks located outside the influence of formal markets and of the bureaucratic structures of the state. In the context of post-independence optimism on the capacity of the states to discipline markets, to guide development processes and eventually to close the gap separating them from the wealthier economies of the Global North, this constituted a problem. Informality challenged the regulatory power of governments and allowed economic enterprises to develop and thrive without contributing to national welfare, or without complying with national regulations – including those supposed to protect workers' rights and safety.

With the crisis of the developmental state and the consolidation of the neoliberal hegemony during the more recent decades, informality began to be understood and framed in new and profoundly different ways: this has been observed by Hart (2009) himself when he revisited the history of the concept and contextualised it in the broader history of economic theory. With the definition of the "Washington consensus" and the enforcement of structural adjustment programmes in most African countries, aiming to reduce state apparatuses and their role in economic planning, the informal economy became a symbol of creativity and vitality of the market, despite or against regulation from above. Furthermore, from the 1990s on, the dominance of bilateral and official aid was increasingly challenged by bottom-up models of development aid based on non-state actors, such as NGOs, community-based organizations, and private companies. Informal businesses and workers came to epitomise the entrepreneurialism targeted by new decentralised forms of aid, which hoped to bypass the mediation of political elites, now represented as corrupt and inefficient.

Both the analyses done in the developmental and neoliberal celebrations of informality, at least in their most simplified versions, shared a relatively static vision: what mattered was primarily the existence of an informal economy – its features, its magnitude, and its impact on the economy at large – and the question of "what to do with it". More recently, criticism of the depoliticising and essentialising effects of the concept led some scholars to focus more on the dynamic processes that constitute informality in different societies. If, on the one hand, many scholars expect a natural process of formalisation along with economic development (Biggeri, 2004), on the other hand it is possible to speak as well of "informalisation" as a historical and political trajectory (see, among others, Castells & Portes, 1989; Meagher, 1995; Tabak & Crichlow, 2000; Verbrugge, 2015) rather than a "natural" subdivision of the economy. Currently, most scholars interpret the informal sector as a realm under constant redefinition in structural relation with its formal counterpart and, more precisely, with the broader political economy that defines the possibilities and obstacles for both unregistered and official economic enterprises to emerge and expand. In other words, as Castells and Portes (1989, 13) observed, "it is because there is a formal economy (i.e. an institutional framework of economic activity) that we can speak of an 'informal' one". In sum, informality can only be understood in light of the nature of state intervention and of the strategies of the formal private sector – including those focused on deregulated or casualised labour – that define its contours.

Starting with the recognition that complex economies and societies face a high degree of interaction between formal and informal domains, and that bi-directional transformation processes are possible, recent theoretical contributions develop taxonomies in order to classify the kinds of interdependencies. In the field of economic sociology, Sciarrone and Storti (2019) argue that the formal and informal spheres may interact following three paths. The first is called "cohabitation", and it occurs when the two domains are both present and active, but remain clearly divided by legal boundaries. The second is "permeation", occurring when one domain collapses into the other for limited sections of a given economic activity or for a restricted period of time. The third is called "hybridisation" and it implies an almost complete overlapping and a combination of the two systems, with the creation of a distinct peculiar setting.[3] A similar reflection has been developed by Kanbur (2009), who classifies the possible reactions of enterprises to changes in economic regulations. According to the choice of the enterprise about how to deal with the formal rules, informalisation may or may not take place. The interaction between formal and informal domains is also extensively investigated in Guha-Khasnobis et al. (2006), who explore the different nuances that it can present.

In the following subsections, we consider in more detail two different theoretical streams for interpreting the formal – informal interplay. They are particularly useful for the explanation of the phenomena reported in the literature on the emergence of mobile money in Kenya and on the Ethiopian micro and small enterprises (MSEs).

Structural approach to the formal–informal relationship

The lack of the expected decrease in the size of the informal sector – supposed to be a consequence of economic growth – questions the dualistic approaches that identify the formal and informal sectors as being insulated and that see the informal sector as residual. The dualist approach finds partial support in La Porta and Shleifer (2014), who claim that the informal sector is underproductive with respect to the formal one and decreases with economic growth, when considering a static observation. Yet, as the same authors point out, the adoption of a dynamic perspective shows a weak relationship between the growth of Gross Domestic Product and the change of the informal sector's size.[4] It also shows that the "absorption" of the informal sector into the formal economy is expected to be very slow. Moreover, the authors argue that registration costs do not appear to play a major role. In disagreement with the common argument – supported for example by de Soto (1989) – according to which informal firms are simply constrained by high registration costs and cumbersome bureaucratic processes and would otherwise thrive as formal businesses, La Porta and Shleifer (2014) provide evidence of the limited impact of formalisation efforts in different contexts. They also indicate that often self-employment is a second choice with respect to wage work (which we will discuss further below).

Still, like most mainstream economic literature, La Porta and Shleifer (2014) overlook structural interdependencies between the formal and informal sectors. The empirical evidence brought to prove the insulation of the two sectors simply indicates a low rate of transitions from informal to formal businesses, but it does not address the broader interdependencies that may link formal and informal economies. By putting an emphasis on these, on the contrary, other scholars have underlined that the relation between formal and informal sectors in a complex economy is more structural, and the boundaries among the two spheres are less strict and limpid. There is an active debate, for example, on how the informal economy is linked to formal firms. According to Chen (2012), few informal businesses work in total isolation from formal enterprises. Most of them buy raw materials from formal firms, or provide finished goods to the formal sector, either directly or through intermediaries that in turn may be informal as well. These processes may take place according to different dynamics, depending on the nature of the production system, which determines "the allocation of authority and risk between the informal and formal firm" (Chen, 2012, 12). Chen identifies three paths. The first is constituted by individual transactions: through standard market operations, informal businesses exchange goods and services with formal enterprises, who are in a dominant position with respect to market knowledge and power and, therefore, control the transaction terms. In the second, the system is organized into sub-sectors: many informal businesses are part of networks that populate different sub-sectors of the production and distribution processes of a given commodity. Transactions with formal suppliers and customers are not only dominated by the dominant formal companies, but they are also influenced by the rules of the sub-sector as a whole, which in turn are determined by the strongest network members. The third sees the appearance of actual value chains: some informal businesses and all their subcontracted workers are embedded in one value chain. The conditions of all the transactions are mostly determined by the lead formal company, which can be national, in the case of domestic value chains, or transnational in the case of global value chains. The main suppliers of the lead enterprise contribute to the determination of the terms of subcontracts to informal enterprises of the chain. According to the same author, globalisation induced processes of "flexible specialisation" (Chen, 2012, 3) that have gone hand in hand with the informalisation of employment and production, for example through outsourcing to small units of production in other countries.

In conclusion, "the informal economy had become a permanent, but subordinate and dependent feature of capitalist development" (Portes et al., 1989, quoted in Chen, 2012, 3). In fact, it is possible to register an increase of the informal economy size during structural adjustment in sub-Saharan Africa and during the 1980s crisis in Latin America (Portes et al., 1989, quoted in Chen, 2012, 3): there is evidence that the informal economy expands during periods of economic adjustment and transition. It represents a resort for people who cannot afford unemployment, because of lack of social protection systems, or who have to complement low wages in the formal sector. Recalling the theoretical taxonomy presented above (Sciarrone & Storti, 2019), the sub-sectors structure may correspond to the "permeation" label, while the value chain structure is the result of a "hybridisation" process. In both cases, formal – informal interactions are very dense, as the two domains are intertwined in the same production process. The literature on the emergence of mobile money in Kenya shows that this case is an example of this kind of relationship between formal and informal.

Approaches that focus on individual agency in moving between formal and informal

A category of theories that analyse the interaction between formal and informal domains focuses on individual trajectories and underlines the agency[5] of individuals in constructing their livelihood strategies across the formal – informal divide. Unlike the "legalist" and the "voluntarist" approaches as defined by Chen (2012),[6] we neither aim to idealise the informal entrepreneur as struggling against unfair regulations, nor define him or her exclusively through their strategies of tax and regulation avoidance. Rather, we observe how individuals shift (more than once in their life) from the formal sector to the informal one and back in order to pursue a "mixed livelihood strategy", pushed by structural constraints and by the need to take the opportunities offered to them, in a discontinuous way, by both sectors.

In this sense, it is useful to consider informality in relation to the concept of poverty, which is another defining element of BOP markets. According to a report of the World Bank (Hammond et al., 2008), "the 4 billion people at the base of the economic pyramid (BOP) – all those with incomes below $3,000 in local purchasing power parity – live in relative poverty". In many streams of literature, poverty and informality are considered to be closely linked. Therefore, formalisation and poverty reduction processes are assumed to be mutually beneficial and necessary to escape undesirable livelihoods. But while poverty and informality are surely related, they do not necessarily overlap: it is important to underline that within the informal sector, there is a wide degree of heterogeneity in terms of income generated and of complexity level of the delivered product or service (Biggeri, 2004). In specific historical and political conditions, entire economic sectors have prospered and generated wealth while remaining essentially informal. An example is the textile trade in Togo, which used to be controlled by the so-called "Nana Benz" – powerful women entrepreneurs who skilfully linked with the elite and established successful monopolies while keeping most of the workforce unregistered (Sylvanus, 2016; Toulabor, 2012). Still, as it is the case for informality, poverty is not a static categorisation that pre-exists economic relations and development patterns; it is, on the contrary, a product of structural interrelations between economic actors, markets, and public policies.

Moreover, the analysis of the link between poverty and informality benefits also from the debate on the relations between "the poor" and "the market". Poverty described as "disconnection from the market" overlooks the many connections between the urban and rural poor with product and labour markets. A number of studies point in this direction, for example, on what concerns commercial versus subsistence agriculture in developing regions: the limited success of promotion of greater commercialisation of agrarian products in the last decades should not be ascribed to "market exclusion", but rather to the costs of using the market and the risks associated, starting from the risks of giving up production for own consumption (see, for example, Jayne, 1994; Barrett, 2008). Rural subsistence production is also exchanged on the market and is often associated with wage work in often fragile and vulnerable conditions (some examples in the case of rural Mozambique are Navarra & Pellizzoli, 2012; O'Laughlin, 2001, 2009; Oya & Sender, 2009). Examples from sectors other than the agricultural one can also shed light on the need to frame the relationship between poverty and markets not in terms of "disconnection", but in a more complex interrelation that can sometimes take the form of "adverse incorporation" (Hickey & du Toit, 2007). One example is artisanal and small-scale mining, a sector that is usually interpreted as poverty-driven, but whose recent success in the Global South may represent another dimension of the expansion of the large-scale mining sector, and may reach those areas where risks of instability or of lower returns do not justify investments from formal companies (Verbrugge & Geenen, 2019).

The evidence of a widespread informal sector has pushed a number of scholars and practitioners to identify small-scale entrepreneurship as the major way out of poverty, by providing market access and credit to informal entrepreneurs, with the goal of establishing a formalisation process. The last decades, which have seen a widespread development of microfinance tools aimed at promoting micro and small enterprises (MSEs), provide interesting evidence and reflections on this issue. Building on a number of impact evaluations of microfinance programmes, the recent Nobel laureates Duflo and Banerjee (2011) put into question the assumption that poor people are "natural entrepreneurs" that just lack the chances to express it. The authors argue that, besides the (real) success stories, most beneficiaries of microfinance do not enter into an entrepreneurial virtuous circle. The main reason is that these projects would need a strong upgrade in scale that is far too big for the size of microfinance loans. The credit needed would be too large, or the assets to build on the business (a plot of land, e.g.) are too small: this means that the problem is not liquidity (that can be solved by credit), but asset endowment or the existence of safety nets against excessive risks. These are among the factors that do not allow a small informal business to shift to more productive technologies, and these observations explain why many businesses are doomed to remain small. Their small size, according to Duflo and Banerjee, is the main explanation of their often very low profitability, despite the high marginal rate of return on investment. In the same line, the United Nations Conference on Trade and Development (UNCTAD, 2015) distinguishes between two categories of small enterprises in developing countries: "entrepreneurs by choice" and "entrepreneurs by necessity" (UNCTAD, 2015), where the former are households with greater asset endowments that pursue accumulation strategies, while the latter use temporary expedients to complement insufficient farm (or wage) incomes. Members of this latter category often run businesses belonging to the informal side of the economy.

Indeed, another limitation in scaling up businesses can be the role that those activities have for the people actually engaging in them, and within their households. According to Duflo and Banerjee (2011), the aim of these activities is to add a small amount of revenue since "every little bit helps", without a real economic and emotional investment in it. Behind Duflo and Banerjee's claim, there is the idea that often, in contexts affected by poverty, informal entrepreneurship may be a second choice because of lack of other options, namely stable employment, that would guarantee stability of income and the possibility to commit to future expenditures. Duflo and Banerjee define these informal businesses as ways to "buy a job" when conventional and formal employment opportunities are lacking, or where they are not accessible. Also Biggeri (2004) states that informal economic activities may contribute to human development and poverty reduction in the strongly segmented economy of sub-Saharan Africa, and that formal and informal domains are coexistent in both urban and rural settings. These views therefore consider informal self-employment and the formal labour market as two separate domains, and this approach may fit the category of "cohabitation" of formal and informal, according to the taxonomy developed by Sciarrone and Storti (2019). The interaction between the two domains lies in the fact that households or single individuals shift by necessity from one to the other, according to the context-specific contingency and to the economic cycles of the society. Empirical research on the labour market and small-scale entrepreneurship in Ethiopia provides a practical example of such a path of coexistence of formal and informal domains in the BOP markets.

Mobile money in Kenya

The development of mobile money in Africa and in Kenya

One important example of the interesting and contradictory interplay between formal and informal economic domains is the mobile banking and mobile money phenomenon in the African continent. In the last ten years, mobile phones started to be used for a broad range of financial services. Examples vary from the simple transfer of money for the purchase of goods and services, to the digitalisation of entire value chains of cash crops, such as coffee and tea, the payment of electric bills from remote and isolated areas, and the transmission of remittances from abroad (Iazzolino, 2017). Since the mobile network operator Safaricom introduced in Kenya the possibility of money transfer through mobile phone in 2007, the sector of development of digital financial services and mobile money has boomed in developing and emerging countries. This generated important consequences on the financial sector dynamics, although quantifying them exactly is challenging (Asongu, 2013). Sub-Saharan Africa dominated the phenomenon, with 350 million mobile phone subscribers (Etzo & Collender, 2010) and hosting most of the 270 mobile money deployments recorded by the industry association of mobile network operators, GSMA (Iazzolino, 2017). In Kenya, over 13 million people subscribed to a digital financial service to send money at low cost (Maurer, 2012).

A wide range of actors such as development practitioners, private enterprises, and academic scholars contributed to an emerging powerful narrative on financial inclusion driven by increased technological advances in the Information and Communication Technology (ICT) and mobile phone domains. The first underlying assumption, which consolidated already during the long diffusion of the microfinance practices, is that improving access to financial services such as credit and insurance strongly contributes to development. The second component of the narrative is that, thanks to digital financial services, it is more straightforward to reach people who are physically distant from banks or who would not have the access requirements for banking services. A network of private and state actors consolidated around this narrative, including local and central banks, international organizations, foundations, mobile network operators, payment providers, and financial technology companies. Large development agencies such as the Consultative Group to Assist the Poor (CGAP), or the World Bank's International Finance Corporation (IFC), provided funding for mobile money as a means to fight poverty through improved access to finance (Maurer, 2012). At the same time, industry actors became extremely interested since they estimated that a high quantity of low value transactions from the poor could become profitable and could lead to increased loyalty for the network provider due to more intense use of the mobile device by the customer (Iazzolino, 2017; Maurer, 2012). Within this framework, enterprises designed products directed to the needs of low-income customers, and institutions facilitated the creation of a favourable environment to this new kind of businesses, in terms of regulation and policies.

The M-PESA service in Kenya is a symbol of success of mobile money technology. It allows people to use mobile phones for money transfer and savings facilities. Starting in 2006, it reached 2 million subscribers just in the first year, and the figure increased to 20 million in 2012 (Meagher, 2018). M-PESA was surely the result of a fruitful interaction between formal and informal innovative actions (Linna, 2012). Local users in Kenya pioneered mobile money by sending "air-time" to each other as a way of shifting money.[7] Various stakeholders at the chain end, such as traders and local shopkeepers, cooperated and allowed users "to convert texted scratch card codes into cash" (Meagher, 2018, 12). The mobile network operator Safaricom obtained funding from Vodafone and from the British international development agency (DfID) for commercializing this practice, previously unregulated and informal. It is interesting to notice that the first pilot project developed mobile payment products for the microfinance domain, and it was not successful (Meagher, 2018). Users began to employ the product as a type of mobile money, and consequently invented additional services such as micro-saving practices. Therefore, it is correct to say that end users were the real innovators in the first project phase (Foster & Heeks, 2013).

Moreover, a broad set of informal institutions played a key role in M-PESA's development and spread as they provided the infrastructures and practices that supported the diffusion of the technology. Examples of these informal actors are remittance networks called *hawala*, informal shopkeepers and rotating credit groups that created familiarity with the mobile money and mobile transfer systems. Furthermore, M-PESA dealers exploited informal commercial practices and networks through which they were able to establish a system of sub-agents who brought the mobile money technology to the whole country, including the slums and rural areas. Arrangements between registered M-PESA dealers and sub-agents were established informally, outside the formal procedure of Safaricom. They rapidly contributed to a further set of both product and process innovations, such as payments for rent and utilities, goods purchasing, bookkeeping, and float management (Meagher, 2018; Maurer, 2012). These innovations were considered successful and were promptly adopted by Safaricom. The wide success of the M-PESA project attracted further investments to Kenya from several foreign companies that opened their African regional R&D centres there, such as Samsung, Nokia, and Google (Linna, 2012).

Reflections on the formal – informal divide for the mobile money phenomenon

General positive aspects and critiques

Regarding the general phenomenon of mobile money in the African continent, many of the evaluations of the digital financial services possibilities highlighted their positive sides and impacts. Benefits are to be found in the reduction of both physical and institutional transaction costs for business operations; improved payment transparency; enhanced possibility to tailor financial services to the needs of the poor; decreased utilisation of commercial intermediaries; improved possibility of control of savings and operations, also by disadvantaged groups, such as women; and creation of local jobs (Iazzolino, 2017; Maliehe & Sharp, 2018). The topic has been included in the stream of literature on business and services for the BOP with enthusiastic considerations. As Maurer (2012) explains, mobile money technology appears as an example of convergence of corporate and public interests. Mobile network operators and the device industry target a large market populated by the world's "unbanked" poorest with the goal of creating revenue. According to many views (Maurer, 2012), the service that is consequently offered increases the degree of financial access for the poor, improving income and triggering development processes. In this framework, the formal actors are represented by the industry and by public institutions that provide a favourable business environment; the informal actors, on the other hand, are seen as a new pool of consumers.

Furthermore, evolutions within the BOP narrative led to considering the poor of the informal sector also as "frugal innovators", that is to say, actors engaged in collaborations with the formal sphere for the "co-creation" of affordable and accessible products (Meagher, 2018). In this view, formal actors take inspiration from existing experimental and innovative practices of the informal sector and scale them up. This formalisation of what has been informal leads to an increase of revenues for the formal sphere, creating an apparent win – win situation. Mobile money enriches this general perspective, since targeted individuals are at the same time consumers, when they utilise the technological service, and product innovators, when they develop new streams of service use and goals, such as creation of micro-savings mechanisms or of markets among subcontracted mobile money agents (Maurer, 2012; Meagher, 2018).

However, scholars also identified a number of shortcomings linked to the mobile money diffusion. The success of this technology for effective improvement of financial inclusion and access is highly context-dependent, and there is still a lack of accepted guidelines for the overall good performance of the service. It is not clear whether the benefits of digital financial services are evenly distributed both on a social and a territorial level, or whether they rather reinforce pre-existing inequalities and exclusion patterns. For example, in some cases, women still lack the formal elements required by regulations for financial service providers. Zins and Weill (2016) find that mobile banking and mobile money use is driven by the same determinants that drive regular banking, and it is therefore positively associated with being a man and having high income and education levels. The gap between urban and rural areas is still present, mainly because private investors need a solid business environment for long-term investments, and these are lacking in remote areas or among customers who would exchange very low amounts of money, such as small-scale farmers. The issue of customer data is also crucial and controversial. The new technology allows to analyse data left by the past track of customers' financial activities. On the one hand, this is favourable for the unbanked poor, since these unconventional information channels for the first time allow formal financial providers to be reassured about the adequacy of the customers placed into the informal economy, and this increases the tendency to include them in the service provision. On the other hand, however, the analysis of customers' data also includes information related to the social surroundings of an individual. If this social environment does not meet the required standards, it may become an obstacle to inclusion in the service, playing a counterproductive role with respect to the customer (Iazzolino, 2017). Finally, cash money is hard to be replaced in contexts in which gifts and money-based contributions play an important role in social interactions (Iazzolino & Wasike, 2015).

Successes and controversial issues in the M-PESA case

The experience of the M-PESA service in Kenya has been widely studied by scholars and corporate managers. It attracted much attention for different reasons. First, it represented a pioneering attempt in the mobile money field, and thanks to its success, it was able to expand to other African countries, and subsequently to countries in Asia and Europe. Second, it offers a particular example to reflect on the interaction between formal and informal spheres in the domain of mobile money development and use, and on its interpretation according to both positive and more critical narratives of BOP markets.

Positive assessments place M-PESA among the success stories of the BOP business models, in a framework in which social needs are seen as stimulus for developing technological solutions that target poor customers in a commercial and possibly financially sustainable way. In this vein, they highlight that M-PESA was launched by a multinational company (Vodafone) and funded by the UK development agency, and they declare that its "primary aim was to contribute to the Millennium Development Goals by offering easy access to micro-loans for the unbanked market segment" (Linna, 2012, 130), therefore promoting the coupling of social and commercial goals. Some scholars focus on the formal – informal sector interaction as one of the key drivers of success. They praise that local enterprises could benefit easily from the so-called "grassroots-level knowledge" as a source for BOP innovation (Linna, 2012, 131), and that local informal hubs and social networks have been effective channels for testing ideas and receiving feedback to be used for business modelling and concept development. Moreover, local knowledge, local organizational networks, and systems of relational contracting of the informal domain were also beneficial for product diffusion in remote areas (Meagher, 2018). Another link which is considered fruitful is the one between local enterprises and multinational companies. Both are considered as winners from the relationship: the former need resources, technical knowledge, additional finance, and access to wider markets. The latter, in turn, could gain smooth access for the provision of tailored products for low-income customers.

One more point in favour of the M-PESA experience is its capacity to reach the economy of scale needed to attain financial viability, as this has not been the case for many other innovative mobile money providers worldwide. This has been possible thanks to the platform technology used to host a wider set of services in addition to the original ones. The new additional software applications were provided free of charge by Safaricom with the aim to generate new demand and strengthen customer loyalty to the provider's primary products. Thanks to this business model, Safaricom could enlarge the partners' network. For example, it has been contacted by actors who proposed ideas for the development of new products, such as Equity Bank, a Kenyan microfinance institution (Linna, 2012).

Other scholars are more critical in their interpretation of the interplay between formal and informal economic actors that generated M-PESA success. With the notion of "adverse incorporation", Meagher (2018) challenges the concept that "frugal innovation" and the vision that co-creation of new ideas for business through collaboration between formal and informal domains always bring win – win situations. In contexts of power and status disparity, agents belonging to the BOP and to the informal sector could be involved in interactions with more powerful actors of the formal sphere with an adverse effect. Control and value extraction could be shifted simply from local informal actors to corporate stakeholders. Meagher argues that narratives on inclusion and collaboration hide a goal of reconfiguring informal institutional and economic systems around the interests of the formal actors, with the aim of reducing costs and increase profit margins. Interactions presented as complementary may actually involve capture of local resources and knowledge. Inclusive engagement could turn out to be highly selective, by picking only the informal actors or institutions that are useful for the need of the business.

Meagher identifies four channels through which adverse incorporation may occur, with the interaction favouring the formal side and leading to actual disempowerment of the informal side. First, copying product or process innovations from informal actors generates a decrease of profits for the channels in which such ideas actually emerged. Second, free-riding on local networks reduces the transaction and marketing costs for the corporate actor. Third, by short-circuiting informal accumulation, selective inclusion may lead to delegitimizing informal commercial intermediaries. As Webb, Kistruck, Ireland, and Ketchen (2010) explain, such intermediaries are often substituted with social enterprises or local NGOs that ally with the formal corporations and act as informal brokers to remote BOP markets of poor customers.[8] Consequently, profit margins of relatively better-off informal actors are eroded, while profits generated along the frugal value chain are concentrated on the side of the corporate partner.[9] Fourth, shifting risks and costs towards informal actors. Often the programmes implemented by large corporations require that the local informal entrepreneurs bear the equipment costs or exploit their social support networks, adding more stress to the system. In this way, local social capital is eroded rather than empowered, while formal corporations avoid the risks and costs of fully formalizing the actors employed in the whole value chain. Moreover, frugal innovators' partnership with development aid divert scarce funding from direct support of local enterprise development or creation of formal jobs.

By applying these reflections to the M-PESA case, Meagher (2018) questions the actual complementarity of benefits between formal and informal actors involved. She argues that the role of informal innovation has not been sufficiently recognised, while the benefits have been captured consistently by the lead firms Vodafone and Safaricom. Meagher (2018) and Maurer (2012) note that, on the one hand, the supposed end users of the M-PESA system actually generated product and process innovations, and on the other hand, their low-cost innovative informal business infrastructure of sub-contractors networks was so crucial for the product diffusion that Safaricom promptly copied the schema at a formal level. After having benefited from the services generated by the informal network, in 2010 Safaricom centralised the control by strongly expanding the role of the cheap sub-agents while reducing the number of better-paid dealers. In this way, it increased both control and profit margins, and allowed "the capture and incorporation of the highly successful informal innovations" (Foster & Heeks, 2013, 206). This process is a demonstration of the four strategies listed above: copying local informal innovations, free-riding on informal retailers' practices, exclusion of "upper ties agents", and shifting costs onto the sub-agents' structures (Meagher, 2018).

Small-scale enterprises: observations from Ethiopia

As we argued in the theoretical section, one of the possible relationships between the informal economy and the formal economic sectors is the observation of the individual strategies across the boundaries of formal labour market and self-employment, especially, but not only, in the BOP markets. Self-employment can be both formal and informal, although the second is the more frequent case. Holt and Littlewood (2014) even overlap the two categories, defining the informal sector as "self-employed working under informal means"; although we have argued that this does not always match the empirical evidence on the informal sector, where bigger businesses may exist, we still observe that, very often, one-person businesses in sub-Saharan Africa are indeed informal.

This section focuses on small-scale entrepreneurship and its role in individual livelihood strategies in a context of an expanding, but precarious, labour market. Ethiopia is a relevant case to analyse the interdependence between the small entrepreneurship sector (MSEs) and the formal labour market.

Economic growth and support to MSEs

Ethiopia is experiencing an unprecedented phase of economic growth, industrialisation, and a drop in unemployment rates. Still, the latter remain quite high, especially in urban contexts: the average urban unemployment rate in 2014 was 16%, with a peak in Addis Ababa (24%), although these figures represent an improvement with respect to 22% nationwide and 33% in the capital city in 2003 (World Bank, 2016). One of the tools put forward by public policies to fight unemployment is the promotion of MSEs. A recent experimental study by Christopher Blattman and Stefan Dercon (2017) followed a panel of nearly 1,000 applicants to entry-level jobs in five industrial firms in different parts of Ethiopia to investigate the relative risks and benefits of industrial and informal work. The experiment randomly assigned jobseekers to industrial jobs, to an entrepreneurship development programme (including a US $300 grant – about US $1,030 in purchasing power parity – and a training programme), and to a control group. After one year, the income of those who entered the entrepreneurship programme had increased by one-third, while the income increase of wage employees was negligible. Moreover, only 32% of the latter group was employed after one year (compared to 20% of the control group), indicating a high turnover. Finally, employees in industrial firms reported a substantial worsening of their health conditions. The authors conclude with a positive view on MSEs as tools to fight poverty and unemployment.

It has to be noted that this experiment did not take place in a political vacuum (Di Nunzio, 2015; Chinigò, 2019): MSE promotion policy in Ethiopia is one of the major policy tools adopted to fight against urban unemployment. The national MSE strategy dates back to 1997 and to the establishment of the Federal MSE Development Agency, but only recently have these instruments received much attention. This strategy aims both at fighting unemployment and at formalizing the peri-urban economy. The targets are especially women and youths, and the promoted MSEs are in a defined number of prioritised sectors (Chinigò & Navarra, 2017). Abebe (2015) and Chinigò and Navarra (2017) focus on these "sponsored" MSEs: both papers find little to non-existent differences in terms of earning and productivity between the formal MSEs and informal self-employment. Chinigò and Navarra argue that this policy, on the other hand, allows groups of people to have access to credit and saving tools, which nevertheless are used more as a substitute for missing income stabilisers than as business development tools.

In a broader analysis of firm size in Ethiopia, focusing on the 2000s, Söderbom (2012) observes that new firms enter the Ethiopian market every year, but they are mostly quite small and characterised by higher death rates with respect to bigger firms. After eight years from their birth, two-thirds of small firms are not operating anymore, meaning that the employment generated has disappeared. The evidence of the relative attractiveness of MSEs found in Blattman and Dercon's paper has to be discussed in light of these works indicating their vulnerability and unstable employment promotion.

Labour market dynamics and informalisation

Beyond the investigation of the performance of the MSE sector, it is relevant to observe the interrelation between small-scale entrepreneurship and the opportunities that can be found on the labour market. According to the World Bank 5th Ethiopia Economic Update (World Bank, 2016), an important characteristic of the Ethiopian urban labour markets in the last decade has been the presence of an increasingly educated workforce, but the little change in the structure of employment and real wages has not reflected the increased level of education. Although improvements are observed after 2012, these do not compensate for previous decreases (see Figure 9.1). According to Ferede and Kebede (2015), there is evidence, moreover, that productivity gains have been higher than wage increases in the last decade. To sum up, there is evidence of wages that are stagnating or experiencing a recent weak growth that does not compensate the decline of the past decade: in most cases, wages do not match the needs or expectations of an increasingly educated and urbanised population.

Inequalities among wage earners are also substantial. Women's wages are 28% lower than men's wages. Real wages of categories with some education suffered the biggest decrease between 2006 and 2014. At the same time, it is low-skilled wages that are clustered around very low levels: the real wage of the 25th percentile of people with no education is below the nominal national poverty line (World Bank, 2016). If we expand the observation beyond wages and look at working conditions, Blattman and Dercon (2017) highlight the worsening effect of industry employment on workers' health in the cases of the employments that were offered to the participants in their experiment. Small businesses (both formal and informal) can therefore be tools to complement low wages or elements of a strategy that switches between labour market and business incomes.

A number of studies, indeed, underline that the earning gap in Ethiopia has been an increasingly important factor to explain the entry into the informal economy. There is a substantial amount of literature on the changes in the Ethiopian labour market in the 1990s and 2000s, after the end of the Derg period and with the country undergoing major economic reforms. In the framework of an important joint project carried out by the University of Addis Ababa, the

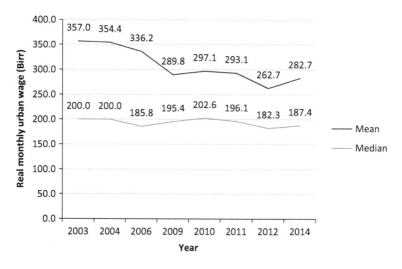

Figure 9.1 Monthly real urban wage in Ethiopia.

Note: we report the years in which the survey was conducted and for which data are available. Figures are in Ethiopian Birr. The mean wage in 2014 would correspond to about 8.8 Euros today.

Source: authors' calculation from data of the World Bank (2016), related to the Urban Employment Unemployment Survey 2003–2014

University of Göteborg, and other institutions, several waves of urban and rural household surveys were conducted, and these allowed researchers to understand major changes in the labour market and in the society (Bigsten et al., 2005). In particular, Bigsten, Mengistae, and Shimeles (2013) highlight that in the decade 1994–2004, segmentation across public – private and formal – informal divides decreased, while mobility across the same lines increased. The sensitivity of sector choice to earning gaps increased overall and is especially important in explaining the selection into the informal sector. Also, in different contexts, several empirical papers try to assess the earnings gap between the formal and the informal sectors (El Badaoui, Strobl, & Walsh, 2008, on South Africa; Nordman, Rakotomanana, & Roubaud, 2016, on Madagascar). The results found are generally mixed, and the size of the gap depends on several characteristics. Especially in Nordman et al. (2016), it appears that low wages in formal wage employment contribute to the attractiveness of employment in the informal sector.

Moreover, there is qualitative evidence (Rossetti et al., 2015) that small informal businesses have also been created by former employees of factories that scaled down the labour forces and laid off workers, thus underlying a process of "informalisation", as highlighted in the conceptual framework of this chapter. Adverse economic shocks can indeed increase informal employment and the size of the informal sector relative to formal employment (Chen, 2012; Colombo, Metta, & Tirelli, 2019).

In conclusion, in the case analysed, informal self-employment does not seem to simply respond to a sort of "natural" preference for entrepreneurship, as it is hypothesised in some streams of the BOP literature. Rather, it is a reaction to changes, opportunities, and conditions on the formal labour market. The attractiveness of the entrepreneurial option in the informal sector increases when the conditions of wage employment deteriorate or are too low for increased costs of living (as it is the case in a growing and rapidly urbanizing economy), or when they do not match the expectations and the needs of the population.

Conclusions

Interactions between formal and informal economic activities in low-income environments of the African continent are complex, and it is challenging to provide single interpretations. BOP markets are often dominated by the informal economy. With our work, we aim to place the BOP debate in the wider framework of the relationship between the formal and the informal sector. Through the analysis of the empirical literature of two selected cases, we show that BOP markets are structurally linked to "upper" formal markets. Nevertheless, this relation may have different shapes, and the specific nature of the connection determines particular consequences for the BOP members and for the system as a whole. Dynamics happening in the formal economy either generate informalisation processes, as it happened in the Ethiopian case, or prevent formalisation paths for BOP working members, as in the Kenyan example.

The Kenyan case study on the M-PESA experience highlights how the strategic interaction between informal stakeholders and private large companies fostered the development and the diffusion of successful technological products in the field of mobile money. This surely increased the access to financial solutions for BOP actors, while becoming financially sustainable and profitable for the internationally supported mobile network operator. However, some scholars demonstrated how the involved formal actors intentionally shaped the interactions with the large pool of informal stakeholders in order to benefit corporate economic interests and *de facto* eroded profit margins of the informal BOP players.

The Ethiopian case study shows that, in BOP settings, the processes linking formal and informal sectors operate in both directions. On the one hand, the government sponsors policies for supporting micro and small enterprises in formalisation processes, with the aim of fighting unemployment and informality. On the other hand, new informal economic activities are started as consequences of earnings gaps or reductions of workforce in companies in the formal sector, thus creating a dynamic of "informalisation". Some of these small informal enterprises receive support from the public programmes mentioned above, which aim to foster their transition towards formal self-employment. In sum, we can say that the attractiveness of (often informal) self-employment is closely linked to the conditions that people can find on the formal labour market.

The cases differ in the dynamics along which the interrelation of formal – informal takes place. Regarding the role of the individual actors, we can observe that in the Kenyan case, the formal stakeholder creates a complex system in which formal and informal are intertwined, and individuals are embedded in this system, with few possibilities to distinguish the two levels. In the Ethiopian case, the formal and informal levels are separated, and the individuals create the connection between the two, through the strategic alternate positioning in one of the two and back.

Some lessons and recommendations can be taken from this research. When studying processes of inclusion from formal to informal players, it is necessary to consider the power relations that are in place. One should analyse the mechanisms along which partnerships produce benefits that are unequally distributed and skewed towards the more powerful actors. If the terms of inclusion do not recognise adequately the interests of the informal actors, the so-called "frugal innovation" schemes may produce adverse incorporation. Moreover, it is crucial to identify when BOP ventures do not have the objective "to draw the poor out of informality, but to benefit from the cost advantages of keeping them informal" (Meagher, 2018, 9). When these cases occur, they should be described in terms of strategic profit extraction from cheap local social capital, rather than of interaction.

It is useful to overcome two kinds of simplistic approaches. One interprets negatively any process different from formalisation, as expression of a backward environment, and it considers the exit from the informal domain as the only path of improvement for BOP individuals and for the society as a whole. The other, on the contrary, idealises the properties of the informal systems in the BOP markets and the opportunities to increase profits from the incorporation of such systems in value chains led by large formal companies. However, such incorporations may produce benefits that are biased towards the formal and powerful side of the system, without pulling BOP stakeholders out of informality.

Future research lines should focus on analysing specific dynamics of formal – informal interactions, with the goal of formulating context-specific policies. On the one hand, practitioners and decision makers should acknowledge the role of informal economic activities for mixed livelihood strategies of BOP members in contexts where diffuse, stable, and affordable formalisation of labour is still absent. On the other hand, it is necessary to assure a fair allocation of benefits in cases where informal BOP actors are embedded in larger value creation processes, including the benefits of formalisation of their work.

Notes

1 Cecilia Navarra writes in her personal capacity. The content of the paper is the sole responsibility of the author and any opinions expressed herein should not be taken to represent an official position of the European Parliament.
2 All authors contributed equally to this chapter.

3 Sciarrone and Storti (2019) focus mainly on the distinction between the concepts of legal and illegal economy. We mention their taxonomy for the application to the broader dichotomy of formal/informal, but we do not restrict our definition of the informal sector to illegal activities only.

4 La Porta and Shleifer (2014) use as a measure of informality the share of labour force that is in self-employment, which, in absolute levels and comparing across countries, has a strong negative correlation with GDP (data from 2013). Still, they show that this correlation substantially decreases when analysing the change in self-employment depending on the change in GDP in a panel analysis (1990–2012, 68 countries).

5 Many definitions have been suggested for "agency" in the social sciences. Stones (2007) proposes the following: "Agency is the ability of individuals or groups . . . to 'make things happen' within given structural constraints and opportunities". For a review of the concept, see also Ahearn (2001), who uses the working definition of agency as "the socioculturally mediated capacity to act".

6 In Chen's taxonomy (2012), the "legalist" school emphasises the burden of cumbersome bureaucratic procedures as a main cause of informality, while the "voluntarist" school stresses the focus on informal entrepreneurs' strategies to deliberately avoid taxation and compliance to formal regulations.

7 Phone companies already sold to people "air-time" (i.e. pre-paid phone credit for communication through voice call or SMS), and they allowed customers to send this credit to other users. Consequently, recipient users spontaneously started to re-sell the received air-time to a local broker, receiving in return either cash, goods, or services. In this way, they transferred purchasing power from the initial sender to the recipient (Jack & Suri 2011).

8 Webb et al. (2010, 650) depict those NGOs as "unique local alliance partners for multinationals to facilitate their entrepreneurship processes, serving society's social needs while positioning the multinationals to gain financial benefits" (quoted in Meagher, 2018, 10).

9 Meagher (2018, 10) reports figures on this process that have been cited by Paunov (2013, 32) in relation to broader studies on inclusive innovation with formal-informal partnerships aiming to reach large, low-income groups and at the same time to provide opportunities for profitable business models: "monopolistic structures in intermediary services, [such as] transporters, traders, commission agents and wholesalers, may take between 30% and 45% of final market values . . . cutting out intermediaries by directly sourcing from lower-income producers and/or relying on them for distribution can be an effective and profitable business model".

References

Abebe, G. (2015). *State-inducement versus self-initiation: A comparative study of micro and small enterprises in Ethiopia* (EDRI Working Paper 13). Addis Ababa: Ethiopian Development Research Institute.

Ahearn, L. M. (2001). Language and agency. *Annual Review of Anthropology*, *30*(1), 109–137.

Anderson, J. L., Markides, C., & Kupp, M. (2010). The last frontier: market creating in conflict zones, deep rural areas, and urban slums. *California Management Review*, *52*(4), 6–28.

Asongu, S. A. (2013). How has mobile phone penetration stimulated financial development in Africa? *Journal of African Business, 14*(1), 7–18.

Barrett, C. (2008). Smallholder market participation: Concept and evidence from Eastern and Southern Africa. *Food Policy, 33*(4), 299–317.

Biggeri, M. (2004). *Growth with development: Informal sector and human development in low-income sub-Saharan economies* (Working Paper No. 140). Florence, Italy: Dipartimento di Scienze Economiche, Università degli Studi di Firenze.

Bigsten, A., Kebede, B., & Shimeles, A. (Eds.). (2005). *Poverty, income distribution and labour markets in Ethiopia.* Uppsala, Sweden: Nordic Africa Institute.

Bigsten, A., Mengistae, T., & Shimeles, A. (2013). Labor market integration in Urban Ethiopia, 1994–2004. *Economic Development and Cultural Change, 61*(4), 889–931.

Blattman, C., & Dercon, S. (2017). The impacts of industrial and entrepreneurial work on income and health: Experimental evidence from Ethiopia. *American Economic Journal: Applied Economics, 10*(3), 1–38.

Castells, M., & Portes, A. (1989). *World underneath: The origins, dynamics, and effects of the informal economy.* In A. Portes, M. Castells, & L. A. Benton (Eds.), *The informal economy: Studies in advanced and less developed societies* (pp. 11–37). Baltimore, MD: Johns Hopkins University Press.

Chen, M. A. (2012). *The informal economy: Definitions, theories and policies* (Working Paper No. 1). Cambridge, MA: WIEGO.

Chinigò, D., & Navarra, C. (2017, August). Small enterprises in urban areas between formalization policies and social protection needs. A discussion on the Ethiopian case. Paper presented at the EADI Nordic Conference, Bergen, Norway.

Chinigò, D. (2019). 'The peri-urban space at work': micro and small enterprises, collective participation, and the developmental state in Ethiopia. *Africa, 89*(1), 79–99.

Colombo, E., Menna, L., & Tirelli, P. (2019). Informality and the labor market effects of financial crises. *World Development, 119*, 1–22.

De Soto, H. (1989). *The other path: the invisible revolution in the Third World.* New York: Harper and Row.

Di Nunzio, M. (2015). What is the alternative? Youth, entrepreneurship and the developmental state in urban Ethiopia. *Development and Change, 46*(5), 1179–1200.

Duflo, E., & Banerjee, A. (2011). *Poor economics: A radical rethinking of the way to fight global poverty.* New York: Public Affairs.

El Badaoui, E., Strobl, E., & Walsh, F. (2008). Is there an informal employment wage penalty? Evidence from South Africa. *Economic Development and Cultural Change, 56*(3), 683–710.

Etzo, S., & Collender, G. (2010). The mobile phone 'revolution' in Africa: Rhetoric or reality? *African Affairs, 109*(437), 659–668.

Ferede, T., & Kebede, S. (2015). *Economic growth and employment patterns, dominant sector, and firm profiles in Ethiopia: Opportunities, challenges and Prospects.* Bern, Switzerland: Swiss Program for Research on Global Issues of Development.

Foster, C., & Heeks, R. (2013). Innovation and scaling of ICT for the bottom-of-the-pyramid. *Journal of Information Technology, 28*, 296–315.

Guha-Khasnobis, B., Kanbur, R., & Ostrom, E. (Eds.). (2006). *Linking the formal and informal economy. Concepts and policies.* New York: Oxford University Press.

Hammond, A. L., Kramer, W. J., Katz, R. S., Tran, J. T, & Walker, C. (2008). *The next 4 billion: Characterizing BOP markets* (Findings No. 292). The World Bank.

Hammond, A. L., & Prahalad, C. K. (2004). Selling to the poor. *Foreign Policy, 142,* 30–37.

Hart, K. (1973). Informal income opportunities and urban employment in Ghana. *The Journal of Modern African Studies, 11*(01), 61–89.

Hart, K. (2009). *On the informal economy: The political history of an ethnographic concept* (Working Paper No. 09/042). Brussels: CEB.

Hickey, S., & du Toit, A. (2007). *Adverse incorporation, social exclusion and chronic poverty* (Working Paper No. 81). University of Manchester: CPRC.

Holt, D., & Littlewood, D. (2014). *The informal economy as a route to market in sub-Saharan Africa –observations amongst Kenyan informal economy entrepreneurs.* In S. Nwanko & K. Ibeh (Eds.), *The Routledge Companion to Business in Africa* (pp. 198–217). London: Routledge.

Iazzolino, G. (2017). Behind the mobile money hype (Newsletter Emerging Economies No. 8). Torino, Italy: Turin Center on Emerging Economies. Retrieved from www.osservatorio-economie-emergenti-torino.it/emerging-economies/08-december-2017.html

Iazzolino, G., & Wasike, N. (2015). The unbearable lightness of digital money. *Journal of Payments Strategy & Systems, 9*(3), 229–241.

ILO. (1972). *Employment, incomes and equality: A strategy for increasing productive employment in Kenya.* Geneva: International Labour Organization.

ILO. (2018). *Women and men in the informal economy: A statistical picture* (3rd ed.). Geneva: International Labour Organization.

Jack, W., & Suri, T. (2011). *Mobile money: The economics of M-PESA* (Working Paper No. w16721). Cambridge, MA: National Bureau of Economic Research.

Jayne, T. S. (1994). Do high food marketing costs constrain cash crop production? evidence from Zimbabwe. *Economic Development and Cultural Change, 42*(2), 387–402.

Kanbur, R. (2009). *Conceptualizing informality: Regulation and enforcement* (Working Paper No. 09–11). Ithaca, NY: Cornell University, Dept. of Applied Economics and Management.

Karamchandani, A., Kubzansky, M., & Lalwani, N. (2011). Is the bottom of the pyramid really for you? *Harvard Business Review, 89*(3), 107–111.

La Porta, R., & Shleifer, A. (2014). Informality and development. *Journal of Economic Perspectives, 28*(3), 109–26.

Lewis, W. A. (1954). Economic development with unlimited supplies of labour. *The Manchester School of Economic and Social Studies, 12* (2), 139–191.

Linna, P. (2012). Base of the pyramid (BOP) as a source of innovation: Experiences of companies in the Kenyan mobile sector. *International Journal of Technology Management & Sustainable Development, 11*(2), 113–137.

Loayza, N. V., & Rigolini, J. (2011). Informal employment: Safety net or growth engine? *World Development, 39*(9), 1503–1515.

Maliehe, S., & Sharp, J. (2018). The digital world and a human economy: Mobile money and socio-economic development in Africa. *Development Finance Agenda (DEFA), 4*(2), 18–19.

Maurer, B. (2012). Mobile money: Communication, consumption and change in the payments space. *Journal of Development Studies, 48*(5), 589–604.

Meagher, K. (1995). Crisis, informalisation and the urban informal sector in sub-Saharan Africa. *Development and Change, 26*(2), 259–84.

Meagher, K. (2018). Cannibalizing the informal economy: Frugal innovation and economic inclusion in Africa. *European Journal of Development Research, 30*(1), 17–33.

Navarra, C., & Pellizzoli, R. (2012, September). Integrating smallholders in rural markets in Mozambique: Empowering women or further marginalizing them? On-line proceedings of the IIIrd IESE Conference: Moçambique: Acumulação e Transformação num Contexto de Crise Internacional, Maputo, Mozambique.

Nordman, C. J., Rakotomanana, F., & Roubaud, F. (2016). Informal versus formal: A panel data analysis of earnings gaps in Madagascar. *World Development, 86*, 1–17.

O'Laughlin, B. (2001). *Pobreza, crescimento e relações de género: liberalização, terra e trabalho nas zonas rurais de Moçambique.* In R. Waterhouse & C. Vijfhuizen (Eds.), *Estratégias das mulheres, proveito dos homens. Genero, terra e recursos naturais em diferentes contextos rurais em Moçambique.* (pp. 35–57). Maputo, Mozambique: UEM.

O'Laughlin, B. (2009). Poverty, AIDS and missing men in southern Africa. *Afriche e Orienti, XI*(II), 151–164.

Oya, C., & Sender, J. (2009). Divorced, separated, and widowed women workers in rural Mozambique. *Feminist Economics, 15*(2), 1–31.

Paunov, C. (2013). Innovation and inclusive development: A discussion of the main policy issues (OECD Science, Technology and Industry Working Paper 2013/01). Paris: OECD Publishing.

Portes, A., Castells, M., & Benton, L.A. (Eds.). (1989). *The informal economy: Studies in advanced and less developed countries.* Baltimore, MD: John Hopkins University Press.

Portes, A., & Haller, W. (2005). *The informal economy.* In R. Swedberg & N.J. Smelser (Eds.), *The handbook of economic sociology* (pp. 403–425). Princeton, NJ: Princeton University Press.

Rossetti, G., Chinigò, D., Navarra, C., & Argaw, T.G. (2015). *Women at work.* Romagna, Italy: Nexus Emilia.

Sciarrone, R., & Storti, L. (2019). *Le mafie nell'economia legale. Scambi, collusioni, azioni di contrasto.* Bologna, Italy: Il Mulino.

Söderbom, M. (2012). Firm size and structural change: A case study of Ethiopia. *Journal of African Economies, 21*(2), (126–151).

Stones, R. (2007). Structure and agency. In G. Ritzer (Ed.), *The Blackwell Encyclopedia of Sociology* (pp. 4869–4872). New York: Blackwell Publishing.

Sylvanus, N. (2016). *Patterns in circulation. Cloth, gender and materiality in West Africa.* Chicago: University of Chicago Press.

Tabak, F., & Crichlow, M.A. (2000). *Informalization: Process and structure.* Baltimore, MD: Johns Hopkins University Press.

The World Bank. (2016). *5th Ethiopia economic update: Why so idle? – wages and employment in a crowded labor market.* Washington, DC: World Bank Group.

Toulabor, C. (2012). Les Nana Benz de Lomé. Mutations d'une bourgeoisie compradore, entre heur et décadence. *Afrique Contemporaine, 2012*(4), 69–80.

UNCTAD. (2015). *Least developed countries report, transforming rural economies.* Geneva: UNCTAD.

Verbrugge, B. (2015). The economic logic of persistent informality: artisanal and small-scale mining in the Southern Philippines. *Development and Change, 46*(5), 1023–1046.

Verbrugge, B., & Geenen S. (2019). The gold commodity frontier: A fresh perspective on change and diversity in the global gold mining economy. *Extractive Industries and Society, 6*(2), 413–423.

Webb, J. W., Kistruck, G. M., Ireland, R. D., & Ketchen Jr, D. J. (2010). The entrepreneurship process in base of the pyramid markets: The case of multinational enterprise/nongovernment organization alliances. *Entrepreneurship theory and practice*, *34*(3), 555–581.

Zins, A., & Weill, L. (2016). The determinants of financial inclusion in Africa. *Review of Development Finance*, *6*(1), 46–57.

Index

Note: Page numbers in *italics* indicate figures and in **bold** indicate table on the corresponding pages.

Printed in the United States
by Baker & Taylor Publisher Services